Good Enough.

A COOKBOOK

Embracing the Joys of Imperfection
& Practicing Self-Care
in the Kitchen

Leanne Brown

WORKMAN PUBLISHING
NEW YORK

Library of Congress Cataloging-in-Publication Data

Names: Brown, Leanne, author.
Title: Good enough : a cookbook / Leanne Brown.
New York : Workman Publishing, [2022] |
Identifiers: LCCN 2021027273 | ISBN 9781523509676 |
ISBN 9781523509676 (ebook)
Subjects: LCSH: Low budget cooking. | LCGFT: Cookbooks.
Classification: LCC TX714 .B786 2022 | DDC 641.5/52--dc23
LC record available at https://lccn.loc.gov/2021027273

Cover by Rae Ann Spitzenberger
Front cover photo credits: Egg: Freezerrr/Adobe Stock;
marble surface: ParinPIX/Adobe Stock
Design by Sarah Smith
Photography by Leanne Brown
Author photo by Evi Abeler

Workman books are available at special discounts when purchased in bulk
for premiums and sales promotions as well as for fundraising or educational
use. Special editions or book excerpts can also be created to specification. For
details, contact the Special Sales Director at specialmarkets@workman.com.

Workman Publishing Co., Inc.
225 Varick Street
New York, NY 10014-4381

workman.com

WORKMAN is a registered trademark of Workman Publishing Co., Inc.

Printed in the United States of America
First printing December 2021

10 9 8 7 6 5 4 3 2 1

For my younger self.
Look, we did it!

CONTENTS

CHAPTER 6: Good Enough Fun 163

In which we work on consciously embracing joy and excitement. Examining some of the ways we stop ourselves from deeply experiencing these good feelings. We make food that helps us deepen our joyful experiences, calm the fears that sometimes come with them, and create happy memories to ground into. Sometimes an all-day cooking project or the magic of seeing bread rising in the oven is just what we need to tap into our spark and share it with others.

CHAPTER 7: Good Enough for You 203

In which we reacquaint ourselves with the concept of rest: taking it easy, making ourselves a priority, and letting ourselves rest to gather fuel for life. By deepening and expanding life's simplest pleasures, and making meals with ourselves in mind, we can focus on celebrating and restoring ourselves—through vegetables, luxurious desserts, and a heroic pasta dish made of whatever was in the pantry.

CHAPTER 8: Good Enough for Others 245

In which we finally accept that the secret ingredient to a great dinner party is emotional vulnerability. Full of recipes that are fun to share. Some are lighthearted and light work, letting the ingredients shine; others are designed to send love and caring out to other human beings. Let's be inspired to do, simply, enough.

END NOTES: After the Meal 279

In which we give leftovers some grace. An invitation to observe what happens to food the next day.

Breakdown/Breakthrough

On the heels of writing and launching my last book, *Good and Cheap*, I was burnt out and exhausted. I was deeply depressed and spent many mornings crying before I got out of bed. Ultimately what got me up and out was a mixture of guilt and fear. I didn't want to let anyone down by not fulfilling my duty, and I was afraid of what I would lose if I didn't complete my obligations. Here I was with my life's dreams—dreams I had never even had the courage to fully voice to anyone—coming true: to be a cookbook author, to have a career spreading the joy of home cooking to others. This was supposed to be it. I didn't understand why I was so miserable.

I began therapy, and it helped. I threw myself into touring, promotion, and the work of launching a book and many other projects. I found pockets of real joy. I could feel proud. But I continued to operate on a cycle of extremes. I would work myself hard to make sure I didn't let anyone down, ignoring my own needs. Once a major deadline passed, I would crash, usually get really sick, sleep, and barely leave the house for days, trying to recover. Guilt would quickly creep in. I didn't deserve a break. What did I think I was doing?

I soon got pregnant and found myself struggling and lonely, with a severe form of morning sickness that lasted throughout the nine months. Being constantly nauseated alienated me from my love of food, making me feel worthless in my chosen career. How could I do my job when food repulsed me? I couldn't seem to get any sustained work done. I was keeping up, but less work was coming my way, so I was keeping up with less and less. The fear and guilt that drove me before were still there, but the energy to get things done was gone.

When my daughter was born, I was elated, but I continued to struggle with loneliness and depression, still unable to get my career looking the way I imagined it should. I preached the joys of cooking and eating. How many times had I said it was a privilege to eat three meals a day? How many times had I said cooking was easy? That the pleasure far outweighed the efforts? I felt like such a fraud as I ate handfuls of nuts over the sink and cold pizza for breakfast.

I know I am not alone in this struggle. I have heard from so many people with similar stories throughout my career.

And I noticed a pattern with folks struggling to feed themselves. Money is often a huge issue, but the deeper issue is believing that they are not worth the effort. I know that feeling intimately. Cooking and feeding ourselves require work, and it is almost impossible to find that energy for yourself when you don't think you are worth it. A sense of worthlessness is an issue regardless of wealth or privilege and can reveal itself at any time in our lives.

So I've decided that I don't want to be motivated by fear and guilt anymore. Although if I'm honest, it's more that I no longer seem to be able to get anything done that way. Beating the hell out of myself just doesn't get the results it once did. I'm working on it. I am trying to connect with the part of me that believes pleasure and strength go hand in hand. I want to be gentle and kind with myself in the same way I hope my daughter will be with herself.

Life is hard. Most of the time I am not my best self. I am often afraid, rushed, stubborn, jealous, caught between what I want to be and what I am. Most of my meals are unremarkable. I write cookbooks and I am an excellent home cook— yet I still struggle to feed myself every day. I almost never meal plan. My fridge is usually disorganized. There are always at least two containers of rotting leftovers in there at any time. I skip lunch and breakfast when I'm busy. I love all kinds of junk food, Doritos especially, but I feel embarrassed when I buy them. I talk about getting everyone into the kitchen, but I rarely let other people help me in my own. I often make cooking sound easier than it is.

Beating myself up for all these things has not made me happier or more productive. It has kept me afraid. Fretting about living up to my own standards has made me feel paralyzed and ashamed, like a fake and a failure. If this is what I do, what I shape my life around, and I can barely cook and eat in the way that I want to, what right do I have to do this work? Fortunately, now I know that is my fear talking. It's not the truth. The truth is much more annoyingly ambivalent. Food is the best and the worst—just like being a person, like being a parent, like loving someone for a long time.

I am no longer going to pretend that cooking is easy, but it is worth it. And editing this book during a pandemic and racial reckoning—with my partner and young child at home in a small Brooklyn apartment for months—crystallized this reality

My intention is for this book to be a gentle hug and a whisper in your ear that you are stronger than you know, and you deserve love and care, wherever you are, whoever you are, and no matter what anyone else might have told you.

in a way that felt like the universe tattooing COOKING IS HARD on my forehead. This book is an exploration of the recipes, stories, and methods that have helped me in this journey to accept and fully honor the beautiful, complex, and meaningful act of cooking for myself and others. It is my effort to integrate my beliefs with reality. I'm sure not there yet, but I think I'm on my way.

From *Good and Cheap* to *Good Enough*

Everyone deserves to eat well every day. I have said this out loud so many times in so many different rooms to so many different audiences. I believe it with every fiber of my being. In my last book, *Good and Cheap*, I explored this concept at the level of physical inequity. Our capitalist system renders some people free to easily meet their physical needs, while others struggle. Not because one person is better or more worthy, but because that is the system. Some have less and some have more. It is not fair; it is simply reality. A reality we can all work to shift through community action. And one that I intend to be involved in throughout my life. My assertion is that our *current* reality does not negate the fact that we all inherently deserve to eat well every day. Some people don't have enough to eat and that is a human tragedy.

But there is so much more to the statement that we all deserve to eat well. Why don't we all eat well every day? The answer is even more complicated than poverty and economic-, social-, racial-, or identity-driven injustice. These are whole system problems, and they affect us externally and internally. They create experiences that leave their mark on us, shaping our ways of thinking and living in the world. Our particular struggles with food, or with anything, are as unique as our own lives.

In this book, I am exploring that idea of deserving to eat from an internal perspective. Yes, each of us deserves to eat well every day, but what are the internal blocks that keep us from eating well? Why do we hurt ourselves or struggle to treat ourselves with the love and care we deserve? Why, when it seems like it should be simple, do we struggle to eat well? We deserve to eat well because we are human, but how do we bring our everyday decisions into alignment with that truth?

My road to healing has brought up all of these questions, quite painfully. Whether you can relate to this experience directly or you notice that something outside of your own self is holding you hostage or affecting your actions, I share this journey with you in the hopes that you can separate your own worthy self from the struggles you've been through and we can look at them together, hand in hand.

Pink Carrots

When I was four years old, I dreamed up a story of my future. I dreamed that I grew up to develop a revolutionary food crop: pink carrots.

These pink carrots had all the nutrition of regular carrots, and they grew in regular soil and required water and gentle tending . . . but they were also magical. When you ate them, the carrots looked deep into your soul, found your greatest flavor desires, and granted them.

The result was that your carrots tasted like cotton candy, steak with blue cheese, cherry pie, or maybe just the best carrots you've ever eaten.

They changed the world, bringing all of us the pleasure we crave and the strength and nutrients our bodies need to thrive.

This grown-up Leanne became very wealthy, and she used her money to buy gifts for her loved ones and help other people fulfill their dreams.

Now, I realize that at some level I have been lucky enough to become that pink carrot purveyor. I share my love of cooking and strive to make it accessible so everyone can benefit from the double impact of joy that good food brings us: pleasure and strength. I believe pleasure and strength go hand in hand. We need both of them to be fully human, to be resilient enough to show our best selves.

How to Use This Book

This cookbook is about the feelings that come up around cooking. It is personal. My hope is that the personal process I share here can guide you to care for yourself in whatever ways are right for you.

It would be absurd to say "This lemon tart can quell workplace rage" or "This meatball dish calms social anxiety." No. We are far too multifaceted for that. But I want the book to help you start a conversation with yourself. As you read it, I hope you'll ask yourself: *Is there anything that resonates? What do I struggle with? How can I show up in kind ways for myself and my most tender parts? And can food, sensory experiences, and memories help heal and soothe those parts? Even in the smallest ways?*

The order of things. Many cookbooks, including my last one, are organized from breakfast to dinner. It's a logical way to set up a practical tool. Here, the chapters are divided into two sections: getting through your day (Preparation, Mornings, Midday, and Weeknights) and getting through your life (When You're Struggling, Fun, For You, and For Others). Essays and ideas start each chapter, followed by recipes (or ideas, in the case of the Preparation chapter) that support the theme. To see a breakdown of the recipes into more traditional categories, please see the Recipe Index, pages 288–289.

TL;DR. Surely you have heard this from other cookbook authors: "Read each recipe all the way through before you make it." Yes, ideally, you would—we all would. But as our attention spans and available time grow shorter, studying a recipe before launching in becomes harder or just something we don't always feel like doing.

With that in mind, I have written a short description of what each recipe entails and tucked it just below the title of each dish—a TL;DR, if you will. In the tech world, TL;DR stands for "too long; didn't read," and the text following "TL;DR" provides a concise summary of a much longer article, essay, rave, or rant.

This summary of general steps is not necessarily a replacement for reading through the entire recipe—please still do that if you can. I hope that a TL;DR for each recipe can help you grasp the general flow of steps so you are not taken by surprise.

Feeling adventurous? These suggestions appear in some recipes and are meant to inspire you with possible variations or additions to throw in if you happen to have them. My hope is that the ideas in this book will help you to substitute, omit, or add ingredients freely, depending on what you have on hand, and in accordance with your own unique taste. If you find yourself hesitant to stray from the path in the kitchen, consider these ideas an invitation to feel adventurous.

Let Go of the Outcome, Embrace the Process

There is a rigidity to recipes because they are instructions for how to do something exactly right. And that is really as it should be. A recipe is like a little contract. If you do these things in the order I have told you, in the way I have told you, you will end up with a successful result. But following a recipe like a robot without engaging with *why* you are doing what you are doing will not make you a confident cook. It will result in you getting food on the table—which is great!—but I want to see you become a confident cook who can look in the cupboard and know you can make something delicious (or at least edible!) out of what you have around.

Fretting about the outcome keeps us from enjoying the process. For many people, cooking feels like an assignment from your least favorite class, which you undertake while dreading the C-minus you are sure you will receive. But the grade doesn't exist and doesn't matter. The process matters so much more than the outcome. It is the connection to, and the enjoyment of, the process of cooking that will keep you coming back, learning, and growing. So let's get rid of the school assignment mentality and try to think of making food like finger painting. The goal is simply to make something approaching the shape of a painting. It can and will be messy, and some paintings will be better than others, but, crucially, you can still have fun making the not-so-great paintings. Home cooking is not going to be all A-pluses—it will have its highs and lows—but if you cook with self-compassion, you can enjoy the experience, appreciate the great meals, laugh at the not-so-great ones, and generally live your cooking life with way less fear. That is my own goal and my goal for you. And my greatest hope of all is that the flexibility we develop in the kitchen will seep into all aspects of our lives, like a gift we give ourselves.

Gateway to Calm Cooking

Before you begin to cook, take the time to go through this little mental checklist, even (especially) if you feel pressed for time. It will help you reframe the process and center yourself on the creation of food. This mindset will help the cooking go more smoothly—and smoother is usually quicker!

☐ Take five deep breaths.

☐ Read the recipe through, taking note of timing.

☐ Check to make sure you have all of the ingredients or are prepared to skip them or make substitutions.

☐ Chop, defrost, or otherwise prep your ingredients so you can have the most harmonious experience of active cooking.

☐ Set your intention to focus on each step in turn and give your energy to the process and the moment. The outcome is in the future, and you can enjoy this time even if the outcome is not perfect.

You have got this!

CHAPTER 1

Good Enough
Preparation

Hold Up, Why Is This So Much Work?

When I first moved out on my own, I was confident about basically zero of it, except for the cooking and feeding myself part. I had worked in a café and been making meals for myself and for family members for years. So when I realized that I had to fill my fridge and pantry and even get kitchen equipment in order to have a hope of the triumphant meals and casual weeknight dinner parties I had imagined . . . I was disappointed. I had a lot of work and learning to do. "Doing the cooking" is so much more than just that time in the kitchen.

And honestly, it continues. I don't want to minimize the amount of work it takes to feed even just yourself each day. No one can give you a map to yourself and your life and your experience. Learning how to feed your unique self takes engagement and effort.

At the most basic level, we require a place to live, a sense of safety, a working kitchen, a source of income, a body that is supported, and emotional well-being. We often ask people to manage their own meals and mental load when they don't have these things we consider basic rights. And of course survival requires some to press on with feeding themselves even when they lack one or more key components—like feeling unsafe in the home or out in the world. Cooking requires a host of other tasks from us besides the time spent in the kitchen, and those tasks require skills and abilities that we often don't talk about:

1. **Deciding what to eat.** Decision-making skills. Knowing what you want. Budgeting. A reasonable understanding of which foods are best for your body.

2. **Procuring the raw goods.** Time. Money. Physical and mental ability. Freedom to move safely in the world.

3. **Storing the raw goods.** Space. Time. Knowledge.

4. **Preparing the ingredients (washing, drying, chopping, and so on).** Knowledge. Time. Organizational skills. Physical and mental ability.

5. **Cooking.** Equipment. Time. Space and ability to focus. Flexibility. Curiosity. Interest. Physical and mental ability.

6. **Serving and eating!** Relationship management. Sense of fun and aliveness, or presence. Social skills.

7. **Cleaning.** Attention to detail. Diligence. Physical and mental ability.

8. **Storing leftovers.** Organizational skills. Knowledge. Equipment. Space to store food within a safe, consistent space to call home.

And there's one important emotional skill that underlies all of these tasks: personal security. That is, cultivating a sense of your own worth and a willingness to actively love yourself.

> Managing meals takes significant mental load.

This chapter addresses points 1 through 4 in the list above, and the following chapters will address 5, 6, and a little bit of 8. For point 7, cleaning, I have nothing for you, other than to approach it with the same self-caring intention as the rest of the process. Ask for help, make it fair, establish some good routines, and do what works best for you.

When you live with others, the items on the list require negotiation. Negotiation with loved ones can be light and easy and fun when things are flowing and you feel connected, but it can be fraught and full of emotional traps and unresolved patterns if you or your loved ones have unmet needs or painful unsaid things. Who is in charge? Who decides what? Who does the work? Who is responsible? I don't have the answers to these questions for your specific life, but if you feel weighed down by the general sense that there is too much to deal with when you enter the kitchen, know this: You are not alone.

Comparison Shopping

A lot of people hate grocery shopping. A lot of people love it. Most people are ambivalent. Sure, taking a list is great. Getting organized is great. Making it a ritual and slowing down a bit with it is great, and we'll talk about all that more, but here I want to acknowledge one of the unspoken pains of grocery shopping: fear of judgment.

Food is so intimate, and the grocery store is a public place where we are making a lot of personal decisions about food. At the same time, we are all looking at each other's shopping carts and—sometimes subconsciously and other times completely consciously—making assumptions about who other people are. And so, of course, we are also carrying around discomfort, or for some, like me, maybe even real anxiety or fear, about what judgments others might be making about us by looking at our carts.

I cannot tell you how many times, whether out in the world or in my email inbox, I hear from often well-meaning people who tell me "horror stories" about what someone else was buying at the grocery store. "They are doing it wrong and I want to save them!" they claim. And all I can suggest is to urge them to focus on themselves and to stop making assumptions about other people's choices. It really doesn't do anyone any good. Yes, we want to see everyone have enough to eat, and yes, we want everyone to eat foods that nourish their bodies and minds and help them live longer, but there is so much we don't know about other people and their needs. Judgment without wisdom is poisonous, both to those we judge and to ourselves.

We might worry about what others think, but chances are that they, like us, are far too wrapped up in their own inner life to notice what we're buying. Even if the aisles *were* full of judgmental jerks, I certainly don't want to make my choices to please them—I already have one of those inside my own head, thank you very much.

I'M HAVING A PARTY, I SWEAR. I'M DEFINITELY NOT JUST GOING HOME TO EAT ALL THESE CHIPS AND TREATS ALONE IN FRONT OF THE TV.

I HAVE 12 BOXES OF OATMEAL. MY MOM SHOULD BE SO PROUD OF ME. WHY DOESN'T SHE EVER SAY SHE'S PROUD OF ME?

I FEEL RIDICULOUS JUST BUYING CAT FOOD AND CHOCOLATE. I'LL BUY THESE CARROTS AND HUMMUS AND SOME BREAD SO I DON'T LOOK LIKE A LONELY CAT LADY.

WOW, BEING HEALTHY IS EXPENSIVE. THIS JUICING THING HAD BETTER WORK.

IF I GET HER FAVORITE CHERRIES, WILL MY MOTHER-IN-LAW FINALLY SMILE AT ME?

I AM SO OVERWHELMED AND TIRED. I JUST WANT TO BE HOME ALREADY.

MAYBE ONE OF THESE TREATS WILL MAKE HIM WANT TO LEAVE HIS ROOM AND SIT WITH ME?

OH NO, AM I GOING TO HAVE ENOUGH MONEY FOR THIS? WHAT IF I MISCALCULATED? I'LL BE SO HUMILIATED AT THE CHECKOUT.

OH GOD, I AM ONLY GETTING CHICKEN, BACON, AND EGGS. I SWEAR I BOUGHT MY VEGETABLES EARLIER. I SWEAR I EAT VEGETABLES. I HAVE SOME FRUIT AT HOME. SMOOTHIES COUNT, RIGHT?

MY CART IS SO FULL OF VEGETABLES, SURELY NO ONE WILL NOTICE IF I SNEAK IN THIS DONUT. BUT LET ME JUST MAKE SURE IT'S COVERED BY THE CELERY AND CHICKPEA PUFFS.

Groceries in the Rain

One day I was sitting in front of my computer at my coworking space. I was miserable, struggling with writing that just wasn't flowing. My baby daughter was in day care, and these hours to think and do my own work felt immensely precious. I let myself drift to thinking about food, and suddenly my mind started churning and bubbling with recipe ideas. I had to get back home to my kitchen ASAP. I could still squeeze some success from this brutal day.

There was one catch: To make the food I was envisioning, I'd have to go to the grocery store first. Unfortunately, as I stepped outside, thick, swampy air enveloped me and I looked up at a darkening midafternoon sky. Thunderstorm weather. Haha! Too bad! *Here goes,* I thought to myself maniacally. I was loaded down with my purse, a bag with my breast pump, and my computer, but I hustled to the subway. It was a lot to carry already and I knew adding groceries would be a struggle, but I decided that I didn't care—I needed this.

A few subway stops later, I walked up the stairs and out into the world again. By then it was actually raining—those big fat droplets that mean this is a real one; this is some serious rain. So I hustled four or five long blocks (New York City long blocks take about three minutes to walk at a brisk pace) to the grocery store, very aware that home was still three long blocks from there. On the way, it began raining hard, soaking me almost immediately. By the time I reached the store, I was running awkwardly with my bags, breast pump banging against my hip, just to get inside and escape the torrent. I was drenched.

My breathing was short and I felt a little panicky. I knew this was an overreaction, but I couldn't seem to calm down. My mind was racing. *I'm really wet already, and I'm not even home yet, and loading myself up with groceries will make it even harder. I can't just wait at the store for the rain to stop, or I'll run out of time to cook because I have to pick up the baby from day care in a few short hours. I could call a car, but it's just three blocks and when it rains, getting a ride becomes impossible since everyone has the same idea.* I was worrying, but I decided to just focus on my first task: getting my groceries.

So I shopped—self-conscious the whole time about looking wet and bedraggled—and then checked out, still unsure how I would get home. Outside, the rain had lightened up a bit. So I thought, *Okay, well, who knows how long this will last, so I'm going to leave NOW.*

I hurried from the store, loaded down with purse, laptop, pump, and two large paper bags full of groceries. I was conscious of the fact that paper bags will disintegrate when wet.

The rain began to thicken again, and my whole body was so tense; my heart was beating wildly. Instead of ignoring the clear panic I was experiencing and hurrying on like I would have done in the past, today I felt curious. Why was I so afraid? Why was my body acting like a pack of wolves was at my heels instead of knowing I was simply on a street corner with some bags in the rain, in no real danger?

I tried to calm my stream of thoughts by starting a conversation. "Why are you so afraid of getting wet?" I took a deep breath. "It's okay, you're just going to get wet, that is totally survivable!" But a voice deep inside me responded, "No, it's not just getting wet, that's not what's so scary." And I asked, "Well, what is it?" as kindly as I could. The voice responded, "Well, we could get so wet—and it's already starting to rain harder—that it could soak these grocery bags and they will disintegrate and all our groceries could fall out onto the sidewalk and be ruined or you just won't be able to get them home and then you can't do your recipes or we'll run out of time to come back and get them and we won't accomplish anything today and all this food will go to waste!" And so I said to the voice, kindly, "Yes, that would be difficult, but I think we can survive that."

I sighed and relaxed a bit, but I still felt so much tension in my body. It wasn't just getting wet or having my groceries ruined or not being able to take advantage of my creative energy. It was something deeper still. So I asked again, "Is there more? What are you so afraid of?" And this last time something in me let go and that voice said, "I'm afraid of how ridiculous we look. Here we are walking in the street with all this stuff getting wet, with our bags about to burst. We look like we made the wrong decision. We look stupid and weak. Who would do this? What self-respecting adult with their life together does this?"

All that fear! That horrible tense feeling! All because I was worried about the judgment of others. Maybe they would point and laugh, but mostly I was afraid that they would look at me and see that I was wrong. I was feeling shame about making a mistake. There I would be, naked for everyone in my wrongness.

This revelation was quickly followed by another. In the past, if I had even let myself get to this point of admitting the truth—that I am deeply concerned with what other people think—

I would have rolled my eyes at myself and said, "That's ridiculous. That is nothing to be afraid of." And the tension would have stayed in my body and I would have hurried home, and then I would have been miserable from this fear of what other people think, as well as my own incredible self-judgment for being afraid of such a ridiculous thing. I wouldn't have helped myself at all—in fact, I would have made my situation worse.

But this time, somehow, in that moment on the street corner with my soaking wet bags, after all the work I had been doing to cultivate self-compassion, trying to treat myself in the same kind way I treat my daughter, things went differently. In that moment when my deepest self revealed that I was afraid of looking "wrong" in public, my first reaction was not admonishment but compassion. I felt genuine lightness and release almost instantly.

> You can be kind with yourself about everyday fears, too—the little ones that you learn to push down, that you don't share, and that you therefore don't heal from.

My stomach let go of its sickening grip, my jaw, shoulders, and spine relaxed, and I grinned and welled up with tears of mirth. And then I was laughing in the pouring rain. I felt incredible. I felt space open up inside me, and it felt like laser beams burst out of me toward the other people around me. I was not alone out here in the rain—I was surrounded by other people who were also stuck in the rain. And there was nothing wrong with any of them, just as there was nothing wrong with me. I suddenly was looking around, noticing everyone, some on the sidewalk with me getting soaked, some in their cars (lucky!), one person walking their dog, another with their children. I could look away from me and the fears I had and out at these beautiful people all around me. Here we were together in the rain just doing the best we could. Some of us are caught in the rain because rain is a part of life. And I felt so connected to those people in that moment. I didn't care if they were judging me, and I couldn't really imagine that they were—because I wasn't judging myself. What mattered was that we were all alive together.

Meeting Antonio

After I had my daughter, Io, I struggled for months and months to find the balance between caring for her, caring for the other people in my life, and caring for myself. For the first many months of her life, balance for me meant complete focus on Io and absolutely nothing for myself or others. This is pretty standard new-parent behavior—that doesn't make it right or good, but it's standard. I told myself that I was caring for myself by caring for Io because I wanted nothing more fiercely than for her to thrive. Looking back, I realize I had serious parent guilt. I thought that if there was any moment when I wasn't focusing on her, I was letting her down. I was putting so much pressure on myself and building up a lot of resentment that ended up being released into my other relationships. My mental state slowly improved as I began to come out of the fog of exhaustion and intensity of early parenthood. I started to notice what I needed: more help, more time to myself, and more time with friends to reconnect to who I was without Io.

One day my husband, Dan, asked me to describe my perfect day, no limits. I surprised myself by describing a day with a personal butler. Someone who knew just what I liked and lived for nothing more than to make me happy. Someone who would follow me around and silently clean up after me, set everything out without being asked, make sure there was mint and lemon in a cold pitcher of water in the fridge, carry me to bed and tuck me in when I fell asleep reading on the couch. You know, just treat me like a queen—and, in an important point for my particular psyche, this butler would be happy to do it! There would be no judgment or annoyance, just desire to give me the space and opportunity to be my best self.

This dream of a perfect day might not seem significant, but it felt important to me. A butler was not my usual fantasy. It reached me in a way that a zillion new-parent articles couldn't. I finally noticed that I needed some serious care. Since long before Io was born, I had been in the habit of doing everything for myself because I didn't think I was worthy enough for anyone else to do it. But lately, I had stopped doing *anything* for myself; not only did I not believe I was worthy of other people's help, I also didn't feel worthy enough for my own help. But as Io's first birthday passed by, I began to realize, with the help of therapy, reading, reflection, and conversation with trusted friends, that I am definitely worthy of my own time. And so my butler appeared.

I decided to do an experiment: I would pretend to be my butler and do all the things I wished he would do for me. While the fantasy could never come precisely true—there is just no way I can carry myself to bed—I realized that there is so much of that caregiving that I can do for myself. *Yes, I am 100 percent about to tell you that playing make-believe helped me take better care of myself.* I'm whimsical, okay?

I wanted my butler to seem like a real(ish) person so I could fully connect to him. Along came Antonio. My Antonio is an older Italian gentleman with wavy salt-and-pepper hair and twinkly, smiling eyes who wears beautiful suits, sings to himself, and has a gentle, fatherly nature. And, of course, he is paid handsomely and feels valued and adored in return.

Antonio loves taking care of me. He is motivated by pure love, never judging my needs as too trite or silly to bother with—unlike what I often do to myself. By

Finding Your Own Antonio

If self-care is something you struggle with, you may need an Antonio, too. So who is your Antonio? Is she a young woman who reminds you of your favorite hairdresser? A huge fluffy teddy bear brought to life? A cute fairy? Mr. Rogers? Think about what feels comfortable for you. I know it might seem childish, but try not to judge yourself, and let your imagination free here. Once you have settled on the right character for your butler, I hope you'll play with the idea and use this persona to figure out what you could do to take care of yourself every day.

inhabiting this persona, I began to practice the art of self-distancing, a technique in which you step outside yourself and observe from a safe distance in order to see things more clearly. As Kristin Neff explains in her book *Self-Compassion*, when you focus on caring for yourself, it allows you distance from the pain you are experiencing. Instead of sitting paralyzed inside the pain, you spend time inhabiting the part of yourself capable of giving care, and that experience is deeply empowering and energizing.

From this safe distance, you see yourself as you truly are: a flawed and utterly lovable human being. As Antonio, I could love myself and find the energy to care for myself. I could care for myself as lovingly as I take care of my daughter and partner.

Antonio would gladly do all the chores I tended to avoid or felt annoyed or resentful about doing, like scrubbing the stovetop, washing and properly storing produce after I buy it, and, yes, putting mint and lemon in a big jar of water in the fridge. He always got my bills and other paperwork done quickly because he didn't want me to worry about expenses and piles of paper. Being Antonio was a transformative experience. And the exciting part was that I could be my own Antonio simply by not judging myself for having needs and not avoiding taking care of them.

Some of you are probably thinking, *Shouldn't her husband have done some of this?* Or *Couldn't they afford a housekeeper or ask friends to help?* And you're right; I didn't need to do it all myself. But I had been stuck in a pattern of not being able to voice my needs for so many years. Remarkably, being Antonio actually helped me to ask for help from others. Antonio would ask for anything on my behalf, even if it was difficult or embarrassing, because he thinks his strong, kind, brave boss deserves it! If she is happy and taken care of, the world is a better place.

We all need and deserve our own butlers, but being Antonio is not about taking on everything yourself. It is about creating the space in yourself to notice the self-care that you can take on, find the courage to ask for the help you need, and accept that some dirty dishes and undone tasks are a part of life.

The Dream of an Infinite, Magically Fresh, Fully Stocked Food Storage System

It is impossible to have on hand every ingredient I might ever like to cook or bake with. The space-time continuum won't allow it. Things would rot before I could eat them all, and my little Brooklyn kitchen would be overwhelmed. But here are the foods I would have available if such petty realities did not exist. These lists are, of course, a window into my own tastes and habits and background. Your dream pantry would look a little different. Nevertheless, thinking about what you love to eat and making a plan to keep it in stock can help you organize your next shopping trip and make meal planning a little more fun. You might imagine your dream pantry kitted out the way your Antonio character would build it for you.

CUPBOARD OR PANTRY

Baking
All-purpose flour
Alternative flours of choice
Baking powder
Baking soda
Chocolate chips
Coconut flakes
Condensed milk
Confectioners' sugar
Cornmeal
Cornstarch
Dates and other dried fruit
Evaporated milk
Graham crackers
Granulated sugar (see note, page 20)
Honey (see note)
Molasses (see note)
Nuts (almonds, peanuts, pistachios, cashews)
Oats
Pure vanilla extract
Seeds (sunflower, poppy, sesame)
Whole wheat flour

Oils and Vinegars
Apple cider vinegar
Coconut oil
Oyster sauce
Rice wine

Sesame oil
White vinegar
Wine vinegars

Dry Goods
Arborio rice
Boxed broth and stock
Boxed mac and cheese
Brown rice
Canned beans
Canned chickpeas
Canned chiles
Canned chipotles
Canned coconut milk
Canned diced fire-roasted tomatoes
Canned soup
Canned whole tomatoes
Cereal
Coffee
Crackers
Croutons
Dried beans
Dried noodles
Dried seaweed/nori
Granola (pages 52–56)
Lentils
Long-grain rice (I like basmati)
Potato chips
Tea
Tortilla chips

Dried Spices and Herbs

Everyday
Black peppercorns
Crushed red pepper flakes
Dried oregano
Fine sea salt
Ground chile powder
Ground smoked paprika
Ground turmeric
Whole and ground coriander
Whole and ground cumin

Sweet
Cinnamon sticks and ground cinnamon
Ground ginger
Whole and ground cardamom
Whole and ground cloves
Whole nutmeg (see note)

Not Essential but Awesome
Black cardamom
Fennel seeds
Lavender
Mustard seeds
Saffron
Sichuan peppercorns
Star anise
Various ground chiles (such as cayenne or ancho)
Whole allspice
Za'atar

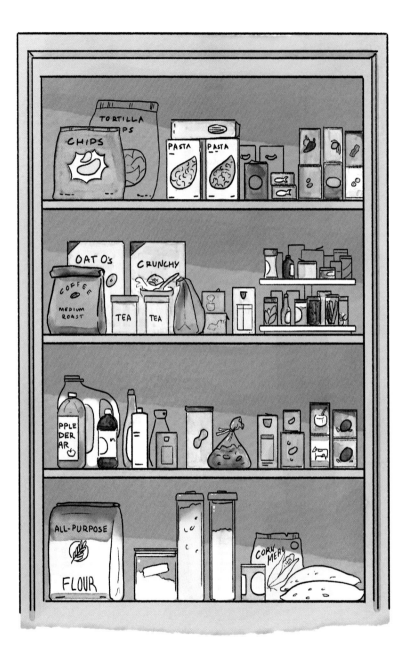

Honey: *I tend to prefer pourable, runny honey because it is more convenient for baking and drizzling. I like my honey dark and flavorful.*

Molasses: *I usually use "fancy" molasses because it is the best for most baked goods. Blackstrap molasses is very strong and has a kind of bitter taste that can be a little unpleasant if you are, say, using it to make chocolate chip cookies.*

Sugar: *I never buy brown sugar, even though I prefer it to granulated (white) sugar and use it all the time. But I don't like the bother of keeping it from going hard, so I just add molasses to granulated sugar in any recipe that calls for brown sugar. The ratio is 1 tablespoon molasses for every 1 cup granulated sugar for light brown sugar, and 2 tablespoons molasses per 1 cup granulated sugar for dark brown or demerara sugar. Molasses added freshly to sugar tends to impart a stronger, more caramelly flavor to the baked goods, and I prefer it!*

Nutmeg: *I massively prefer whole nutmeg over ground nutmeg. You can easily grate whole nutmeg with a Microplane, and the aroma is amazing! So much is lost when it is preground.*

FRIDGE

Hardy Fruits and Vegetables Drawer
Apples
Cabbage
Carrots
Leeks
Oranges
Summer squash

Tender Vegetables Drawer
Asparagus
Bell peppers
Broccoli
Cauliflower
Celery
Chiles
Cucumbers
Dark leafy greens
Eggplant
Green beans
Herb bundles (see note)
Lettuces
Mushrooms
Scallions
Snap peas

Meat/Cheese/Deli Drawer
Cheddar
Fresh mozzarella
Parmesan or romano
Ricotta or feta
Any other favorite cheeses
Salami
Smoked salmon
Smoked turkey
Tofu

Side Door
Beer
Chile paste
Hot sauces
Jams/jellies
Ketchup
Kimchi
Miso
Mustards
Pickles
Soy sauce or tamari
Sparkling water
Sparkling wine

Dairy and Eggs
Butter
Cream
Eggs
Milk
Nondairy milk
Yogurt

Main Fridge
Berries
Chicken
Fresh ravioli or fresh noodles
Homemade sauces and dressings
Hummus
Leftovers
Maple syrup
Salsa
Sliced mango
Sliced pineapple
Tortillas

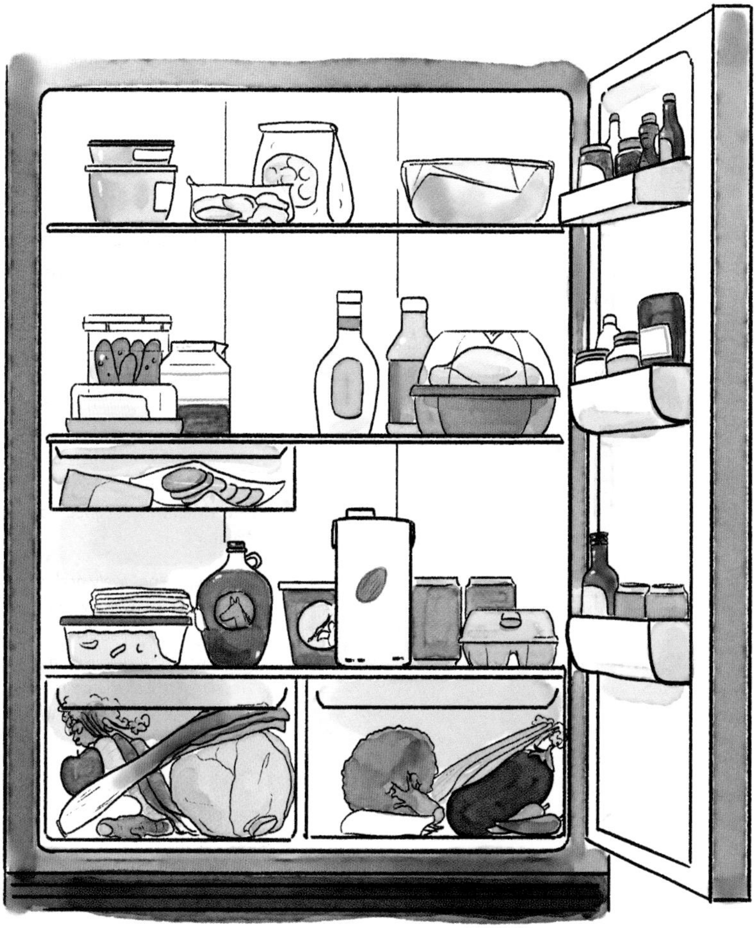

Herb Bundles: *When you buy fresh herbs, wash them, wrap them in moist paper towels or tea towels, and store them in the fridge to keep them fresh for as long as possible. One exception is mint, which doesn't keep long. I almost always use it the first day or two after I buy it, and if I don't, then the next day I just put the mint in a jug of drinking water for flavoring.*

FREEZER

Bacon
Bagels
Burger patties, premade
(see page 105)
Chopped spinach
Corn
Edamame
Ginger (see note)
Ground beef

Ground pork
Hot dogs
Ice cream
Packaged fruit
Peas
Popsicles
Presliced bread
Puff pastry

Ready-to-bake chocolate chip
cookie dough (page 200)
Ready-to-bake toffee cookie
dough (page 193)
Salmon (see note)
Sausages
Shrimp (see note)
Whitefish (see note)

Ginger: *Keeping whole ginger in the freezer is great because it lasts for ages and is much easier to grate while frozen. I only leave mine out on the counter if I want big chunks of ginger for making tea.*

Seafood: *Frozen fish is often the freshest you can get. In the vast majority of cases, the "fresh" fish at your supermarket or fish vendor was shipped frozen and then thawed. Once defrosted, fish should be eaten soon, and it shouldn't be frozen again, so this "fresh" fish is convenient if you are planning to cook and eat it on the same day that you buy it. But frozen fish can be kept in the freezer and thawed right when you are ready to eat it, so it is as fresh as possible. Truly fresh, straight-from-the-water, never-frozen fish is wonderful, but rare. I like to be in control of when I thaw fish, so I buy frozen.*

OUT ON THE COUNTER

Avocados
Bananas
Bread
Garlic
Lemons
Limes
Ripening fruit (kiwi, stone fruit,
    mangoes, and so on)
Tomatoes

IN A COOL, DARK PLACE

Onions
Potatoes
Shallots
Sweet potatoes
Winter squash

BY THE STOVE

Crushed red pepper flakes
Fine sea salt (see note)
Neutral cooking oil (see note)
Olive oil
Pepper

Fine sea salt: *The salt called for throughout the book is fine sea salt, which is significantly lower in sodium than other varieties, particularly kosher salts like Morton's.*

Neutral cooking oil: *These oils have a high smoke point, so you can cook with them over high heat, and they won't overpower a dish with their flavor. Avocado oil is not neutral, but generic vegetable oil is.*

Assembly Only

Cooking is great, but eating is essential. Sometimes you can't take the time to prepare food, and you need something quick to eat that will get you through the next meal or bedtime or these last emails or this conversation. Or maybe you're in the middle of a pandemic (as I have been, while creating this book) and you have been making sourdough daily for three months and you just need a break from the kitchen. Times like these call for a good reserve of no-cooking-required sweet and savory snacks that don't always come out of a bag. If prepared snacks serve you and your body well, that's great, but I prefer a wider variety of nourishment. Some of the items below can be eaten just as they are; others you can prep (quickly and easily) ahead of time so you'll have them on hand when you need them. Take what works for you and leave the rest.

Zero to Low Effort

What satisfies your cravings but takes little effort? Here are some assembly-only foods that I rely on. They require very little to no cooking, but are satisfying enough to nourish me in a moment of need.

Cheese

Chocolate

Dates (plain or stuffed; see page 26)

Dips and spreads (hummus, salsa, bean dip, tzatziki, and so on)

Fresh fruit (apples, grapes, oranges, and so on)

Nuts (plain or seasoned)

Pickles, olives, or pickled vegetables

Popcorn (I keep kernels and microwavable popcorn on hand. Season with pepper and parmesan, maple syrup and cardamom, or honey and ginger.)

Tortilla chips and crackers (pair with dips and spreads for maximum effect)

Yogurt (see Morning Stretch Yogurt Bowls, page 50, for some serving suggestions)

Thoughtful but Still Low-Stress

If you have a little more time and feel inspired, a bit of creativity can make snack- or mealtime feel extra special. These basic snack recipes are just a starting point for your imagination—make what feels good and eat it when you feel hungry, whether that's in between meals, after school with kids, or for dinner.

Oranges

Break into segments, slice, or halve the oranges, then top with:

- Crumbled feta and herbs
- Ricotta and honey
- Dark chocolate drizzle
- Pistachios, olive oil, and salt

Honey Roasted Nuts

Coat raw whole nuts (almonds, cashews, peanuts, pecans, pistachios, or walnuts) with a light layer of honey and spices. My favorite combinations include:

- Honey, cocoa, cinnamon, and salt
- Honey, cinnamon, cayenne, and salt
- Honey, ground ginger, turmeric, and salt
- Honey, tahini, matcha powder, and salt
- Honey, coconut, cardamom, and salt (best paired with pistachios!); add the coconut in the last few minutes of cooking as it toasts more quickly

Roast the nuts at 350°F for 10 to 15 minutes, stirring or shaking them every 5 minutes, until they are evenly toasted. Sprinkle them with a bit more of the spices and salt just after they come out of the oven. Let cool, then store in an airtight container.

Hard-Boiled Eggs

Make a big batch of hard-boiled eggs to keep in the fridge. When you're ready for a quick snack, peel one, halve it, and serve:

- Sprinkled with salt
- Drizzled with sriracha or soy sauce
- Dipped in salad dressing
- Wrapped in a piece of smoked salmon
- Wrapped in nori
- Wrapped in lettuce with a pickle

Dates

Dates are sweet and full of energy, with a natural pocket for stuffing with flavor once you pull out the pit.

- Stuff with goat cheese
- Stuff with or dip in nut butter
- Stuff with a folded piece of salami
- Stuff with an olive

Snack Mixes

- Popcorn, peanuts, pretzels
- Small crackers, cereals, dried fruit
- Almonds, coconut flakes, dried cranberries
- Pretzels, dark chocolate chips, peanuts
- Pumpkin seeds, raisins, banana chips

Going the Extra Mile

The idea of meal prep for the week can be overwhelming, and not everyone has hours to commit to cooking the week's food on Sunday. However, if you are motivated to do some of the work in advance, these ideas (again, they're meant to kickstart your creative thinking) might add some oomph to your daily routine.

Roasted Potatoes

Or sweet potatoes! They're perfect for a side dish, in salad, or with other leftovers throughout the week. (And this would work for almost any roasted vegetable.)

Fruit Bowl

Arrange grapes, berries, or any ready-to-eat fruit in a nice bowl and set it on your counter (or in the fridge, depending on the temperature and your fruit fly situation).

Bacon

Cook a whole package of bacon. Store the cooked bacon wrapped in a paper towel in the meat drawer of your fridge or freeze it in a storage bag. Throughout the week, you can use it to make a breakfast sandwich or crumble it onto a salad without having to splatter your kitchen with grease.

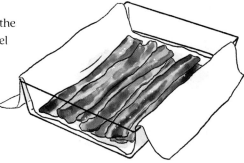

Luxury Water

Spa water, fancy water, whatever you want to call it . . . It's also known as: What to add to a pitcher of water to make you feel special. (Bonus: You may drink more water.)

- Apple slices
- Berries
- Cinnamon stick
- Citrus (lemon, lime, orange, grapefruit) wedges or slices
- Cucumber slices
- Edible flowers
- Fruit juice frozen into ice cubes
- Grapes, sliced in half
- Mint sprigs
- Pineapple slices
- Rosemary
- Thyme
- Used tea bag (for a super light tea flavor)

Grocery Shopping as Ritual

I gather my bags. I walk a short distance while looking around, experiencing the weather and life around me. If I am stuck in some pattern of thinking, the walk will jolt me back to the present moment and remind me that everything is okay. I arrive at the grocery store. When I get there, I have a list and a general plan. I allow myself to be inspired. Looking at fresh food and seeing what people are interested in or what looks good. Watching the seasons change and the holidays make their mark on the store's landscape. Noticing that sometimes I want to buy flowers, sometimes pastries, chips, sausages, watermelon. And how those impulses and cravings relate to how I'm feeling or the vibe or the season. It makes me feel like I'm in sync with my humanness.

While I have just described my ideal shopping ritual, there is simultaneously another side to the grocery shopping experience. It's not always fun. It frequently feels like a chore. It seems to take up a lot of time, and I resent it. When I am particularly busy, fitting in the grocery shopping is difficult, and every slow walker is an obstacle designed to infuriate. Or it's as silly and simple as just not wanting to do it or not wanting to have to interact with people. I'll procrastinate getting going and then feel guilty, and that puts me in a bad mood, and suddenly I am mad at myself and nothing is fun. And this is me with all my privilege—for anyone with more obstacles to grocery shopping, the journey to a good experience is longer and harder.

I tend to go grocery shopping every two or three days—except during a pandemic, when I follow public health advice to go as infrequently as possible. I love how the grocery store forces you to negotiate space with others. How you can see people having a bad day, dealing with screaming kids or a tense conversation on the phone, or just hurrying to get something done on their lunch hour. I love how some people are focused on working through their list, while others just wander through the store. I love how some people look lost and uncertain, while others pace the aisles with an almost fierce determination. I love the careful, awkward dance of deciding which line to wait in and making small talk while you pay. It's all so banal and at the same time so rich with emotion and drama and all the beauty of being human.

Grocery shopping is an important grounding experience for me. It has been since I lived away from my family. It feels grown up. It feels productive. It brings a kind of peace because it is necessary, yet there can also be an indulgence to it.

I usually plan to give myself one treat, like a pastry or chocolate milk or potato chips. But by the time I am nearly finished, I often realize that I don't actually need the treat. That makes it special. I give myself a treat when I need it, not just because that is what I do. It feels like freedom, and I'm grateful for the privilege to enjoy these simple pleasures. Then I walk home with my heavy bags, put the groceries away, and get excited about all the food I am going to make.

I find that it's even easier to make shopping at a farmers market feel like a ritual. It's less frequent, and it's outside. Compared to the supermarket, it is less mission driven. I don't have an exact list, just a sense of what I need in broad categories, like fruit and eggs. At the supermarket, it's easy to fall into the mindset of wanting to get in and get out with our stuff as quickly as possible, so it sets us up to see other people as obstacles rather than a part of the experience. But at the farmers market, we are usually aware that it is a leisurely shopping experience and the amblers and artisans are part of what we are there for. So, we can give ourselves permission to have a shared human experience. And we experience it not at the level of our conscious brains, but in our nervous systems. Our hearts know that we are sustained by food, and we are all in this surviving, living, thriving game together. This sensory experience reminds us of our shared humanity, which is so healing and connecting. It's not a day to "get yours" and survive at the expense of someone else.

Grocery shopping is an important grounding experience for me. It has been since I lived away from my family. It feels grown up. It feels productive. It brings a kind of peace because it is necessary, yet there can also be an indulgence to it.

Procuring food, let alone making it and eating it, is an essential part of our lives. Like every task we have to do, it can be a delight or an obligation depending on how we feel. If we can set ourselves up to enjoy it at least some of the time, that is good for us and good for everyone we touch.

Good Enough Mornings

On Waking Up Sad

I had hoped to write a different essay than this one. I thought that, after years of personal struggle, this book would be the push I needed to solve the morning problem once and for all. This essay would be a victory lap. It might begin with a sentence like "Mornings used to be so hard for me until I learned the power of positive thinking and egg eating!" But no. There has been no such change or revelation. Breakfast has remained my least favorite meal. The food is great; it's the timing that stinks.

Our culture is saturated with the image of the superior morning person. These "good" people wake up early, bright and chipper. They are successful and industrious, get things done, and are living in the light, metaphorically and literally. Conversely, people who stay up late are bad. Lazy and cowardly and undisciplined— and best kept in the dark. From my teenage years onward, I waited to turn into a morning person. "Please, sir, I'm ever so good, pick me to be a morning person! I'll make the most of it, I will!" But I was never blessed with this particular privilege. I got jobs that required early rising and had a baby, so I do get up earlier and go to bed earlier than I would by nature, but it's a matter of necessity. I am still a filthy night-dweller at heart.

And yes, of course, night people are not monsters. Of course. I wish our culture made more space for those with different sleep patterns, but there are far more pressing injustices, and with a little insight, we can shed the nasty stories about ourselves. My sleep preferences are not tied to my fitness as a parent, my productivity, or my value as a friend. I know that if I start getting up at 5 a.m. to go to the gym before work, I will not magically become less anxious and start my own successful business.

In the morning, I am my saddest and smallest self. I don't want sleep to be over. I don't feel ready. I don't feel powerful and strong. Lying there in bed, I feel vulnerable, like I will never get enough rest to feel whole. Next I am hit with a wave of disappointment, because I want so badly to be the kind of person who wakes up and gets moving and is excited to take on her day. I have so much to live for and so much to give; how dare I lie here feeling sorry for myself? I feel the immediate weight of responsibilities and obligations. It feels impossible that someone as small and weak as me could possibly accomplish my many goals. Getting out of bed is the first step in the march toward failure.

I get out of bed with guilt weighing me down. I should be with my daughter. I should make breakfast. I should want to make breakfast. I should be grateful for what I have. I should be excited for the day of work, for the opportunity to do the work I love. Or the opportunity to spend the weekend with my family. But instead, I mostly feel tired.

> **Getting out of bed is the first step in the march toward failure.**

There is no morning ritual that will make the sadness go away. It's there before I open my eyes, from the moment when my physical senses break into my dreams and I am wrenched from that world into the disappointment of my waking life, where everything seems ambivalent and the love and connection I long for exist on the other side of risks I'm not sure will pay off.

What I have come to realize is that this is okay. It's okay to be sad. It's okay to be tired. It's okay not to be a morning person. It is not a problem to be solved. And that acceptance helps, because the rest—all that guilt and worry and longing to be different—only makes the situation much worse. I'm trying to let go of that shiny idea that I should be feeling great in the morning and instead welcome the sadness, which of course won't actually hurt me and is only a temporary state.

There is nothing wrong with being sad. Sometimes the reality that we can't do everything we dream of, that we can't connect with everyone, that we can't solve the world's injustices—that is sad. And the sad reality of those things tends to come to me in the morning. Whenever it comes for you, it's okay to feel it. To process the information.

So I don't know how not to wake up sad. It's not a choice. But I can definitely choose to be kinder to myself and not shame myself for feeling sadness, or for how that feeling might slow me down. Going out into the world is hard and scary, and hard, scary things need love and tenderness. I start by putting one foot on the floor, eating something, hugging someone, or petting some creature. Those things start to move the fog a little. I try my best not to let my mind run away with all the things I "should" do and simply care for myself first, noticing that I am hurting and tending to it gently. In the doing and caring, I can move forward through this wave of feeling and find the calm blue ocean beyond.

Gratitude Is an Experience, Not a Performance

Prayer before a meal was a practice I grew up with. Over time, as with so many everyday rituals, I lost the connection—if I ever had one—to its meaning. It felt like an obligation. I knew that taking a moment to be thankful could be a nourishing practice, but the premeal prayer just made me feel fake. And years later, despite reading and hearing about the benefits of gratitude practices, I just couldn't get into one. It reminded me of all the many times I'd been lectured about gratitude as a child.

In my experiences growing up, the concept of gratitude mostly came in the form of the phrase "you should be grateful." Adults use this phrase as a weapon to cut away children's emotions that they find inconvenient. But gratitude is not that moment around the Thanksgiving table when it's your turn to speak and everyone is looking at you, but you don't want to talk in front of your mean, drunk uncle, and you still feel like crying because your brother told you that you look ugly in your new shirt, and you don't want to say the wrong thing and be chastised. That's not being ungrateful, that is being scared.

Growing up, I was not a big fan of school. I did okay, and I wasn't bullied especially hard, but I was scared a lot of the time. So scared that I would often throw up in the mornings. If anyone had asked me what was going on and genuinely wanted to know, I would have said I was terrified. I was scared of the kids and the teachers, of the pressure and expectations and evaluations. Afraid I would do or say something that would be pointed out and ridiculed or punished. These are good reasons to feel reluctant to go to school, and you would think that they would invite deep compassion. Yet the message I got again and again was to hide the fear because it was ingratitude. But I wasn't ungrateful for school. I was scared.

For me, gratitude—or its opposite, ingratitude—became bound up with the shame of being afraid. The shame of a feeling I wasn't supposed to have. I felt alone and afraid and unable to show it to anyone because, instead, I had to perform my gratitude, or else I would be rejected. So it makes sense that I was resistant to gratitude practices even in other, more healthy, grown-up forms. Sometimes, when you're told what you should feel rather than having your real feelings acknowledged, your feelings get a little tangled up. When I was young and deeply afraid and needed to be seen and understood, I had been told that I should be feeling gratitude instead. As an adult, I had to notice that I misunderstood gratitude. I had to recategorize it—from the feeling of being alone in my fear or embarrassment, to the feeling of being connected to all the good in my life.

I wish I could go back in time and tell that little girl that it's okay to be scared. That you can be scared and grateful at the same time. And that it's okay if you don't feel grateful right now! We can get through this together and feel the gratitude later, on the other side of some deep breaths and some time.

Once I realized that gratitude was a good feeling, I was better able to turn toward it. Gratitude, I learned, is that connected feeling of "Wow, I am so lucky." So, so, so lucky to be here on this planet, alive and breathing, with the chance to love and connect and feel pleasure. Sometimes it's "Man, my bed is just so comfortable" and other days it's "My friends are so strong and make me feel so loved" or "The little bags under my daughter's eyes make me want to kiss them." That gratitude is for me. It's not here to be performed so others will accept me. It's for me to feel happy!

Reframing Gratitude

Resting has always felt uncomfortable to me. My personality has always led me toward being a perpetual advocate. When I see injustice, I feel compelled to act. This drive has created an interesting and meaningful career, but doesn't always serve me well in my personal life and in the resting state of my own mind. What feels like advocacy to me—critiquing, correcting, and perfecting my parenting, my relationships, my attitude—rounds the corner into perfectionism. And perfectionism is poison. It can trick me into thinking everything is awful when there is so much that is good.

Focusing on the imperfections steals the joy from all the rest. The small problems will always be there. They are not important. And most of the time it's not in our power to change them. I don't mean the conscious areas of powerlessness, like how we can't make our friend stop drinking or cure cancer or ensure that every child has a loving home. I mean foundational areas of powerlessness, like how we didn't choose to be born into our body or our family or our country. There is so much in our lives that we have no control over. We certainly do not choose the traumatic experiences that shape us and change our brain. For some people, a social interaction is as hard as running a marathon. That is not a choice! It's a situation you find yourself in. And if we can choose to be grateful in our reality, with all its baggage, then we are choosing to make the most of our time on this planet.

It's a delicate balance. Being grateful is a choice, and it can be a hard choice, because the things to be angry or upset or worried about can seem very large indeed—but being grateful doesn't mean you forget them or ignore them. Gratitude simply helps you have a fuller picture of your reality. Bad experiences can have an outsize impact, but thinking about the good things in your life can interrupt those painful thoughts, as if your best friend just danced into the room with great news for you. It's like a hug from the inside out. You can't help but smile. And it's not a performance, it's genuine! It seems to me that thinking about what we are grateful for is the closest thing we have to being able to feel happy whenever we want. It is a feeling of love for your life, for others, and for what you have, and leaning into that feeling is emotionally gratifying, touching, and profound.

A Gratitude Practice

Sit down with a snack or meal in front of you.

Relax your neck, shoulders, and jaw.

Take a deep breath into your belly and then exhale.

Look at the food in front of you.

Think about the ingredients, and see which stands out.

What is its history? How did it get here?

Think about the land where it was grown or raised.

All the people who worked to bring it to you—those who tended it and picked it and shipped it.

The work that you and perhaps other members of your family did to pay for it.

The work you did to prepare it.

Try to feel a connection to all of those people taking care of you.

The love of strangers fills this bowl in front of you.

We are never really alone. We're in this together.

Designing Your Everyday Smoothie

This feature is inspired by Jamie Stelter, an organization goddess whom I greatly admire. Jamie is an early-morning traffic reporter in New York who has a fairly punishing schedule that requires her to be awake and alert when most of us are not. She manages this by eating hearty, healthy meals that keep her going—and since it's so early when she eats her first meals, she can rely only on herself to prepare them. She has shared her smoothie practice and her various routines many times on social media. She is grounded in reality, and she loves and takes great care of herself so she can thrive in her unusual circumstances.

Define the practice, and take what works for you. Have a go-to smoothie that you can consume every weekday morning (or every morning, for that matter). You buy the ingredients for at least a week's worth of the smoothie, prepare them ahead of time, stash the mixture in bags or jars in the fridge or freezer, and simply pull one out in the morning to blend and go.

Learn the basic ratio. For a sweet-tasting green smoothie, I fill my blender one-third full with greens. I top that off with chopped, frozen, sweet yellow or orange fruit, like banana, orange, pineapple, and mango. Apple is good, too. Then I add just enough juice, milk, or water that I can blend the mixture; usually that means adding enough liquid to rise up to about three-quarters of the height of the fruit. If the smoothie is too thick to blend thoroughly, I add more liquid. If I'm going to drink the smoothie later on in the day, I'll make it a little extra thick, knowing that it will thaw and loosen up a bit over time.

Smoothie Basics

Banana. For sweetness and bulk.

Pear, nectarine, peach, pineapple, and/or mango. Adds sweetness and juiciness.

Berries. Strawberries add sweetness and bulk, but raspberries, blueberries, and blackberries also add tartness. They can be used fresh or frozen.

Lemon, lime, orange, and/or ginger. To cut the sweetness and brighten the flavor.

Almond butter, peanut butter, or tahini. For protein and bulk.

Yogurt or coconut milk. For protein and bulk.

Milk, juice, or water. For liquid!

Ice. Optional; only if you have a high-powered blender. For temperature if you're using fresh ingredients.

Spinach and/or kale. For earthiness and vitamins. (Other varieties of greens are a bit weird in smoothies!)

Honey. You usually won't need extra sweetener, but sometimes it's nice.

Pure vanilla extract. Vanilla lifts the flavor profile and makes a smoothie feel special. It's especially nice if you are doing a simple combo; in a more complex smoothie, it can get lost.

Creamy Hands-Off Scrambled Eggs

TL;DR: *Cook whisked eggs over lowest heat, mainly leaving them alone for 20 to 30 minutes. Add cheddar, scallions, or leftovers to serve.*

Serves 2

1 tablespoon butter

4 large eggs

½ teaspoon fine sea salt

¼ cup shredded sharp white cheddar cheese (optional)

2 scallions, finely chopped (optional)

Up to 1 cup of any leftover vegetables, cooked meat, or a combination (optional)

Freshly cracked black pepper

Buttered toast, for serving (optional)

To me, these are the best of all egg worlds. I used to think scrambled eggs were awful since I'd always had them in the tough, lumpy form that comes from overcooking. But these eggs have the creaminess of a French omelet without the stress and perfectionism required. They seem almost dangerously rich even when you don't add cheese. And you barely have to do anything and can blearily prepare toast and coffee while your eggs cook slowly. The final result is the fluffiest and smallest-curded mountain of creamy, salty egg deliciousness. It will make you feel like some kind of magician. When I serve these, people always assume I have added cream or so much cheese or *something*. It is the magic of that low heat and breaking up the egg into the smallest curds possible so it retains its natural richness.

1. Melt the butter in a small pan over the lowest heat possible.

2. While the butter melts, crack the eggs into a bowl, add the salt, and whisk with a fork briefly just to break up the yolks—don't worry about aerating them.

3. Pour the eggs into the pan with the melted butter and let them sit on that super low setting, stirring occasionally to lift up the slowly cooking eggs from the bottom and break up the curds, until they're all cooked, 20 to 30 minutes.

Note: I know, it's sooooo slow. I pull the pan from the heat when the eggs are still just a little loose and moist. Some might call them undercooked, but I call them perfectly creamy. Cook your eggs less or more according to your taste.

4. Toward the end of the cooking time, stir in the shredded cheddar, scallions, and leftover vegetables or meat, if using, just to warm them through and incorporate. Finish with a grind or three of fresh black pepper and serve immediately with toast, if desired.

Note: You can also scramble your eggs faster over higher heat (though only ever medium heat, at maximum); that just means you'll need to stand at the stove, stirring constantly to break up the curds as they form. Basically you want to never let any chunks of larger curds form, always breaking them up into the loosest, smallest bits possible to create a creamy mountain. But try it once with low heat so you understand the final look you're aiming for.

Salty Coconut Melon Refresher

TL;DR: *Drizzle cut melon with coconut cream, honey, salt, and vanilla.*

I know it's a good idea to drink water in the morning. I always feel better when I do. But my insatiable love for coffee means that I usually forget a tall glass of water. In the spirit of proper hydration, I started to serve myself watermelon first thing in the morning.

Melon—especially watermelon, but fresh cantaloupe and honeydew are wonderful also—for breakfast is straight up fantastic, but giving it the fruit salad treatment with coconut, honey, and a pinch of salt? This makes even a disappointing, underripe watermelon worth shoveling into your gob at 7 a.m. It's best made fresh; left overnight, the juices seep from the melon and combine with the dressing to create a kind of melon cereal milk. It's a bit weird, but I've slurped it down a few times. This dish also makes a truly incredible part of a spread when you have guests over on a lazy afternoon.

1. Cut the melon as you prefer, but I usually cube it. If you are pressed for time or lack motivation, skip to Step 2 and just dip your slices in the coconut dressing as you cut them.

2. Combine the coconut cream, honey, salt, and vanilla in a large bowl. Add the melon and toss it all together until the melon is evenly coated. Voilà!

3. Serve immediately, with a wedge of lime and a drizzle of extra coconut cream, if desired, or refrigerate overnight and embrace the cereal milk—watermelon juice lifestyle.

Serves 4 as a bowl or 2 as a smoothie

- 2 pounds melon, such as watermelon, cantaloupe, or honeydew
- 2 tablespoons coconut cream or ¼ cup coconut milk, plus more for drizzling
- 2 teaspoons honey
- ½ teaspoon fine sea salt
- 1 teaspoon pure vanilla extract
- Lime wedge, for serving (optional)

SMOOTHIE VARIATION

Cut the melon and blend it, then add the coconut cream, honey, salt, and vanilla. Blitz for a minute or so to get the smoothie nice and frothy and fully incorporate the honey, then taste and adjust to your preference. If your watermelon is at room temperature, consider chilling the smoothie for 10 minutes before drinking it.

Zucchini, Pistachio, and Lemon Muffins

TL;DR: Mix wet ingredients and dry ingredients, then combine them. Bake in muffin pan at 350°F for 20 to 25 minutes.

I wasn't sure I was going to put these muffins in the book until I served one to my two-year-old and she shimmied her shoulders and said "So yummy!" and "So good!" over and over again. I mean, it's the law now. Everyone has to have these. Zucchini adds texture and moisture, and these muffins have an incredibly floral, bright, sweet aroma and flavor. My senses always feel dull and far away in the morning, and these muffins smell and taste like stepping into a quiet garden, with the gentle breeze on your skin bringing a light scent. They gently and lovingly awaken your senses to the undeniable truth: They are so yummy.

1. Preheat the oven to 350°F. Line a standard 12-cup muffin pan with silicone or paper liners.

Note: I highly recommend investing in silicone molds if you bake muffins or cupcakes often. They are reusable so you cut down on waste.

2. Place the zucchini, ground pistachios, sugar, lemon zest, egg, and yogurt in a large bowl and mix well.

3. Place the flour, baking powder, baking soda, and salt in a medium bowl and whisk to combine.

4. Sprinkle the flour mixture over the zucchini mixture and gently mix until the flour is just incorporated. Don't overmix, or the muffins won't be as tender.

5. Fill each muffin cup about three-quarters of the way full with batter. Bake until a knife inserted into the center comes out clean, 20 to 25 minutes. Let the muffins cool to room temperature before enjoying. Store them in a sealed container at room temperature for up to 4 days.

Makes 12 muffins

1 cup grated zucchini

½ cup ground pistachios (see note)

½ cup sugar

Zest of 1 lemon

1 large egg

½ cup plain yogurt

1 cup all-purpose flour

1 teaspoon baking powder

1 teaspoon baking soda

½ teaspoon fine sea salt

Note: Take a heaping half-cup of shelled pistachios and grind them in your food processor, adding more until you get a half-cup ground. I like them to be crumbly but not powder-fine.

Delicate Dill and Cheddar Omelet

TL;DR: *Whisk eggs with salt and dill, pour them into pan, and swirl them around. Sprinkle cheddar into middle. Roll and serve.*

Serves 1

2 large eggs

⅛ teaspoon fine sea salt

1 tablespoon chopped fresh dill, plus extra for garnish, if desired

2 teaspoons butter

¼ cup shredded white cheddar cheese (see note)

Buttered toast, for serving (optional)

FEELING ADVENTUROUS?

I sometimes substitute Boursin or cream cheese for the cheddar. It ups the creaminess inside the omelet if that is something you enjoy.

Falling in love is a lot of fun. When I look back on it, it has a kind of dreamy quality—the edges of my memories are both blurry and bright, like the light on a perfect autumn day. In my early years of adulthood, I fell in love with cooking. I remember walking back home from the farmers market, anticipating making this omelet, satchel full of fresh eggs, dill, seasonal vegetables, and usually some fresh carrot juice for my Saturday morning hangover. The world felt warm and inviting. I made this almost weekly for my now-husband and myself, so there is also that kind of falling-in-love memory mixed in here. Life has changed a lot since then, but when I want to reconnect with that warm feeling and those simple times, I make this omelet, and the particular flavor of dill sends me back, like a hug from my twenty-year-old self.

1. Crack the eggs into a small bowl, add the salt and dill, and whisk with a fork just long enough to break up the yolks, maybe 5 seconds.

2. Heat a medium nonstick pan (I like cast iron best) over low heat. Add the butter, let it melt, and swirl it around the pan to coat.

3. Working quickly, pour the eggs into the pan and swirl them around or use a spatula to move them around until they cover the pan. Once the pan is coated, sprinkle the cheese in a line along the center of the eggs. By now the eggs should be looking a little dry in some areas and mostly cooked through. I like a little bit of gooeyness in some places. The cooking time should last 30 seconds to 1 minute. It's fast if your pan is warmed fully!

4. Once the eggs are cooked to a slightly dry consistency, but with just a wee bit of runniness, turn off the heat and roll up the eggs like a rug with a gooey cheese center. The omelet might be a little brown in places. That's okay. Transfer the omelet to a plate, sprinkle with more dill or gently lay it over buttered toast, if you like, and serve.

Breakfast Apple and Orange Crisp

TL;DR: *Layer apple slices and crisp ingredients. Bake at 375°F for 35 to 40 minutes.*

Serves 6 to 8

Butter, for greasing the dish

4 large apples (your favorite variety)

1 large orange

1 tablespoon all-purpose flour

3 tablespoons packed brown sugar

½ teaspoon fine sea salt

1 teaspoon pure vanilla extract

TOPPING

1 cup old-fashioned rolled oats

½ cup all-purpose flour

¼ cup packed brown sugar

½ teaspoon freshly grated nutmeg (optional)

1 teaspoon ground cinnamon (optional)

½ teaspoon fine sea salt

½ cup (1 stick) unsalted butter

I'm really into the whole dessert-for-breakfast thing, can you tell? This crisp might seem decadent and wild, but actually it's a pretty reasonable amount of sugar per serving, and even the butter comes out to not that much more than you might have on toast. It's really okay. It's a good breakfast. This comes together quickly and easily but does require a little baking time, so it's nice to prepare it the night before. It's delicious served at any temperature—cold, room temperature, warmed in the microwave, or crisped up in a 375°F oven.

1. Preheat the oven to 375°F. Butter a 13 x 9-inch baking dish.

2. Cut the apples in half and remove the stems and cores. Slice the apples into thin pieces.

Note: There's no need to peel the apples unless that's your preference. I find I get between 24 to 32 slices per apple, but go as chunky or as thin as you like.

3. Place the apples in the buttered baking dish. Use a Microplane or small grater to zest the orange and sprinkle it on top. Juice the orange directly over the apples (use a sieve if your orange has seeds). Add the flour, brown sugar, salt, and vanilla. Using your hands, toss the apples, coating them evenly.

4. Make the topping: Combine the oats, flour, brown sugar, nutmeg and cinnamon (if using), and salt in a medium bowl. Stir the topping a few times with a wooden spoon or your fingers, just enough to roughly disperse everything. Cut up the butter into tablespoon-size (or smaller) pieces and add them to the bowl. Use your hands to roughly squish the butter with the dry ingredients until you have a crumbly, relatively even mixture. Sprinkle the oat mixture all over the top of the apples.

5. Bake until the apples are cooked and bubbly and the topping is browned, 35 to 40 minutes. Serve immediately, or cover and store in the fridge for up to a week.

While this crisp is baking, your house will smell like the platonic ideal of autumn.

Morning Stretch Yogurt Bowls

Just as you need to gently move your body to transition it from sleep into wakefulness, a little low-stakes creativity in the morning can help you reconnect with yourself. Think of pulling together this breakfast bowl as your morning mental stretch. Simply grab some plain yogurt and take a look around at what flavors you might try this morning. Here are some suggestions, based on leftovers from other recipes or combinations I particularly enjoy. Remember, if an experiment is not to your taste, that's okay! Innovation requires flops, and after all, it's just a bowl of yogurt and you can try again tomorrow. Rather than "Ugh, what a gross mistake," try telling yourself, "I admire your original thinking, and we can learn from this."

Mango with cardamom syrup: Combine ½ cup sugar and ½ cup water in a small pot with 6 crushed cardamom pods or 1 teaspoon ground cardamom. Simmer and stir until the sugar dissolves and the mixture thickens, about 5 minutes. If you used cardamom pods, strain the syrup. It makes about ½ cup and keeps well in the fridge—drizzle a little on top of chopped mango and yogurt, to taste.

Jalapeño and honey: Adding hot peppers to your morning routine might sound weird, but spice and sweet are a classic combo, and combined with the cooling yogurt? It's like an alarm clock for your mouth. Simply slice a few rings of fresh jalapeño, throw them into your yogurt, and drizzle honey over the top.

Triple Citrus Custard Cream and Lemon Tart Granola: One of my favorite ways to eat the Triple Citrus Custard Cream (page 242) is swirled into yogurt with a hefty sprinkling of Lemon Tart Granola (page 52) on top.

Tahini, date, and banana: Swirl a heaping spoonful of tahini into the yogurt, then top with sliced banana and a few finely chopped dates. A heavenly combination.

Key lime pie: Swirl a few spoonfuls of Lime Tart Spritzer syrup (page 135) into the yogurt, then top with a sprinkle of lime zest and some crumbled graham crackers for crunch.

Tomato, cucumber, and hummus: Add chopped cucumber and tomato and stir a swirl or two of hummus into the yogurt.

Apple with cider syrup: Chop an apple and cook it with ½ cup apple cider over low heat. Let the cider thicken until it coats the apple slices, then nestle the saucy apples on top of yogurt.

Strawberry, blueberry, and basil: Top the yogurt bowl with blueberries, strawberries, and little strands of chopped basil.

Tahini, date,
and banana

Triple Citrus
Custard Cream
and Lemon Tart
Granola

Key lime pie

Jalapeño
and honey

Strawberry,
blueberry, and basil

Mango with
cardamom syrup

Apple with
cider syrup

Tomato,
cucumber, and
hummus

You're Set for the Week Granola

TL;DR: *Mix oats and granola additions together.*
Bake at 300°F for 45 minutes, stirring a few times.

Why make granola for yourself? Made-ahead breakfast makes mornings tolerable, that's why. Did I mention I hate mornings? Here we have the convenience of cereal paired with the yumminess of pretty much anything else, prepared in advance. Transferring some of that late-night energy and industriousness to my morning self feels like a real kindness.

The granola will seem soft when you take it out of the oven, but once cooled, it becomes very crisp. If you like big granola clusters, let it cool completely on the sheet pan, then break it up. For less chunky granola, stir it when it comes out of the oven. All three of these granolas should last for at least a month, stored in an airtight container at room temperature, but I go through them quicker than that!

Lemon Tart Granola

Makes 6 cups

6 cups old-fashioned rolled oats

½ cup coconut oil, melted

½ cup honey

Zest of 4 lemons

Juice of 2 lemons

1 large egg

½ teaspoon ground cardamom (optional)

2 tablespoons poppyseeds (optional)

Some people drink lemon juice and water in the morning to wake up. I will never be that person because coffee is way too good. This lightly sweet and bright granola is inspired by those lemon-water morning people. If you like lemon with cardamom (I do!) or poppyseed (who doesn't?) and have them around, throw them in. Pair this granola with leftover Triple Citrus Custard Cream (page 242), yogurt, and blueberries for a truly remarkable experience.

1. Preheat the oven to 300°F. Line a sheet pan with parchment paper or a silicone baking mat.

2. Place the oats in a large mixing bowl. Measure the coconut oil and then the honey in the same measuring cup (see note, opposite) and add them to the oats. Add the lemon zest, lemon juice, egg, and ground cardamom and poppyseeds, if using, and mix with a spoon or your hands until the oats are evenly coated.

3. Spread the granola out on the prepared sheet pan. Cook until it's lightly browned all over, taking it out every 15 minutes to stir so that the edges don't get too dark, about 45 minutes total. (If you don't do the 15-minute stir, the edges will burn and the middle will be pale and soft instead of crisp!)

4. Let the granola cool. Store it in an airtight container at room temperature.

I have strategically asked you to measure out the coconut oil before the honey for a reason: When the grease from the coconut oil coats the measuring cup, it's much easier for the honey to slide out of that cup. If necessary, heat the coconut oil in a microwave in 30-second intervals until it's a liquid.

Baklava Granola

Makes 6 cups

4½ cups old-fashioned rolled oats

1½ cups chopped mixed nuts

6 dates, pitted and chopped (optional)

Zest of 1 navel orange (optional)

4 teaspoons ground cinnamon

1 teaspoon fine sea salt

½ cup coconut oil, melted

½ cup honey

It's got nuts, orange, cinnamon—what could be more breakfasty? But also, that's what's in baklava! You can have a bowl of nourishing granola that tastes like the most heavenly treat out there. It's really happening, everybody. The orange zest is optional, but highly recommended if you keep oranges around. Bonus: While it's baking, your house smells like baklava!

Choose whatever nuts you like or have around—salted or unsalted, raw or roasted (a double roasting never hurt anyone). Almonds are great. I love to add a few pistachios and cashews when I have them around. Chop the nuts roughly into whatever size you like; go as chunky or as fine as you prefer.

1. Preheat the oven to 300°F. Line a sheet pan with parchment paper or a silicone baking mat.

2. Place the oats, nuts, dates (if using), orange zest (if using), cinnamon, and salt in a large mixing bowl. Measure the coconut oil and then the honey in the same measuring cup (see note, page 53). Mix everything together until the granola is moist throughout.

3. Spread the granola out on the prepared sheet pan. Cook until it's lightly browned all over, taking it out every 15 minutes to stir so that the edges don't get too dark, about 45 minutes total. (If you don't do the 15-minute stir, the edges will burn and the middle will be pale and soft instead of crisp!)

4. Let the granola cool. Store it in an airtight container at room temperature.

Chocolate Macaroon Granola

Makes 6 cups

4½ cups old-fashioned rolled oats

1½ cups unsweetened coconut flakes

¼ cup unsweetened cocoa powder

½ teaspoon fine sea salt

½ cup coconut oil, melted

½ cup honey

FEELING ADVENTUROUS?

• Add 1 teaspoon ground cinnamon and ½ teaspoon freshly grated nutmeg in Step 2.

• Stir in 1 cup chocolate chips in Step 4, after the granola cools.

This is the granola that I lived on during my first few months with my daughter. I would make a huge batch and have it for breakfast and as a snack throughout the day. It's sweet and very much feels like a treat, but it still has much less sugar than most store-bought granolas and is much cheaper. You can add nuts or other grains, but make sure that you lessen the amount of oats or coconut so that all the dry ingredients add up to 6 cups.

1. Preheat the oven to 300°F. Line a sheet pan with parchment paper or a silicone baking mat.

2. Place the oats, coconut, cocoa powder, and salt in a large mixing bowl and stir to combine. Measure the coconut oil and then the honey in the same measuring cup (see note, page 53). Mix everything together until the oats and coconut are moist throughout and the cocoa powder is evenly distributed.

3. Spread the granola out on the prepared sheet pan. Cook until it's lightly browned all over, taking it out every 15 minutes to stir so that the edges don't get too dark, about 45 minutes total. (If you don't do the 15-minute stir, the edges will burn and the middle will be pale and soft instead of crisp!)

4. Let the granola cool. Store it in an airtight container at room temperature.

Good Enough
Midday

Sometimes Self-Care
Just Means Chores

Being a person is really hard. You are constantly confronted with what you want to do and the limited time and energy you have to do those things. You have to work to earn money to live; you have to work in your home and on your relationships and projects. You also need to rest and have fun or you grind yourself down and can't do any of those responsible things anymore. Being engaged as a person means constant work and constant growth. It is *exhausting.* I frequently feel overwhelmed by my responsibilities, and never more so than in recent years, when I was pregnant and during my daughter's first year of life.

During my pregnancy, I was hit with an extreme form of morning sickness that lasted throughout the nine months. Cooking and preparing food is my passion—it's how I relax, it's how I connect with myself, it's what I do when I want to feel competent, organized, and good at something. As it's become my career, cooking has become central to my identity. So I wasn't prepared for what it would feel like when my happy place became my disgusting and frightening place. Days were spent cycling between vomiting and simply enduring the gnawing discomfort of nausea. Food was utterly repulsive, but my body was building a human from scratch and needed sustenance, even though it was rejecting most forms of it. Feeding myself every day became extremely hard, painful, disheartening work.

My stomach was like my own personal volcano. It had to be carefully managed or it would explode. I couldn't drink water on an empty stomach or it would erupt, so each morning I forced myself to eat bread, crackers, a bagel—whatever inoffensive carbohydrate was at hand. I could then drink water safely. I had to maintain this careful balance between water and carbohydrates all day. Food was no longer pleasure or culture or human connection; it was volcano management.

The experience taught me what it must be like for people who truly find no joy in food. I have always wanted to welcome even the staunchest non-cooks and food agnostics into the kitchen and help them feel some sense of belonging there. But for the first time in my life, I was inhabiting the body of a non-cook—and understanding the experience viscerally rather than intellectually. I wondered if everything I stood for was wrong.

I felt lonely and ashamed, like a fraud. I felt like I had lost myself. My body had betrayed me and I didn't recognize it. I felt worthless because I couldn't do the one thing I believed I was truly good at. My memory of that time is a haze of simply surviving. But I am so grateful for the experience now because it made me realize

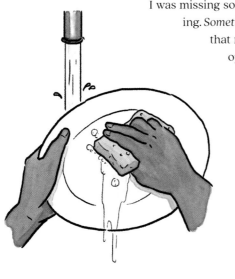

I was missing something in the way I talk about cooking. *Sometimes cooking is just hard work.* I realized that my philosophy—that every meal is an opportunity for pleasure—was great in theory, but in reality it was smothering me. It was too much pressure. If every meal is an opportunity for pleasure, then I was failing quite a bit of the time.

This lesson—that not *every* meal is precious—hit me even harder after I had my daughter, Io. Yes, I had my taste and desire for food back, hooray! But I had no time to think about it or prepare it like I'd used to. When I did cook, I was harried and resentful. I started cooking after Io went to sleep. Nothing involved or time consuming, but anything instead of takeout each night (though of course there was still plenty of takeout). I had to guard my time carefully, almost like I got time rations and I was learning how best to spend them. I was so exhausted that spending a time ration on making dinner sometimes felt like punishment. If it wasn't the best dinner, I would beat myself up for it and then beat myself up more when I realized that the dishes also had to be done.

Eventually, I learned to calm my inner perfectionist and just make something. The fact is that when I make something—even if it's some kind of Franken-bowl of leftovers—I don't regret not ordering pizza. I feel proud of myself for using up what I have, proud of my decisiveness, and generally proud that I can take care of myself. I have come to realize that, often, 90 percent of the goal of a meal is just to get fed; the last 10 percent is very nice to have but sooo not worth stressing over.

This attitude became essential during the COVID-19 pandemic that left all of us stuck inside our homes, hearing sirens and making sourdough if we were lucky, or losing jobs, people, and housing if we were not. Cooking became *it*. People loved and hated it, engaging with it in a way they may not have before or had not in years. It was overwhelming, and heartwarming. Cooking is an essential skill. But it amplifies the feelings we bring to it. Throughout the pandemic, people used cooking to calm themselves and cope with chaos. As a project to distract themselves. As a way to find pleasure. Their anxieties and insecurities were acted out through the food they were making and eating (or not eating). The lessons to be drawn from such a hard time are numerous, and I am so far from processing them all at the time of this writing that I couldn't bear to try. I *can* say this: Like all acts of caring, cooking sometimes flows so easily and feels so right, and other times it is only pure necessity, habit, or discipline that brings you to the cutting board.

Finding the time and energy to cook is still hard work, whether in my volcano body, as a parent, in a pandemic, or at any other time. There are a lot of times when pleasurable things can feel like hard work. Sometimes I wish I could pause time and take a break from all the caring that being alive requires. But we can't. And it's okay to feel any kind of way about that.

Food Is a Necessity

We might grow up with candy as a reward for good behavior or for doing a chore, and we might, consciously or unconsciously, reward our own children or friends with food. It's a completely normal and accepted part of relating to each other. But it's important to remember that food is not a reward. I am often guilty of denying myself food until I "get this one thing done." I was doing it just now, while writing this book, about to work straight through lunch when I remembered the truth: Food isn't something that you can earn or that you sometimes don't deserve. You deserve food because you are a human. You deserve to live. You deserve the life you want.

That is definitely what I believe. And yet. My habits say differently.

Self-care is a habit. And the habit of taking ourselves and our bodies for granted is built up over a lifetime. So it makes sense that when we give more of our attention to ourselves in an uncritical way, perhaps for the first time, we might notice some habits of thought that are pretty incongruent with what we think or how we might treat others. One of the patterns of thought I noticed early on, which has been very tricky to unlearn, is rewarding myself with food. I'm not even talking about the reward of a special treat like a pastry or fancy cocktail, but actually just *lunch*. I would feel hungry, notice I was hungry, and then, based on where I was in my workflow, decide whether or not I would tend to the hunger. If I hadn't been as productive as I wanted, I would automatically keep working instead of letting myself eat. But what do we know about hunger? It does not help our productivity! Hunger pangs have one purpose and one purpose only—to tell us to eat, please. To refuel so we can keep going. But at some point we receive the message that being able to put aside our physical needs to work harder or longer is impressive. "Successful people are successful because they don't let their petty physical needs stop them!" We conflate willpower (a term that I hate, anyway) with the ability to dismiss ourselves.

Denying yourself food when your stomach rumbles will not help you get your work done. It will rob you of your strength and guarantee a crash. It's practically the definition of self-defeating behavior.

For me, I think this habit comes from a childhood misunderstanding of what strength really is. I'd learned to define strength as some kind of superhuman ability to go without sleep, food, connection, and fun for as long as it takes to accomplish something. Sure, you can get things done this way. I have done it many times. But I have paid an enormous price. You may get it done, but you snapped at your kid every day this week. You may get it done, but you didn't notice that you missed your mom's birthday. You may get it done, but when you get it done with self-punishment, you are going to be miserable—and that comes at a cost to you and your relationships. It doesn't have to be that way. Motivation does not come only through fear of punishment, I promise.

> Like all acts of caring, cooking sometimes flows so easily and feels so right, and other times it is only pure necessity, habit, or discipline that brings you to the cutting board.

Shifting into motivating myself differently has taken time and tons of compassion. Self-punishment is an old habit and one that served me well for many years. I shifted through the process of becoming aware of what self-punishment costs me, and that meant feeling the pain of all that loss. It's desperately sad for me to think of all the ways in which I was unintentionally cruel to or dismissive or neglectful of myself. But because I feel sad about that, it also tells me that I *want* to act differently, and I know I can.

Since childhood, I have learned to focus on other people for motivation and for inspiration. I have looked to the needs of others and listened to what I was told to guide me in how I should spend my time. It might not have been satisfying, but at least it was safe. Of course, that left the critical and imaginative part of me stewing with frustration, so I hid her away. Now I'm working on my relationship with that part of myself, and we're still building trust. One of the best ways to build trust is to care for her. When we get hungry, we take a full stop and feed ourselves. It can be difficult to get quiet enough to hear what your body is really saying to you. A million times I have interpreted a growing feeling of discontent as something else and gone into full problem-solving mode before realizing I'm just hungry. Rather than fear of punishment or self-deprivation, I now motivate through deep connection with the life I want to have and the person I want to be. I want to take a creative risk and be brave because I want to be seen and to connect. I want to connect with others so I can keep healing and growing and support others in their own healing and growing. When I feel alone and afraid, I connect with that deep truth. And as long as I have eaten recently(!), I can find my courage.

How to Love Salad

It took me a long time to realize how much I loved salad. Our culture is not nice about it. Poor salad is almost always the least fun, least celebratory thing on the table. It's what you eat when you are "being good," "making the better choice," or "getting some balance." *Ugh.* Not to mention the fact that *The Simpsons* has burned "you don't win friends with salad!" into our brains.

If salad were a person, she'd be the boring cousin that your parents said you had to eat lunch with, and she'd drone on about how much better her old school was and casually insult your shoes. But really salad is just misunderstood. If you get to know her, you'll realize she's the best friend you've always wished for, who always has your back, tells the best stories, and compliments your look. You just never got to know her. Give her a chance!

Find your friendly salad. If you're still not convinced (and you want to get into salad—if you don't, then skip this whole thing), try the following exercise: What salad do you like? Chances are there is at least one kind that you will order and do enjoy. Caesar? Wedge? Anything slathered in ranch dressing? Eat that salad sometime soon, and think about what you like about it. Remember it. Try to hold on to that memory so that, at some future lunch, you remember that it's a great option that will bring you delight. This is your friendly salad. It's not judging you because you don't like it. It doesn't think it's better than you because it's soooo healthy. It's just your friend, who happens to be a salad.

Once you figure out your friendly salad, you can start venturing out a bit—add a new ingredient, maybe something you're unsure about, to your friendly salad. Give your friendly salad a makeover by switching up the greens or the dressing. As you eat more salad and enjoy it more often, your stubborn brain will start to realize that salad is just another type of meal option and not a punishment or a source of shame. It's just a big bowl of stuff you like to eat all mixed together!

Figure out your favorite greens mix. Be sure you like the taste well enough that you'll be happy when you get a bite of only the greens. Make sure you always have those greens on hand.

Use pretty bowls. A salad is almost always naturally beautiful because it's so colorful, and piling it into a bowl you love gives an added layer of aesthetic pleasure.

Dress your salad effectively—toss, toss, toss. There is nothing worse for me than dressing on the side. I'm never going be able to get dressing all over every leaf in this little bowl with my little fork. You need a big bowl and tongs! Honestly, vegetables are delicious, and dressing is seasoning. Season enough and salad will taste good, full stop.

Have one premade dressing ready to go. Whether it's store-bought or home-made, make it one that you love.

Building Blocks (of Your BFF)

These are the elements that make up a great salad. Consider each of these categories to find balance in your bowl.

CRUNCHY—the greens when they are nice and fresh, or croutons, bacon bits, crunched-up tortilla chips, crisp radish chunks, and so on

PROTEINY OR OTHERWISE HEARTY—meat, tofu, egg, or cheese

FATTY AND SALTY—oil, cheese, anchovies, nuts, or creamy dressing

ACIDIC OR BRIGHTENING—dressing (like a classic vinaigrette), citrus juice, fruit (like tart raspberries), or capers

How to Make Weekday Lunches More Intentional

- Make a workday meal plan and rotate through it. Be flexible with it. It's nice to have as a fallback even if you don't use it, because it reduces cognitive load.

- Do a lot of cooking on Sunday so you can put together lunches during the week.

- Bring lunch ingredients to your office (even if it's at home) and make it on-site.

- Find a lunch buddy—a coworker or a friend—to chat with for ten minutes or so to make sure you take a real break and connect. If it's in person, offer to bring lunch for them sometimes, and let them do the same for you.

- If you work in an office, try having a potluck once a week, assuming your coworkers are people you like being around. If you don't, try the lunch buddy idea above, or expand it to have a picnic with a couple of neighbors, nearby colleagues, or friends.

- Create a treat routine to look forward to, like a meal you have every Wednesday that you love.

- It's okay to buy lunch! Celebrate the break. It's not a defeat. You're storing up some energy for next time.

Choose Your Own Lunch-venture

Creating the right conditions for you to cook and take care of yourself and your family is so important. Of course, the reality is that you may never have the perfect setup, and most days the best-laid plans will blow up and you'll need to be flexible. That being said, you won't be successful if you don't even know what you need! For a long time, I thought that I just had to live with life as it is, and that I would simply have to adapt to the situation and space where I found myself. Once I started paying attention to myself and how I felt in different spaces—what gave me energy, what made me anxious, what made me feel calm and at peace—I realized that while I couldn't control a lot of things, I could try to create situations and spaces where I could be my best and most productive. It wasn't a pointless battle; it was showing up for myself.

I needed to first let myself daydream. What would my ideal day be like? What would my ideal space be like? What would I do if money, time, and other factors were not a consideration? Would I be in a French castle or on a beach? In a giant room-size bed with an open window letting in the breeze? In the middle of a fairy grove? When I return to reality, is there any little bit of that daydream that I can bring into my day? Can I go have lunch in bed or sit in nature? Or can I just sneak into the bathroom to be away from my kid for a moment? In letting myself dream and be truly honest about what I would like, I learned so much about what I needed, and there was a lot I could apply to real-life situations!

Cauliflower-Cheese Pita Sandwich

TL;DR: *Chop cauliflower, roast, then sprinkle with cheese. Scoop into pitas.*

Personally, I find that striking a balance between enough food and too much at lunch is genuinely difficult. You want to be satisfied and have enough to get you past the inevitable afternoon lull and through to dinner, but also not find yourself so full that you end up with your head on the desk. Big ol' salads work for me, but so does this sandwich, with its crispy and vibrant, mustardy cauliflower and gooey cheese and spinach. It is definitely not the "roasted vegetable sandwich" that will make any old-school vegetarian cringe.

1. Preheat the oven to 450°F. Line a sheet pan with parchment paper or a silicone baking mat.

2. To prepare your cauliflower for roasting, cut away the green leaves, core, and any woodier white parts of the stem. Break the cauliflower apart into florets and spread it out on the prepared sheet pan.

3. Drizzle the olive oil and dijon mustard over the cauliflower florets and sprinkle them with the salt. Using clean hands, toss the cauliflower until every floret is coated.

4. Roast the cauliflower until the florets are a nice deep brown, 30 to 35 minutes. Remove the sheet pan from the oven and turn off the oven. Sprinkle the shredded cheese over the cauliflower and place the pan back in the oven to let the residual heat melt the cheese, about 5 minutes.

5. Cut or tear the pita bread in half lengthwise and spoon a tablespoon or so of yogurt into each pita half. Fill the pouch with a handful of spinach leaves and then scoop in the cheesy cauliflower. Sprinkle with scallions, if using. Serve hot or let cool and eat when ready.

Makes 2 or 3 sandwiches

1 head cauliflower

1 tablespoon extra-virgin olive oil

1 tablespoon dijon mustard

2 teaspoons fine sea salt

1 cup shredded sharp white cheddar cheese

2 or 3 white or whole wheat pitas

Yogurt or sour cream

Fresh spinach

Chopped scallions, for garnish (optional)

Note: If you're doing meal prep, you can roast the cauliflower ahead of time and store it, covered, in the fridge for a few days until you're ready to make sandwiches.

Spicy Miso Broccoli Melt

TL;DR: *Roast broccoli. Toast buns, melt mozz on them, slather in gochujang mayo, and top with roasted broccoli.*

Serves 4

2 heads broccoli

1 tablespoon white miso

2 teaspoons soy sauce or tamari

1 teaspoon plus 1 tablespoon gochujang paste (see note)

4 soft hamburger buns

Sliced fresh mozzarella, to cover the buns

¼ cup mayonnaise

Note: Gochujang is a spicy and sweet chile paste that can be found in the hot sauce aisle of most grocery stores, as well as at Korean and other Asian markets.

This sandwich has broccoli rabe vibes, but rabe
is hard to find in many parts of the country, and *ahem* it has some haters in my house. The gochujang and miso are not fridge staples for everyone, and if that is the case for you, then sure, skip this one, until the day you try the miso dish that makes you feel all the feels and you launch yourself into the fridge section of your grocery store to get yourself a little tub. This melt is sweet and salty and amazing and reminds me of every broccoli rabe or broccoli sandwich that has ever been the best sandwich on a given menu.

1. Preheat the oven to 425°F. Line a sheet pan with parchment paper or a silicone baking mat.

2. Cut the broccoli into florets. Place the miso, soy sauce, 1 teaspoon of the gochujang, and 1 teaspoon of water in a small bowl and whisk to combine.

3. Tumble the broccoli onto the prepared pan and pour the sauce over the top. Use your hands to rub the sauce all over the broccoli. Roast until the ends of the broccoli are crispy, with some brown bits, and a fork can be poked through easily, 10 to 15 minutes.

4. Slice the buns in half and toast them in a toaster oven (or a full-size oven, if that's all you have). Place the sliced mozzarella on the top half of each bun, slide the buns back into the toaster oven, and let warm until the mozzarella is oozy, 2 to 3 minutes.

5. Mix the remaining 1 tablespoon of gochujang with the mayo and slather it on the bottom half of each bun. Top with a generous amount of roasted broccoli and squish the mozzarella-y other half of the bun down on top to try to encase it. Eat the sandwiches immediately or wrap them in paper and take them on the road (they're great for a picnic!). If you have excess broccoli, store it separately in the fridge and enjoy the leftovers.

Simple Cheese Sandwiches

Cheese sandwiches are a staple in many households. They might seem almost boring, yet with slight tweaks of cheese choice or jelly or bread, they can start to feel sophisticated. A cheese sandwich reminds me of picnics and travel and time off on a warm summer's day. It elicits a vacation feeling—that beautiful experience of walking through a gorgeous neighborhood, exploring a city, or hiking a new path for the first time. You're fully present, noticing, witnessing the beauty of your surroundings, and something that may be everyday for someone else is new and marvelous to you. There is no hurry. Your job is simply to be. You realize it's possible to make memorable moments anytime you feel fully present in your life. These sandwiches and the memories they carry bring me a little closer to that, even if I only have a twenty-minute lunch break. They're little reminders that stress is temporary.

Smoked gouda, pesto, thin cucumber medallions, and basil. This combo is a favorite of my sister. She likes to put it on croissants to take on picnics. It has a real tea-party-with-my-girls vibe.

Brie and jam. Here you have the feeling of a European train station. You're eating something practical on the go as you wait for the train, but it's also so delicious. You've chosen a simple baguette sandwich and you're savoring it in the bright rays of midmorning summer light.

Cream cheese blitzed with jalapeños or berries. You're sitting on the bank of a river under a tree with a notebook at your side and a blanket under your knees, a sandwich half eaten at your left. You breathe deeply.

Sharp cheddar and pickle slices with a drizzle of honey. "Wow, what is that you're eating? It looks incredible. Wait . . . really? That's what's in it? I'll, um, have to try it sometime. Oh gosh, no, I couldn't impose. No, but thank—well, actually. Really, if you aren't going to eat it . . . I wouldn't want it to go to waste. Oh. Oh my god, this is better than it smells. You just eat this, like, on a Tuesday?"

October Farro

TL;DR: *Cook farro. Sauté sweet potato, red onion, and spinach. Serve the farro in bowls topped with the veggies and goat cheese.*

Serves 4

1 cup farro, rinsed and drained

1 tablespoon extra-virgin olive oil

2½ teaspoons fine sea salt, plus extra as needed

1 medium sweet potato

1 large red onion

2 tablespoons unsalted butter

1 package (16 ounces) frozen chopped spinach

Freshly cracked black pepper

1 small package (4 ounces) goat cheese

Squeeze of fresh lemon juice (optional)

This is a great make-ahead meal because the farro and vegetables can be cooked separately, refrigerated, and then easily put together in a bowl and warmed up when you're ready to serve. Sweet potato and spinach are a more unusual combination, but I'm not sure why—they taste great together, especially alongside the random little pockets of creamy, tangy goat cheese. For an alternative, swap out the farro here for the miso-dressed quinoa from the Miso Salmon Taco Bowl (page 74).

1. Combine the farro, olive oil, and 1 teaspoon of the salt with 2 cups of water in a medium pot over high heat. Bring to a boil, then lower the heat and let simmer, covered, until the farro is tender, 10 to 30 minutes. Turn off the heat and let the farro sit, covered, until the vegetables are ready.

Note: Cooking times for farro vary depending on whether or not it is hulled (a.k.a. pearled), which is not always marked on the packaging. But the package will usually give you an estimate for the cooking time.

2. While the farro cooks, chop the sweet potato and red onion into small (½ inch or smaller) pieces.

3. Melt the butter in a large skillet over medium heat. Add the sweet potato and stir to coat. Sprinkle a heaping ½ teaspoon of the salt over the top. Cover the skillet and let the sweet potato cook undisturbed for about 5 minutes. Uncover and continue to cook, stirring occasionally, until the sweet potato is just getting tender, another 5 minutes.

4. Add the red onion, spinach, and remaining 1 teaspoon of salt, and stir. Let everything cook, stirring occasionally, until all the water from the spinach is cooked off and everything is tender and smelling delicious, about 10 minutes. Season to taste with pepper and more salt, if needed. Crumble the goat cheese over the top and stir gently just to disperse.

5. To assemble, drain the farro and divide it among four bowls. Top with the vegetables and, if desired, a squeeze of lemon.

Note: *If you are saving any portions for lunches throughout the week, let the farro and the vegetables come to room temperature, then store them separately in sealed containers in the fridge for up to 5 days, and assemble when you're ready to eat.*

The goat cheese is delicious when you have little pockets of it throughout, so you don't want it to melt too much.

Miso Salmon Taco Bowl

TL;DR: *Cook quinoa. Shake up dressing. Salt and cook fish.*
Crush some tortilla chips, grate some carrots, then assemble.

Serves 4

QUINOA

1 cup quinoa, rinsed and drained

2 cups vegetable or chicken broth

1 tablespoon white miso

SALMON

Fine sea salt

4 fillets salmon, thawed if frozen

1 tablespoon canola, grapeseed, or vegetable oil

2 teaspoons white miso

2 teaspoons extra-virgin olive oil

1 teaspoon hot sauce

DRESSING

1 jalapeño, stemmed and seeded (for less heat, if desired)

¼ cup chopped fresh cilantro

¼ cup extra-virgin olive oil

Juice of 1 very juicy lime

1 teaspoon fine sea salt

Wee squirt of honey

SALAD

4 to 6 cups arugula or other salad greens

½ cup crushed tortilla chips

2 carrots, grated

Ideal for meal prep, this taco bowl can all be done in advance, stored separately, and easily assembled. Just mix up the salad without dressing, in the morning or the night before, and when you're ready to eat, add the dressing, toss, and you're good! It's also so varied in texture (crunchy, silky) and taste (savory, spicy, tart, sharp) that having it for lunch a couple of days in a row will not lead to boredom.

You'll have leftover quinoa, which you can use in place of farro in any dish (try it in October Farro, page 72), add to bowls, or eat for breakfast.

1. Combine the quinoa, broth, and 1 tablespoon miso in a small pot over high heat. Bring to a boil, then lower the heat and let simmer, covered, until the quinoa is fluffy, with a curly tail encircling each grain, about 15 minutes. Turn off the heat and let the quinoa sit in its steam with the lid on, the way you would with rice.

2. While the quinoa cooks, sprinkle salt all over the salmon fillets. Then make the dressing: Place the jalapeño, cilantro, ¼ cup olive oil, lime juice, salt, and honey in a food processor and blitz until smooth.

3. To cook the salmon, warm the canola oil in a large cast-iron pan over medium-high heat, swirling it around. Place the salmon skin-side down in the pan, cover, and cook until the fillets are done to your preference, 6 to 8 minutes. Remove them to a plate.

4. Combine the 2 teaspoons miso, 2 teaspoons olive oil, and hot sauce in a small bowl and mix well with a fork. Slather this glaze all over the top of the cooked salmon.

5. Combine the arugula, tortilla chips, and grated carrot in a large mixing bowl. Add the dressing and toss.

6. Add the salmon and about half the quinoa to the mixing bowl with the greens and toss again to break up the warm grains and the salmon. Serve immediately. (Save the rest of the quinoa for another dish. The salad components will keep, separately, in the fridge for up to 3 days.)

Best Friend Salad

TL;DR: *Roast delicata squash, toast macadamia nuts, and make dressing. Chop kale, assemble the salad, dress, and toss.*

This salad is inspired by that person whom you love unconditionally, for whom doing something helpful comes easily because it flows from the energy of your love. You want them to have joy and pleasure, but also strength and well-being. I often share baked goods with people—everyone loves a gooey treat, so they are an easy win—but, for me, making a healthy, nourishing, delicious, and balanced meal for someone is a more intimate and deeply caring act. It says, "I want us to connect over this food, but I also want you to walk out of here knowing that your body is stronger and that I want you to be well in your whole life, even when we aren't together." With this salad, I try to apply that same sentiment—the easy, thoughtful, warm love you have for a best friend—to myself. I hope you'll treat your beautiful self that way, too.

1. Follow the instructions on page 222 to make the roasted squash and toasted nuts from the Macadamia-Crusted Delicata Squash. Whip up a double batch of the Maple Mustard Tahini Dressing.

2. Slice the kale into ribbons or bite-size pieces, according to your preference. Shuffle them into a mixing bowl and toss with the dressing.

3. Grate the gouda with the small, rough holes on a box grater or a Microplane. I like to be pretty generous with the cheese here, but if you aren't so sure, hold back a bit and add more to your plate as desired.

4. Add the roasted squash, toasted nuts, and gouda to the bowl with the kale and toss. Serve, adding more gouda if you like.

Note: This salad is just as lovely the next day, so if you are making it just for yourself, save some for tomorrow's lunch. If you put it in the fridge before dressing it, it will keep for up to 3 days.

Serves 2

1 recipe Macadamia-Crusted Delicata Squash, with a double batch of Maple Mustard Tahini Dressing (page 222)

1 bunch dinosaur kale, stems removed (see note)

Small hunk of aged gouda

Note: Remove the stems from the kale by pinching the stem at the bottom and pulling the leaves up to release them from the stem. Discard the stems or freeze them for stock.

Days and Days Salad

TL;DR: *Make dressing. Chop veggies. Mix veggies and dressing.*

Serves 6 to 8

DRESSING

¼ cup peanut butter (see note)

Juice of 1 lime, plus extra as needed

1 tablespoon honey

1 teaspoon sriracha or sambal oelek

½ to 1 teaspoon fine sea salt, plus extra as needed

3 tablespoons extra-virgin olive oil

1 tablespoon water, or as needed

Note: I use a very lightly sweetened peanut butter, but any kind will work well. If yours has a lot of sugar, taste the dressing before you add the honey to gauge how much extra sweetness it needs.

SALAD

1 can (15½ ounces) chickpeas, drained and rinsed

½ small red cabbage, shredded

1 English cucumber, chopped

¼ to ½ cup chopped fresh cilantro or mint

4 to 6 dates, pitted and finely chopped

¼ cup salted nuts, roughly chopped (I like almonds best!)

I ate this a lot during my first three months as a new mother. It's delicious and refreshing and filling and comes together quickly. It's often hard to eat enough veggies when you are rushed because it takes time to wash, chop, or otherwise prepare the produce before eating it. This salad feels worth the effort (even if it takes you three hours with interruptions) because you are chopping big, hearty vegetables and it makes a huge batch. If you make it just for yourself, you will have lunch all week—for days and days. If you have the ingredients, make a double batch of dressing; it's also good on noodles, on chicken, as part of a rice bowl, or as a dip for cut vegetables.

1. Make the dressing: Place the peanut butter, lime juice, honey, sriracha, and salt in a large bowl and whisk to combine. Slowly drizzle the olive oil into the mixture, whisking as you drizzle. Add enough water to thin it to your preferred consistency; a tablespoon is usually all I need. Once the dressing is smooth and well mixed, taste it. Add more lime juice or salt according to your preference. (Alternatively, huck everything into a little jar and shake until smooth.)

2. Add the chickpeas, cabbage, cucumber, cilantro, dates, and nuts to the bowl with the dressing. Toss the salad together and enjoy.

Note: If you want to eat this salad throughout the week, save the dressing in a separate container and assemble the salad ingredients in a separate bowl. The undressed salad should keep in a container in the refrigerator for up to a week, and even when it's dressed, it will keep until the next day.

FEELING ADVENTUROUS?

- Add 1 fennel bulb, finely chopped, in Step 2.
- Add 2 scallions, finely chopped, in Step 2.

Brooklyn Breakfast Salad

TL;DR: *Make dressing. Boil eggs. Toast bagel croutons. Mix dressing with greens and toss with croutons, eggs, and salmon.*

Serves 1 hungry person

2 ounces (¼ package) cream cheese

Juice of ½ lemon, plus extra as needed

1 tablespoon extra-virgin olive oil

1 teaspoon dijon mustard

2 scallions, finely chopped, plus more for serving (optional)

½ teaspoon fine sea salt, plus extra as needed

Freshly cracked black pepper

2 large eggs

½ large bagel, cut into cubes

3 cups salad greens, such as arugula, spinach, or a mix

2 to 3 slices (about 1½ ounces) smoked salmon, torn into pieces

1 tablespoon everything bagel topping or sesame seeds (optional)

This is what I make with the bits of leftover breakfast foods I have in my fridge. Even though it's basically just leftovers mixed together, it feels super special and delicious and kind of luxurious, all the flavors of lox and bagels, but with greens. It's filling and comes together quickly. There's no need to use the everything bagel topping or sesame seeds, but if you have them, add them for fun. Bread instead of bagels works, too, of course.

1. Fill a medium pot half full with water. Bring it to a boil over high heat, then turn the heat down to maintain a simmer. Combine the cream cheese, lemon juice, olive oil, mustard, scallions (if using), salt, and pepper to taste in a big metal bowl. Place the bowl over the pot of water, so that the warmth from the hot water melts the cream cheese. Whisk the dressing together until smooth. Taste and add more salt or lemon juice, if desired. Take the dressing off the heat and set it aside.

2. Place the eggs in the simmering water—if it doesn't cover the eggs, add more water—and turn up the heat until the water comes to a boil. Set a lid on the pot, turn off the heat, and let sit for 5 minutes. Then drain the hot water from the pot and run cold water over the eggs. Let them cool while you assemble the salad.

3. Place the bagel pieces in a toaster oven or a dry pan over medium heat and toast until they are light golden brown, 4 to 6 minutes per side.

4. When the eggs are cool enough to handle, peel them and cut them into quarters.

5. To assemble the salad, drop the salad greens and toasted bagel pieces into the large bowl with the dressing and toss. Pile them high in the center of a plate. Nestle the egg pieces in among the greens. Artfully lay the salmon pieces over the top and sprinkle with more scallions and everything bagel topping, if using.

If you are making the salad ahead of time, store the elements—the greens, bagel croutons, dressing, eggs, and salmon—separately, tossing them together only when you are ready to serve. The dressing will keep, covered, in the fridge for a few days.

Leftover Potato and Pesto Salad

TL;DR: *Cook potatoes and meat in butter, then mix in the rest of the ingredients. Put away half for lunch the next day.*

Fast, delicious, and satisfying, this amped-up potato salad feels indulgent and exciting, but refreshing and healthy at the same time. I first made it on a swelteringly hot Brooklyn evening when the humidity was bonkers. I didn't cook the potatoes with the salami—I just mixed leftover potatoes with all the rest of the ingredients cold from the fridge. I had an amazing evening to myself after the baby was asleep, and I sat drinking cold mint-infused water and eating this on the couch while I did small computer tasks and watched comedy. Bliss. But this recipe is in the lunch section because I made such a large quantity that I stored half of it in a container for later. It was even better the next day because the pesto had a chance to penetrate the potatoes.

1. Melt the butter in a large pan over medium heat. Add the potatoes; if they are not already seasoned from a previous use, salt them generously. Let them cook, stirring just once or twice, until lightly browned, about 5 minutes.

2. Sprinkle the chopped soppressata, if using, over the potatoes. Stir and cook until everything is a little crispy, another 2 minutes. Taste and add salt, if desired.

3. Transfer the warm potatoes to a large bowl. Add the chickpeas, pesto, ricotta, and greens. Toss it all together until everything is coated with pesto and ricotta and serve. If you don't eat it all the first night, portion the leftovers into a sealed container and enjoy in the next day or two (but no longer or the flavor starts to fade).

Serves 2

1 tablespoon butter or extra-virgin olive oil

1 pound baby potatoes, quartered and cooked (see note)

Fine sea salt (optional)

4 to 6 big slices soppressata or salami, chopped finely (optional)

1 can (15½ ounces) chickpeas, drained and rinsed

1 tablespoon basil pesto

1 tablespoon ricotta cheese

3 cups baby kale or other salad greens

Note: This is meant to be a leftovers salad, but if you don't have leftover potatoes, it doesn't take long to make some. Just scrub the baby potatoes, place them in a pot with water to cover, and boil them; they should be fork-tender in about 15 minutes. Once cooked, cut them into smaller pieces depending on their size—half-inch to an inch works well (more edges to get crispy).

How to Get a Girlfriend Salad

TL;DR: *Cook bacon, chop kale, toast bread in the bacon grease. Cook corn and crumble the bacon into it. Toss the kale with lemon juice and pesto. Toss everything together and shower with grated romano.*

Serves 2 as a meal or 4 as a side dish

4 strips bacon

1 large bunch dinosaur kale

2 cups day-old bread cubes (from about 4 slices of bread)

1 to 1½ cups corn (fresh, canned, or frozen and thawed)

3 tablespoons to ¼ cup basil pesto, plus extra as needed

Juice of 1 lemon

Finely grated romano cheese

FEELING ADVENTUROUS?

Serve with one or more of the following:

• ½ to 1 cup cubed fresh mozzarella

• 1 cup halved baby tomatoes

• ¼ cup kalamata olives

• 1 cup shredded or diced roasted chicken

• 1 boiled egg per person, halved or quartered

When I first met my husband, Dan, he tried cooking as a means to impress me several times—and while I was impressed, it was definitely not by his cooking. After an ill-fated jambalaya featuring liquid smoke, he settled into a standard rotation. My favorite was his "low country pasta"—taken directly from the pages of a mid-1990s GQ—featuring pesto-smothered wagon wheels with corn, kale, and olives for me and bacon for him (I was vegetarian at the time). I still love it. It's hearty and salty and sweet in just the right way. Here is the salad version of that Dan classic. It comes together quickly and tastes great at lunch the following day.

1. Line a plate with paper towels. Cook the bacon in a cast-iron or heavy-bottomed pan over low heat, flipping it once or twice until it's crispy, about 20 minutes. Transfer the bacon to the towel-lined plate to soak up the grease. Leave the bacon fat in the pan.

Note: You can crank the heat at the end to finish the bacon quickly, but it's nice to let it cook slowly, without having to worry about burning it.

2. While the bacon cooks, remove the tough center stems from the dinosaur kale and cut the leaves into thin ribbons.

3. After the bacon is cooked and removed from the pan, drop the bread cubes into the pan with the bacon fat and turn up the heat to medium. Cook, tossing occasionally, until the cubes are browned and crispy, about 10 minutes. You now have croutons! Remove them from the pan and set aside.

4. Toss the corn into the pan and cook over medium heat just until warm, 2 minutes. Crumble the bacon back into the pan with the corn. Once it is warmed through, remove the pan from the heat.

5. Combine the kale, pesto, and lemon juice in a large bowl and toss. Add the warm, bacon-scented corn and toss again. Add the croutons, top with finely grated romano to your taste, and toss a final time before serving.

Take your time and enjoy making kale confetti. The bacon is cooking slowly and there is no rush.

Hearty Summer Vegetable Salad
with Sausage Croutons

TL;DR: *Cook sausage croutons while you chop vegetables and drain chickpeas.*
Toss all ingredients together with salt and lime juice.

*Serves 2 as lunch or
4 as a side dish*

1 tablespoon butter or extra-
virgin olive oil

1 sausage of your choice
(see note)

1 cup cubed bread
(approximately)

1 cup corn (fresh, canned, or
frozen and thawed; see note,
page 87)

1 can (15½ ounces) chickpeas

2 tomatoes (your favorite
kind)

½ English cucumber

1 avocado

1 ounce feta cheese

Fine sea salt

Juice of 1 lime, plus extra as
needed

Note: Use breakfast sausage,
lamb, chorizo, or whatever you
like! For a vegetarian version,
skip the sausage and cook the
croutons in butter.

FEELING
ADVENTUROUS?

Use radishes or snap peas
for the cucumber, or black
or cannellini beans for the
chickpeas.

The dressing on this salad has only salt and lime juice
because so much flavor already comes from the mingled tomato and
cucumber juices and the hit of meatiness from the sausage croutons.
Summer produce is such a joy—it's all wonderfully flavorful and
nutritious and goes together so well. All you have to do is chop and
put it together. In the hot summer months, preparing this salad can
feel like a meditative gratitude practice. As the croutons cook and I
chop and layer vegetable upon vegetable, I am here in this moment,
thankful.

1. Melt the butter in a large pan over medium heat. Cut the sausage into
slices if it's precooked, or crumble it out of its casing if you're using
fresh. Add the sausage to the pan and cook until it is lightly browned
and cooked through, 3 to 5 minutes.

2. Add the bread cubes to the pan and mix to coat them with the butter
and sausage grease. Cook, stirring occasionally, until the cubes are
golden brown, about 5 minutes.

3. While the croutons cook, add the corn to a large salad bowl.
Drain and rinse the chickpeas and add them in. Chop the tomatoes,
cucumber, and avocado and add them as well.

Note: *I like to chop the veggies into smaller pieces so you can have a
mingling of all the ingredients in each bite. But if you are in a hurry or like
your salad chunkier, by all means cut larger pieces.*

4. Once the croutons are golden brown, let them cool for a minute or
two, then add them and the sausage to the bowl with the vegetables.
Crumble in the feta with your fingers and sprinkle salt all over the
salad, starting with ¼ teaspoon and adding more to taste. Sprinkle
with fresh lime juice and toss. Taste the salad and add more salt and
lime juice until you are happy with the flavor. Serve immediately.

Fresh corn will be a little less sweet and more grassy-tasting if added to the salad raw. If you like, you can cook fresh corn, with the husk still on, in the microwave until it's brighter yellow and aromatic, 1 to 2 minutes, to steam it.

Two Dressings That Are Good on Everything

Making your own dressing is a chance to taste and adjust the salty, sweet, and acidic qualities that make any dish taste good, like you're a magician and a potion maker. The first dressing below is creamy, yet also zingy, sweet, salty, and complex enough to elevate simple vegetable salads. The second is the tongue-tingling trio of lemon, lime, and orange—found in three forms in this book: dressing (below), pasta (page 155), and custard (page 242). It's that good.

Creamy Dill and Date Dressing

TL;DR: *Soak dates, then process them with yogurt, dill, and lemon.*

Makes 1 cup

4 dates, pitted

¼ cup warm water

½ cup plain yogurt

¼ cup chopped fresh dill

Juice of 1 lemon, plus extra as needed

1 teaspoon fine sea salt, plus extra as needed

1. Soak the dates in the warm water for 2 minutes.

2. Pour the dates and water into a small blender and process until smooth. Add the yogurt, dill, lemon juice, and salt and process again until smooth. Taste and add more salt or lemon juice as desired.

3. Serve over your favorite salad or store in an airtight container in the refrigerator for up to a week. Shake well before using.

Triple Citrus Dressing

TL;DR: *Juice citrus and whisk with olive oil.*

Makes about 1 cup

1 lemon

1 lime

1 small to medium navel orange

⅓ cup extra-virgin olive oil, or as needed

Fine sea salt and freshly cracked black pepper

1. Set a sieve over a medium bowl and juice the lemon, lime, and orange over it to catch any seeds or pulp.

2. Add ⅓ cup olive oil (or an amount equal to the citrus juice) to the bowl, along with a healthy sprinkling of salt and pepper, and whisk. Taste and adjust with more salt, pepper, or olive oil, if desired.

3. Serve over your favorite salad or store in an airtight container in the refrigerator for up to a week. Shake well before using. If it starts to taste dull, an extra squeeze of citrus will revive it.

Good Enough Weeknights

To Cook or Not to Cook, That Is the Question

I used to really worry about my choice to cook or not—we're talking Hamlet-level musings on a cold, dark night. Imperfection scared the hell out of me.

If I had the thought "I don't want to cook," I was doomed. If I chose to get pizza, I couldn't enjoy it because I felt selfish, slovenly, or spendthrift. If I chose to cook but I didn't do the greatest job, or I rushed, or I didn't clean up properly, it was not good enough. If the meal was great but my attitude was bad, even that was enough to condemn me. Sometimes it took some creativity, but my brain would find some criticism to throw at me, negating any good I might have done. Clearly, I was a fraud, my cooking was garbage, and I was a monster for leading others to believe it is anything but.

Because I say things like "every meal is an opportunity for great pleasure" and "cooking doesn't need to be a chore," I thought that I had to live by those statements 100 percent of the time or I was a liar. When I'm at my best, I do connect with those ideas. They are true. But there are so many days when I am not my best self, when I am grouchy, tired, short on time or patience—and that version of me is no less worthy than the expansive and joyful me. This me is deserving of compassion. She doesn't deserve to be shamed for feeling the way she does.

In all my experiences of cooking, and having the opportunity to speak with so many people about their experiences of cooking, I have come to realize that the most important indicator of whether or not you will enjoy your meal is not how good the food looks or tastes. It's in that moment when you're thinking about your meal. It's in that moment when you might think, "I know what I want to cook" or "Oof, I don't want to cook," and you make a decision—to make something, to order in, to eat leftovers or an apple and some cheese—and you accept that decision as valid and good enough. It's in being kind to yourself.

It's not about the meal itself, how you prepare it, or how you eat it. The outcome is not the measure; it's how you feel during the process that matters.

Perfection Is a Liar

For perfectionists, the phrase "good enough" is deeply unsettling, even threatening. For most of us trying to make it in this high-pressure culture, it sends a chill down the spine: Not overachieving can feel like failing on purpose. How dare you give up at good enough? I am here to tell you that perfection is a fantasy—so it doesn't make a great goal.

Good enough is not settling; it is your best. And your best is a real standard. Your best is always enough. This is not some kind of "in defense of mediocrity." It is deeply fulfilling to try your best, and to give your all is life-affirming. You can be proud of your best, fulfilled by your best. But your best looks different from day to day. Sometimes getting out of bed and eating dry toast is your best, and sometimes it's hosting a ten-person dinner. Perfection is a delusional standard. We think of it as a benevolent yardstick that drives us to do our best. But at what cost? Do we want to live a life of achievement without a sense of ever having reached a destination? Always working and planning and never able to sit back and be proud? Never peaceful, always criticizing? And in pursuit of a fantasy?

Wrenching ourselves out of the fantasy of perfection can be unsettling. There is a lot we have to face if we are to live in reality: The pain of the time we have wasted worrying and scheming for perfection when we could have been loving and creating. The life we missed. The fact that we are not in control of how others see us. We are not even in control of what our best is. We are not in control of the talents we are born with, our personalities, or how we grow into who we are through the experiences we have. We are the products of so many factors outside our control.

But good enough has a higher meaning than imperfect. It is also a declaration of belonging. I am good enough. What I have to give is good enough. What I have done is good enough. It is revelatory and celebratory and human to accept that you are good enough. We are good enough. *So it is.*

Good enough is being free to do things in the way that feels truly right to you. For most people, that means taking care of yourself and the needs of others, especially those that you love. Freedom means that a good life, or a good meal, doesn't look one particular way. It is all about what works for you.

The work is in letting go of the rules, judgments, and standards of your society, family, friends, and colleagues and really figuring out what you need. There is no such thing as a bad home cook. Unlike a restaurant chef, you are not subject to the whims of an audience whom you must please in order to pay your bills. There is no critic that could make or break the restaurant. There is only you. You decide

Good enough has a higher meaning than imperfect. It is also a declaration of belonging. I am good enough. What I have to give is good enough. What I have done is good enough. It is revelatory and celebratory and human to accept that you are good enough. We are good enough. So it is.

what kind of critic you want to be. Lead with the standards of others, harsh judgment, and impossible expectations and you will avoid cooking. Lead with curiosity and compassion for yourself, and pleasure and ease await in the kitchen.

And yes, sure, you do have an audience if you have a family! They live in your house. But your family is not a paying public; they are your partners and collaborators. Your successes and failures are all shared. Leaning into that shared ownership of preparing and eating food can bring freedom and fun to what might otherwise feel like subjugation.

Caring and being cared for are both such nourishing experiences, but if you have fallen wildly out of balance toward one or the other, it doesn't feel so great—and I say this as someone who has spent a lifetime caring for others and resisting being cared for. If you live with anyone and you eat together, then you need to share the process of feeding one another. I can't tell you how to do that, and have no business trying. But with all my heart, I wish you lightness and joy and ease.

Overwhelmed

When I see a big stack of paperwork, I feel overwhelmed. When I am in a room filled with people and no set purpose, I feel overwhelmed. And sometimes at 5 p.m. after a long day, when I think about what's next and I remember I have to make dinner, I feel overwhelmed.

Why? It's just dinner. I've done this a thousand times. But there is just so much I want.

I want it to be delicious.

I want it to be satisfying and comforting.

I want to end the day on a high note.

I want it to be nourishing and (my definition of) healthy.

I don't want to go to the grocery store.

I want to eat it with my family.

I want it to be timely, before we're all hangry.

I don't want to have to make a meal plan.

I want cleanup to be easy.

I want to connect with friends and family.

I want it to be in step with my values.

That's a lot for one dinner to accomplish. So when I get overwhelmed, I name as many of these things as I can, and I choose one or two to focus on—for example, this uses up leftovers and will be quick. After all, one dinner will not come together to meet all of my desires. If it did, what would I do with the rest of my life? Instead, I take a deep breath, send a hug to the sweet person inside me with the big, ambitious desires, and notice what I do have right here and now. It's enough.

Pato's Weeknight Farro

TL;DR: *Cook farro with a parmesan rind. Sauté vegetables and beans. Combine, stir, season, and top with feta.*

Serves 4

2 cups farro, rinsed and drained

1 parmesan rind (see note)

3 tablespoons extra-virgin olive oil, or more as desired

3 cloves garlic

1 pint cherry tomatoes, quartered

Zest and juice of 1 lemon, plus extra juice as needed

1 bunch asparagus, woody ends removed, chopped

1 can (15½ ounces) chickpeas or white beans, drained and rinsed (optional)

4 ounces feta cheese, plus extra as needed

Fine sea salt

Freshly cracked black pepper (optional)

Note: The parmesan rind adds salty richness to the farro. If you don't have one, just add 2 teaspoons of salt to the water.

FEELING ADVENTUROUS?

This is the cardinal version, but I also love it with butternut squash and red onion, or with a sweet potato, spinach, and goat cheese combination (like the October Farro on page 72).

My dear friend Pato hates cooking but sincerely loves to place a plate of food in front of you. He loves the caring part, the nourishing part, if not the chopping and sautéing part. This recipe contains a few of his favorite things (except the beans, which I've added) that come together quickly enough for him to feel good. It's a nice way to change up the weeknight pasta routine, and it's great cold the next day, unlike pasta, which is always hard to bring back to life.

1. Place the farro, parmesan rind, and 5 cups of water in a medium pot over medium heat.

2. Bring to a boil, then lower the heat and let the farro simmer, covered, until it is puffed and tender, 10 to 30 minutes (see note, opposite).

3. While the farro cooks, place a large skillet over medium heat and add a generous amount of olive oil—about 3 tablespoons, but a little more doesn't hurt. Slice your garlic cloves into lovely thin little wafers and add them to the warm oil. Let them cook until they're fragrant, about 1 minute, and then add the quartered cherry tomatoes and lemon zest. Cook, stirring occasionally, until the oil takes on a hint of orangey red from the cooking tomatoes, about 4 minutes.

4. Add the asparagus and beans, if using, to the skillet and stir. Let everything cook together, stirring occasionally, until the asparagus is just tender and bright green, about 4 minutes.

5. Once the farro is cooked, drain off all but about ½ cup of the cooking water. Remove the parmesan rind, if you used one. Toss the farro and reserved cooking water into the skillet with the vegetables. Mix it all up and let simmer just until some of the liquid has boiled away and the farro soaks up some of the delicious juices, 2 to 5 minutes. Drizzle with lemon juice, crumble in the feta, and stir. Taste and adjust with salt and more lemon juice or feta as desired.

6. Sprinkle with black pepper, if desired, and serve.

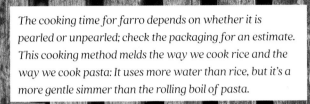

The cooking time for farro depends on whether it is pearled or unpearled; check the packaging for an estimate. This cooking method melds the way we cook rice and the way we cook pasta: It uses more water than rice, but it's a more gentle simmer than the rolling boil of pasta.

Fast White Bean, Chorizo, and Hearty Greens Stew

TL;DR: *Sauté vegetables, then chorizo and tomato paste. Add beans and water and cook until thickened and flavorful. Add greens and eat.*

It has taken maturity to embrace the glorious simplicity of this kind of dinner. My inner critic is prone to telling me that it's not creative enough or new enough or whatever overachieving mark you might expect from a perfectionist fantasy. But this stew is made of pantry staples, comes together in 20 minutes, and is delicious, nourishing, and balanced. It's a dream of a meal—fun to make, fun to eat, and proof that simple is wonderful. Like all stews, it gets better with a few days in the fridge. It also works well as a side dish for a larger barbecue meal and as a potluck dish.

1. Melt the butter in a medium pot over medium-high heat. Add the shallots, bell pepper, and ½ teaspoon of the salt to the pot and cook, stirring occasionally, until the shallots are translucent, 3 to 5 minutes.

2. Add the chorizo and tomato paste, using a wooden spoon to break up the chorizo. Cook until the chorizo is cooked through and beginning to brown, another 3 minutes. Then add the beans, 1½ cups of water, and the remaining ½ teaspoon of salt. Put a lid on the pot and let it cook for about 10 minutes.

3. Taste the stew and add more salt if you think it needs it. Squish a few of the beans with the back of the spoon to thicken the broth. Turn off the heat, add the greens, and stir them into the stew until wilted.

4. Dollop the stew into bowls over farro, pasta, or rice, or serve with bread for dunking.

FEELING ADVENTUROUS?

- Use any sausage, ground meat, or meat alternative in place of the chorizo in Step 2. Try sweet Italian sausage, finished with parmesan or romano, for a different experience, or lamb sausage with harissa, coriander, and fennel seed for a North African take on the dish.
- Add chile powder and/or chopped chiles along with the chorizo in Step 2.

Serves 4

2 tablespoons butter

2 shallots, chopped

1 bell pepper, stemmed, seeded, and chopped

1 teaspoon fine sea salt, plus extra as needed

5 ounces fresh chorizo or other sausage, casing removed

1 tablespoon tomato paste

2 cans (15½ ounces each) white beans or chickpeas

Handfuls of hearty greens, such as spinach, kale, chard, or collards

Farro, pasta, rice, or hearty bread, for serving

Relaxed and Romantic Risotto

Whenever I make risotto, it tends to be the highlight of the week. It feels special and a little fancy, but it is actually a one-pot, one-bowl meal, so it's not too bad to clean up. I deeply enjoy the process of making it. It simply must be made while listening to music and drinking a glass of wine—especially since you need the wine for cooking. It really has that "I'm a sophisticated grown woman" vibe. You chop, then sauté, add the rice, and relax, occasionally stirring and adding more broth as the rice plumps up and gets creamy and starchy and delicious. Finish with a flourish of cheese and pepper and you're ready to eat.

Leek and Squash Risotto with Goat Cheese and Honey

TL;DR: *Cook leeks and squash, then add rice, wine, and broth in stages. Serve with goat cheese, pepper, and honey on top.*

Serves 4 to 6

1 tablespoon butter

2 leeks, sliced into thin half-moons

1 medium delicata squash, seeded and sliced into ½-inch pieces

1 teaspoon fine sea salt, plus extra as needed

1 cup arborio or carnaroli rice

½ cup dry white wine (optional; see note, page 101)

4 to 4½ cups vegetable or chicken broth

Freshly cracked black pepper

1 small package (4 ounces) goat cheese

2 tablespoons honey, or as desired

This risotto is a celebration of sweetness in its many forms, but still achieves balance from the tartness of goat cheese before the final honey drizzle.

1. Melt the butter in a large heavy-bottomed pot over medium-high heat. Add the leeks, squash, and salt and stir. Cover the pot and cook, stirring occasionally, until everything has softened, about 10 minutes.

2. Pour in the rice and stir to coat with the vegetables and butter. Turn the heat down to medium-low, pour in the wine, and stir. Let simmer until the wine has been absorbed, 30 seconds to 1 minute.

3. Add 1 cup of broth to the rice and let it cook, stirring occasionally, until it is absorbed, about 5 minutes. Continue to add broth 1 cup at a time, letting each cup cook until it is absorbed, and the rice is tender and fully cooked, about 20 minutes. It should be thick but still a bit soupy. Taste and add more salt, if you think it needs it, and a generous grind of pepper.

4. Turn off the heat and crumble small chunks of goat cheese (see note, opposite) all over the risotto. Serve in bowls, drizzling each bowl with a generous ½ tablespoon of honey, or more if you like.

I like to stir the goat cheese in just a bit so you still come across pieces of creamy, tangy cheese, rather than having it completely incorporated into the dish. It's more fun that way!

GOOD ENOUGH

Bacon and Kale Risotto with Fried Eggs

TL;DR: *Cook bacon, then add onions, rice, wine, and broth in stages.*
Fry eggs in butter. Serve risotto topped with parmesan and fried eggs.

There is something sexy about this elevated breakfast for dinner creation, as if you are enticing your partner to stick around for breakfast the next day.

1. Place the bacon in a large pot over medium-low heat and cook, stirring occasionally, until crispy, 5 to 10 minutes. Pour off most of the bacon fat (see page 258 for how to deal with it).

2. Add 2 tablespoons of the butter to the pot with the bacon and turn the heat up to medium. Quickly toss in the onions and 1 teaspoon of the salt. Let cook, stirring occasionally, until the onions become translucent, about 5 minutes.

3. Pour in the rice and stir to coat with the onions, bacon, and butter. Add the white wine and stir. Let simmer until the wine has been absorbed, 30 seconds to 1 minute.

4. Add 1 cup of broth to the rice and let it cook, stirring occasionally, until it is absorbed, about 5 minutes. Add 2 cups more of broth, just 1 cup at a time, letting each cup cook until it is absorbed, about 5 minutes for each addition. Taste the rice and add more salt, if you think it needs it, and a generous grind of pepper.

5. Add the kale to the risotto and stir until it wilts, about 1 minute. The risotto should be thick but a little soupy—if it needs more liquid, add the remaining ½ to 1 cup of the broth. Continue to cook and stir until the rice is cooked through but still has a little bite to it, about 5 minutes more.

6. Meanwhile, melt the remaining 4 teaspoons of butter in a small skillet over medium heat. Crack in the eggs, 2 at a time, and fry until they're crispy on the bottom, 2 to 3 minutes. Cook them to your taste—sunny-side up, over easy, whatever!

7. Turn off the heat under the risotto, add the grated parmesan, and stir. Serve in bowls, topping each one with a fried egg and a bit more parmesan.

Serves 4 to 6

4 strips bacon, chopped into small pieces

2 tablespoons plus 4 teaspoons butter

2 medium onions or large leeks, chopped

1 teaspoon fine sea salt, plus extra as needed

1 cup arborio or carnaroli rice

½ cup dry white wine (optional; see note)

3½ to 4 cups vegetable or chicken broth

Freshly cracked black pepper

1 bunch dinosaur kale, finely chopped (see note)

4 to 6 large eggs

½ cup grated parmesan or romano cheese, plus more to taste

Note: If you stay away from wine, or don't have any, you can just use broth instead. However, you will lose out on the acidity wine provides, so if you can, squeeze a bit of lemon juice over everything at the end or add a tablespoon or so of wine vinegar along with the broth to bring out all the flavor.

Note: If you substitute curly kale, use less because it doesn't wilt as much when cooked.

Saucy Spiced Chicken
with Tomato, Goat Cheese, and Mint

TL;DR: *Brown chicken thighs. Cook onion, garlic, cinnamon, and cumin with canned tomatoes and chipotles. Add chicken and simmer until thickened. Top with goat cheese and mint.*

Serves 6 to 8

2 pounds boneless, skinless chicken thighs

2 to 3 teaspoons fine sea salt, plus extra as needed

2 tablespoons extra-virgin olive oil

1 large red onion (or any kind of onion)

4 cloves garlic

1 can (28 ounces) whole tomatoes

2 teaspoons ground cinnamon

2 teaspoons ground cumin

2 chipotles in adobo, blitzed or finely chopped (see note)

4 ounces goat cheese

Handful of fresh mint leaves

Note: To skip the spiciness of the chipotles, substitute 2 teaspoons smoked paprika, adding it with the cinnamon and cumin in Step 4.

Cooking in a big pot always feels like culinary potion-making—building flavor, layer by layer, until, magically, you've created something that is more than the sum of its parts. Because it's a stew and magical, the flavors in this dish meld and get yummier the second and third day it's in the fridge. The only way I can think to describe it is that it's like if Indian butter chicken was trying to make your Moroccan friend feel more at home at a house in France. You follow me? If you make this amazing stew early in the week, it can lead to several fantastic meals with minimal work on the other days. Option 1: with fluffy rice, crusty bread, or some kind of pita or garlic-brushed flatbread. Option 2: in a taco with some chopped cabbage or whatever vegetables you like. Option 3: with farro or tossed with pasta, butter, and a bit more cheese. Option 4: dolloped over roasted potatoes or cauliflower.

1. Cut the chicken thighs into bite-size pieces and tumble them into a bowl. Sprinkle liberally with 2 to 3 teaspoons of the salt and toss to coat. Let the chicken rest with the salt for a few minutes.

2. Warm the oil in a heavy-bottomed pot over medium-high heat. Place half of the chicken in the pot and let cook until lightly browned all over, about 5 minutes per side. If the chicken sticks to the pot, pour a bit of water into the pot to help loosen it. Remove the cooked chicken to a clean bowl to rest, leaving the juices in the pot. Repeat with the second batch of chicken.

3. As you cook the chicken, chop your onion into small pieces and slice the garlic into thin chips. Prepare the canned tomatoes: Drain the tomato juice into a bowl (but don't throw it out!!), then dump the tomatoes onto your cutting board and roughly chop them.

4. When all the chicken is cooked and resting, turn the heat down to medium. Add the onion to the chicken juices in the pot, along with

½ cup of water. The water will help deglaze the pot, so use a wooden spoon to quickly scrape up any chicken bits stuck to the bottom. Add the cinnamon, cumin, and a dash of salt and cook until the onion is light brown, 5 to 10 minutes. Add the garlic and cook for another 2 minutes. The sauce should be dark brown, aromatic, and juicy looking!

5. Add the chopped tomatoes to the pot, squishing any really big chunks, and cook until the tomato begins to caramelize and develop flavor, about 5 minutes. Pour in 1 cup of water (see note below), the tomato juice, and the chopped chipotles. Return the chicken to the pot, then bring the stew to a simmer, still over medium heat. Once it's simmering, turn the heat down to low and place a lid on the pot, slightly askew. Let the stew cook over low heat for at least 20 minutes, but longer if you can, up to 1 hour 30 minutes, to allow the flavors to meld. Taste and adjust the salt and other seasonings, as needed. The sauce should coat the chicken loosely and be a little smoky and spicy.

Note: *Incidentally, I usually measure this water into the empty tomato can to get any lingering tomato bits.*

6. Before serving, stir in the goat cheese and let it melt and mingle with everything. Taste and add more salt as needed. Sprinkle the top with the mint leaves and serve. This stew will keep in the fridge for up to a week or in the freezer for up to a month.

Favorite Summer Burgers

TL;DR: *Butter buns. Prepare toppings. Form meat and spices into patties. Grill burgers. Toast buns. Assemble.*

Juicy, smoky, simply delicious burgers. These burgers have become a favorite of my husband. They came about one day when I wanted to make chorizo burgers (the obsession is strong, as I'm sure you can tell if you look up chorizo in the index of this book), but I couldn't get my hands on chorizo and so decided to make something vaguely emulating it. The meat is half beef and half pork, both just 80 percent lean (meaning 20 percent fat!), for the most tender and juicy burgers. The addition of paprika is subtle, but it makes the burgers a little more smoky and savory. It can be tempting to add onions or other things to homemade burgers, but I think the best ones are simply well-seasoned meat—leave the onions for the topping. These are best cooked on an outdoor grill, but smashburger-style in a hot pan is great, too! Serve with any of the offerings from the Vegetable Celebration (pages 210–227) to round out the meal.

1. Set out a large tray or plate. Split the buns and butter both sides for toasting on the grill. Spread out the cheese slices, if using, so you can have them on hand to top each burger. On a separate tray or plate, set out the other toppings and condiments so each diner can customize their own burger to their personal delight. Set aside to serve with the cooked burgers. Cut 8 squares of parchment paper approximately 3 inches in size.

2. Place the beef, pork, salt, pepper, and paprika in a big metal bowl. With clean hands, mix it all up, just until the beef, pork, and spices are well mingled and there are no big pieces of one kind of meat. Don't smash the mixture or work it too hard or your burgers will be tough.

3. Divide the meat mixture into 8 equal portions. Take one portion and press it gently and firmly into a thin patty about 3 inches across. Press it down extra thin in the center to keep the patty from shrinking up into a charcoal briquette shape as it cooks. Place the patty on one piece of parchment paper and then place another piece of parchment

Makes 8 burgers

8 potato or brioche buns

Butter, for buttering the buns

1 pound ground beef (preferably 80% lean, 20% fat)

1 pound ground pork (preferably 80% lean, 20% fat)

1 tablespoon fine sea salt

1 teaspoon freshly cracked black pepper

2 teaspoons ground smoked paprika

TOPPINGS (YOUR CHOICE)

Meltable cheese

Crispy fresh lettuce leaves or shredded iceberg

Sliced tomatoes

Sliced pickles

Thinly sliced onions, somewhere on the scale of raw to pickled to caramelized according to your preference

Condiments!

paper on top. Continue to make patties, stacking them in a pile with parchment in between each layer to keep them from sticking.

Note: *If you're not going to grill the patties right away, cover them tightly with plastic wrap and leave them in the fridge for a few hours or up to a day. Raw patties, sealed airtight, should keep in the freezer for up to 2 months.*

4. When you're ready to eat, heat the grill to medium-high heat. Place as many patties as can fit on your grill and cover with the lid. Grill until the patties are cooked on the bottom and looking brown and delicious on the edges, 2 to 3 minutes. Flip and cook, with the lid closed, for another minute or so. If you're making cheeseburgers, add cheese to each patty after you flip.

Note: *If you don't have a grill, heat a cast-iron pan over medium-high heat and cook the burgers, covered, for 2 to 3 minutes. Flip and cook, adding cheese if desired, until both sides are dark brown and the cheese is melty, another 1 to 2 minutes.*

5. Once you flip the patties, place the buttered buns on the grill and cook until they are lightly toasted, 10 to 20 seconds.

6. Flip each finished burger onto a bun and serve with the prepared tray of toppings and condiments.

Sweet and Spicy Chicken Dinner

To me, the orangey redness of chile oil, where you can see the jammy, dark oil slick, is the yummiest look there is. With these chicken dishes, I wanted to create glazey, deeply brown-sugary, but also spicy, salty, and caramelized flavors.

Chile, Garlic, and Date Chicken Tacos

TL;DR: *Make chile-date paste and cook chicken in it. Toast tortillas and top with glazed chicken, diced tomatoes, and scallions.*

Makes 6 to 8 tacos

2 red chiles, stemmed and roughly chopped

4 dates, pitted

4 cloves garlic

2 tablespoons extra-virgin olive oil

1 pound boneless, skinless chicken breasts or thighs, chopped into bite-size pieces

1 teaspoon fine sea salt, plus extra as needed

6 medium or 8 small flour tortillas

Chopped fresh cilantro, as desired

1 small tomato, diced, for serving

Chopped scallions, for serving

If you prefer less of a bone-and-sinew experience in your chicken dinner, go for the tacos! They are packed with flavor from the chile paste, but are still quick enough to serve on a weeknight.

1. Combine the chiles, dates, and garlic in a small food processor or blender. Add ¼ cup of water and blend until you have a fine paste.

2. Warm the oil in a pan over medium heat. Add the chile-date paste and ½ cup of water and cook, stirring occasionally, until the mixture smells wonderful and darkens slightly, 5 to 10 minutes.

3. Add the chicken and salt to the pan and stir well to coat the chicken in the chile-date paste. If the paste seems dry, add more water; you want all that deliciousness on the chicken, not stuck to the pan. Turn the heat down to medium-low and continue to cook, tossing occasionally and adding more water as needed, until the chicken is cooked through, 10 to 15 minutes.

4. As the chicken cooks, toast the tortillas in a dry pan, one at a time, just to make them warm and pliable (see page 115), with a couple of golden brown spots, about 1 minute per side.

5. Once the chicken is cooked, sprinkle with cilantro, to taste. The chicken should be a little juicy still; add a bit more water if it seems dry. Taste and adjust the salt, if needed.

6. Pile the chicken into the tortillas and top with the tomato and scallions to serve.

Chile, Garlic, and Date Butterflied Roasted Chicken

TL;DR: *Blitz chile-date paste. Butterfly a chicken. Slather chicken in paste. Roast at 400°F for 45 minutes. Let it rest and then serve.*

If you are a roasted chicken family, try it in place of your usual bird, and try the butterfly method! Once you've learned to butterfly, it's easy, and the chicken cooks more quickly and evenly. If the idea of sticking an entire chicken in the oven scares you, I understand. It feels like such a risk! But it really is easy. I know we have these images of people pulling perfect roasted birds out of their ovens and imagine they have esoteric knowledge, but it's just salt and heat. You can do it! (Dare I say that a roasted chicken makes a great centerpiece for a dinner party or a holiday dinner as well.)

1. Preheat the oven to 400°F. Place an oven rack in the middle position.

2. Combine the jalapeños, dates, garlic, oil, and ½ teaspoon of the salt in a small food processor or blender. Add 1 tablespoon of water and blend until you have a fine paste.

3. Butterfly the chicken: Cut along the right side of the spine, starting at the tail and cutting all the way through to the top. (Sturdy kitchen shears make this quite simple.) Then cut along the left side of the spine to remove it completely. Save the spine for stock or throw it away. Flip the chicken over and press down hard on the middle of the breastbone to crack it so the bird will lie flat.

4. Pat the chicken dry. Sprinkle the remaining 4 teaspoons of salt all over it. Rub the chile-date paste all over it, too, and under the skin as much as possible. Lay the bird flat in a large roasting pan and tuck the wing edges under the body. Roast until the biggest part of the thigh registers 160°F, about 45 minutes.

5. The roasted chicken will smell richly caramelized as the chicken fat mingles with the chile-date paste and the skin browns. Let it rest at room temperature for 10 minutes before cutting and serving.

Serves 4 to 8

2 red jalapeños or other fresh red chiles, stemmed, seeded (for less heat, if desired), and chopped

4 dates, pitted

4 cloves garlic

1 tablespoon extra-virgin olive oil

4½ teaspoons fine sea salt

1 whole chicken (4 to 5 pounds)

Shrimp Scramble with Rice

TL;DR: *Cook rice. Sauté shrimp, then scramble eggs in same pan with peas. Serve with scallions and/or hot sauce.*

Serves 2

½ cup medium- or long-grain white rice

½ teaspoon fine sea salt, plus extra as needed

2 tablespoons butter

6 to 8 ounces small (41 to 50 per pound) frozen shrimp, thawed, peeled, tails off, and deveined (see note)

4 large eggs

2 teaspoons soy sauce

½ teaspoon toasted sesame oil

¾ cup frozen peas

Chopped scallions, for serving (optional)

Hot sauce or chiles, chopped or sliced, for serving

Note: To thaw the frozen shrimp, place them in a sieve and submerge it in a bowl filled with cold water. The shrimp should thaw in 20 to 30 minutes. If you are in a hurry, you can run the cold water through the sieve to make it go faster.

This is a pretty classic Chinese dish done in a pan instead of a wok. It's fast and bright and full of flavor, and it comes together as quickly as a grilled cheese sandwich. Frozen shrimp are a freezer staple in my home, and they thaw quickly in a bowl of cold water in the sink. I especially like to make this dish when I have a carton or two of leftover rice, so I don't even have to wait the extra 10 minutes for the rice to cook. I throw the old rice in the pan at the last minute and toss it all together to warm through and get a little browned on the bottom. It's all pantry ingredients here, and more interesting than the sum of its parts.

1. Pour the rice into a sieve and run it under water until the water runs clear. You are trying to rinse off the excess starch and any debris clinging to the grains. Combine the rice, salt, and 1 tablespoon of the butter with 1½ cups of water in a medium pot over medium-low heat. Bring to a simmer, then reduce the heat to low and let the rice simmer gently, covered, until it is tender and can be fluffed with a fork, about 20 minutes.

2. About 10 minutes into cooking the rice, melt the remaining 1 tablespoon of butter in a medium pan over medium heat. Add the shrimp and cook, stirring occasionally, until the meat is just pink and the tails begin to curl, 3 to 5 minutes.

3. While the shrimp cook, crack the eggs into a bowl and add the soy sauce and sesame oil. Whisk briefly with a fork.

4. Pour the eggs into the pan with the shrimp and move them around briskly until the eggs are fully cooked, about 2 minutes. Taste and adjust the salt as needed. Just as the eggs are nearly done, add the frozen peas and toss them around the pan with everything else. Cook until the peas are warmed through and bright green, 1 to 2 minutes.

5. Serve the scramble in bowls with the rice, topped with scallions, if using, and hot sauce or chopped chiles.

Skillet Tilapia Tacos
with Mango Salsa

TL;DR: *Make salsa. Season tilapia. Toast tortillas in pan and keep them warm in oven while fish cooks. Assemble tacos and douse in salsa.*

I was truly devastated when our favorite neighborhood taco place closed because I could no longer get their amazing fish tacos whenever I wanted. For my at-home version, I don't make my own tortillas fresh to order like they did, but these are awfully close. If you have helpers, the tacos can come together even faster because someone can do the fish and tortillas while the other person makes the salsa. The preparation might seem complicated the first time you make it because there are three components, the tortillas and fish have to be done quickly, and you want everything to be ready at the same time and eaten right away so moisture doesn't wreck the tortillas . . . you know, tacos! But they are fast and easy and yummy and feel so nourishing, so just lean into it. You can do this.

1. Make the salsa: Combine the mango, shallot, bell pepper, cilantro, lime juice, and salt in a medium bowl, stir, and set aside to let the flavors mingle. It helps if they get to know each other.

2. Make sure your tilapia fillets are fully thawed, then pat them mostly dry with a paper towel. Place the salt, cumin, paprika, and pepper in a small bowl and stir to combine, then lightly coat the tilapia on both sides with the seasonings. Set the tilapia aside while you deal with the tortillas.

3. Preheat the oven to 125°F.

4. Heat a dry cast-iron skillet over medium heat. Working in batches, toast the tortillas in the pan until they puff up and develop a few brown spots, 1 minute or so per side. As you finish toasting them, place the tortillas in the warm oven on an oven-safe plate, under a towel. This should keep them warm and pliable until you are ready to assemble the tacos.

5. When you're done with the tortillas, turn the heat under the skillet up to high. Once it is nice and hot, add a tablespoon or so of the

Makes 8 tacos

MANGO SALSA

1 large mango, peeled and finely chopped

1 shallot, finely chopped (half a red onion works well, too)

½ red bell pepper, finely chopped

½ cup chopped fresh cilantro

Juice of 1 lime

1 teaspoon fine sea salt

SKILLET TILAPIA TACOS

4 large or 8 small fillets tilapia, skin removed and thawed if frozen

1 tablespoon fine sea salt, plus extra as needed

2 teaspoons ground cumin

2 teaspoons ground paprika

1 teaspoon freshly cracked black pepper

8 to 16 corn tortillas (see note)

2 tablespoons neutral cooking oil, such as canola

Freshly squeezed lime juice, for finishing

Note: If your corn tortillas are small and a little flimsy, you will want to have 2 per taco (for a total of 16), but if you have larger, sturdier ones, you should need only 1 per fish fillet (for a total of 8).

cooking oil. Working in batches so you don't crowd them, gently place 2 or 3 pieces of tilapia in the pan, cover, and let cook for 2 minutes. Flip and cook until they are just cooked through, beginning to flake apart, and ideally have a few brown spots, about 2 minutes more. Remove to a plate and place in the warm oven. Repeat until you have cooked all of the tilapia; replenish the oil in the pan as needed.

6. Taste the fish. Sprinkle with more salt, if you like, and squeeze fresh lime juice over the tilapia to finish.

7. To assemble the tacos, place 1 or 2 tortillas on a plate (see note, page 115) and top with 1 large piece of tilapia or 2 small ones (don't worry if they break up; that just means they're lovely and tender) and a generous spoonful of mango salsa. I recommend two tacos per person.

Smoky Cauliflower Enchiladas

TL;DR: *Panfry chorizo and vegetables. Cook chile sauce briefly, then blend it. Assemble enchiladas in a baking dish, top with sauce, and bake at 375°F for 20 to 25 minutes.*

This meal is versatile. Are you a planner? Assemble this the night before (keep the sauce separate from the enchiladas), cover, and keep in the fridge, then pull it out and bake it the next evening. Need quick gratification? Make these into tacos instead of baking— just assemble the filling on warm tortillas. Do you like to get the active cooking done and then have some time to connect and set the table and chill while it bakes? Then do the whole shebang in one evening.

I like the flavor here unmuddled by the cheesy richness, but it's true that enchiladas are usually extremely cheesy, and if you miss that, shower these in a melty cheese before baking them. Of course, if you want a vegetarian meal, omit the chorizo. Please, please go with what you most enjoy.

1. Preheat the oven to 375°F.

2. Warm 1 tablespoon of the oil in a wide pan or Dutch oven over medium heat. Add the onion and crumble the chorizo into the pan. Let cook, occasionally breaking up the meat with a wooden spoon, until the chorizo is lightly browned and the onion has softened and just started to brown, about 5 minutes. Add the cauliflower, 1 teaspoon of the salt, the cumin and paprika (if desired), and about ½ cup of water, cover, and cook, stirring occasionally, until the cauliflower is soft, about 20 minutes.

3. While the chorizo filling cooks, warm the remaining 1 tablespoon of oil in a small saucepan over medium-low heat. Add the garlic and cook until it smells great, about 1 minute. Add the tomatoes, green chiles, and remaining ½ teaspoon of salt and stir. Remove the pan from the heat and use an immersion blender to blend the sauce until it's smooth. Put it back over medium-low heat and bring it to a gentle simmer, with the lid slightly askew to allow steam to escape. Let the sauce bubble away until you're ready to add it to the enchiladas. Stir occasionally.

Serves 3 or 4

- 2 tablespoons extra-virgin olive oil
- 1 onion, chopped
- 8 ounces chorizo (about 2 links)
- 1 head cauliflower, finely chopped
- 1½ teaspoons fine sea salt
- 1 teaspoon ground cumin (optional; see note)
- 1 teaspoon ground smoked paprika (optional; see note)
- 3 cloves garlic, sliced
- 1 can (28 ounces) fire-roasted diced tomatoes
- 1 can (4.5 ounces) chopped green chiles
- 3 to 4 cups chopped dinosaur kale (cut into ribbons)
- 6 medium or 8 small tortillas (flour or corn is fine)
- Chopped scallions, for serving
- Chopped fresh cilantro, for serving

Note: If you have cumin and smoked paprika on hand, use them to amplify the chorizo flavor, but don't buy them just for this recipe—it's still delicious without them.

4. Add the kale to the chorizo filling and stir until it's just wilted, 1 minute. Taste and add a bit more salt if you'd like. Remove the pan from the heat.

5. Spoon a layer of enchilada sauce over the bottom of a wide casserole or baking dish. Fill a tortilla with a few spoonfuls of filling, roll it up, and place in the pan, seam side down. Continue with the remaining tortillas and filling until the pan is full. Spread more sauce generously over the enchiladas.

Note: *I find that I use about half the sauce per pan of enchiladas. If you have leftover sauce, you can put it in the fridge for another use or freeze it to use with your next batch of enchiladas.*

6. Bake until the tortilla edges start to brown and the enchiladas are warmed through, 20 to 25 minutes. Sprinkle with chopped scallions and cilantro and serve. Store any leftovers in the fridge, where they will keep for 3 to 5 days; reheat them in the oven so they can recrisp.

Sambal Shrimp Lettuce Wraps

TL;DR: *Defrost shrimp. Process and cook sambal. Cut mango.*
Put out butter lettuce. Sauté shrimp and add half the sambal.
Serve on a big platter and make little lettuce wraps.

Serves 2

SAMBAL

4 shallots

4 cloves garlic

5 red jalapeños (any fresh red chile will do)

1 teaspoon fine sea salt, plus extra as needed

¼ cup vegetable oil

1 tablespoon tamarind paste, plus extra as needed

1 tablespoon sugar, plus extra as needed

LETTUCE WRAPS

2 mangos, peaches, or nectarines, chopped

1 head butter lettuce

2 tablespoons butter or vegetable oil

1 pound small (41 to 50 per pound) frozen shrimp, thawed, peeled, tails off, and deveined (see note)

Note: You can, of course, cook this dish with larger shrimp or prawns; just adjust the cooking time accordingly in Step 4. To thaw the frozen shrimp, place them in a sieve and submerge it in a bowl filled with cold water. The shrimp should thaw in 20 to 30 minutes. If you are in a hurry, you can run the cold water through the sieve to make it go faster.

Spicy food makes me feel good, so when I first encountered a version of this dish at a local restaurant, the dark-red jammy-looking sauce made my heart soar. The restaurant has since closed down, so I have to make it myself. Sambal is an amazingly spicy, sweet, and complex sauce or condiment popular in Southeast Asian cuisines, and very much worth the effort. Once you have made it, it keeps in the fridge for a couple of weeks, which can be such a help on a tired night—you can make it ahead of time, and then all you have to do is cook shrimp, cut up mango, and put out lettuce cups for a beautiful weeknight dinner. With the crisp, fresh lettuce and juicy fruit, this dish is stunning.

This recipe makes twice the amount of sambal you need for the shrimp, but it's so good that you will want to make the shrimp again, or toss the sambal with noodles, drizzle it on vegetables, or mix it with sour cream and dip cucumber into it. Make wild or brown rice to serve alongside the wraps for a larger meal or to feed four people.

1. Make the sambal: Trim and peel the shallots and garlic and place them in a food processor or mortar and pestle. Cut the tops off the jalapeños and cut them in half. For full heat, add the jalapeño halves to the shallots and garlic, or for less heat, remove some of the seeds and the white ribs. Add the salt, then grind up the shallots, garlic, and jalapeños a bit. Add a tablespoon or so of the oil and keep grinding until you have a uniform paste.

Note: Wear gloves when chopping hot chiles to avoid getting that chile burn on your fingers. You can also oil your hands to protect them. Whatever you do, keep your fingers away from your eyes!

2. Warm the rest of the oil in a small pan over medium heat. Add the jalapeño paste and cook, stirring constantly, until it darkens and the oil breaks from the paste, 10 to 15 minutes. You are basically caramelizing the shallots, garlic, and jalapeños. Once the jalapeño paste has darkened,

take the pan off the heat and stir in the tamarind paste and sugar. Taste and add more salt, tamarind, or sugar if you think it needs it. Set the sambal aside until you are ready to cook the shrimp.

3. Peel the mango and chop it into long or bite-size pieces, according to your preference. Arrange the mango on a large serving platter or board, and nestle the leaves of butter lettuce next to it.

4. Melt the butter in a large pan over medium heat. Rinse the shrimp and shake them as dry as you can without being too obsessive. Add them to the pan with the butter and cook until they release some of their juices, about 1 minute. Add half of the sambal paste and stir to coat the shrimp. Cook, stirring occasionally, until the shrimp are pink, curled, and cooked through, 3 to 5 minutes.

Note: *This dish is very juicy and rich and generously sauced, but if you don't think it needs all that sauce, by all means use less sambal. Using less sambal will also reduce the heat of the dish.*

5. Serve the sambal shrimp alongside the lettuce and mango, either spread out on the platter or in a bowl. Ask diners to fill a lettuce leaf with shrimp and mango and eat it like a small wrap.

Good Enough When You're Struggling

Cooking for Self-Worth

Looking back, I realize that I fell in love with cooking during a bittersweet time in my life. I was functional, but feeling extremely depressed. Cooking was the one thing I let myself do that I really enjoyed. But I could only get away with letting myself cook because I told myself it was work that needed doing.

I had graduated from college and was working a job that was, by all accounts, an incredible opportunity. I worked at city hall in my hometown of Edmonton, and I worked every day to help and support other people. The job was hard. I was a young woman, and as is the case for so many young women, it was difficult to get people (mainly men) to respect me. And I craved respect because I myself didn't think I belonged there. I had gotten into a pattern of thinking where all I allowed myself to do was work. Whether it was the work I was paid for, work around my home, volunteer work, or the emotional work of listening to and supporting my friends and partner, I always had to be working—and working for others, never myself. If I stopped working, I would have to sit with myself, which meant sitting with a sense of worthlessness.

I had no clear sense of direction. I didn't see myself as someone who was good enough at anything to have a clear path. I wasn't creative enough, smart enough, driven enough—I felt there was nothing about me that was interesting or powerful enough to do anything in particular. So I directed my energies toward service to others. Other people's needs and dreams would bolster my self-worth.

With my salary, my partner and I were able to buy a condo, and I suddenly had an amazing kitchen and space, enough money to buy groceries, and time to teach myself to cook whatever I wanted. I felt so free in my kitchen. I let myself experiment and play, and I had confidence. I knew what I was doing when I was making food; it was a language that came naturally to me, and the information stuck in my head like little else did. I felt so excited and proud when people said they liked my food, and I felt equally as excited to be able to tell them how to make the food they enjoyed so much.

Cooking gave me a little gateway into self-care, but the rest of my life was worse than ever. I was afraid all the time of making a mistake. Because my sense of self-worth was wrapped up in what I did, I felt I had to say yes to everything—that I had to keep working in order to be a moral person. I felt that if it were possible for me to contribute and I chose not to, I would betray my values. Who did I think I was to say no? I wasn't better than anyone else. Everyone was struggling, and I thought I had a duty to contribute anywhere I could. It was impossible to keep up with. I burned out hard.

This pattern of working too hard and burning out had been going on for years. It was all I knew how to do. As far as I knew, the only way to accomplish anything was to grind myself down until I limped over the finish line, sick and unable to enjoy my victory. Those victories weren't even mine—they belonged to the people whose acceptance I was working to earn. Each effort felt like an attempt to keep just enough ahead that no one would find out I was worthless. And each time the anxiety seemed to return sooner and with more power. If my worth was contained solely in what I did for others, I couldn't rest or I risked losing everything.

Eventually, I found the courage to quit that job so I could figure out what to do next. But it really wasn't the job itself that had made me unhappy. More than anything, I needed a break. I was relentlessly cruel to myself. My inner voice was like the stepmother in *Cinderella*, saying I was nothing, and unfortunately, when I quit my job, she didn't leave me. Lucky for me, I was able to trick my inner stepmother, telling her that cooking was work. She didn't need to know that I was secretly having fun in the kitchen.

My breakthrough came when I was talking to a friend who asked me why I loved cooking so much. I found myself saying, "It's the one time I don't feel guilty and can just have fun." As he talked, telling me about a project he was doing and how he thought I might get involved, the weight of what I'd just said sank in. I realized I was sick of feeling only as good as the work I did, only as good as the things I said yes to. Some deep-down, hurt part of me was saying, "Help, I am more than this." So when my friend finally asked me to get involved in his project, I said, with grief and shock, that I couldn't. I said that I simply could not do another thing for other people without first doing something for myself.

From that moment began a long and painful journey of putting myself back together, slowly and quietly deciding to follow my own dreams, moving to New York, getting my master's degree, and writing cookbooks.

But the battle with the evil stepmother will never be truly over. Over the years, I have realized that her voice is not an evil voice, but a terrified one. She is afraid that if I stop doing what everyone else wants, they will abandon me—that I have nothing to offer but my service. I try every day to soothe her fears and show her that while it is hard, and I may get rejected and misunderstood and even fail, I am still worth fighting for.

Now, when I am at my lowest, cooking is there for me still. I love the feeling of a rough, shaggy dough transforming into a smooth, elastic dough under my spirited kneading. I love the sense of control I feel as I blast around the kitchen, efficiently moving from one task to the next in the service of a meal. I love to watch for the moment when garlic starts sizzling in the pan, bubbles of oil popping around it as the edges begin to curl and turn light brown, its inviting aroma filling the kitchen. When I am cooking, the mistakes of the past melt away and the fears of the future grow fuzzy, and there is only now. This beautiful little life. This wonderful body that works so well. This bright mind noticing and connecting. And I am free.

Making Something Is One Way to Say I'm Here

Tough times and overwhelming feelings come and go. We all experience them. It can help to remember that this moment and these feelings will pass. But for those of us who have ever gotten stuck in difficult feelings that lead to depression, they can get very scary. Sometimes caring for yourself enough to eat, let alone to do the work of making food, can feel impossible. I don't have a cure or a strategy that works consistently—I am not a mental health expert, and if you are feeling any of these things, please, please tell someone because we absolutely cannot deal on our own. You are valuable and we want you here. But speaking for myself, my own process of feeling painful emotions goes something like this: First there is a spiral of grief, sadness, and fear—the sort of devastating, wracked with sobs, barely able to function, panic attack realm where you wonder if you can live. But you do. Somehow you bear it, like when you stub your toe or crack your head on the corner of a piece of furniture, and the pain mounts and mounts, and you breathe and grimace, maybe shout an expletive or two, and know that it will pass. Ideally—and I will say that I am still very much learning to do this one—you let someone witness your pain. Someone who loves you. Someone who can show you compassion and kindness and let you know that you are lovable. But then, after that acute time has passed, when you are in the hangover stage, still working through pain and sadness and lack of energy . . . well, that's tough, because sometimes you can get stuck.

For me, the best way to get unstuck is to create something. Anything. Making anything is the first step on the path out of the dark. Sing a little tune. Take a picture. Make a little flower out of the tissue you were using to wipe away your tears. Write a few sentences on paper. Draw something. Make a joke. Put something out into the world. It sends energy to that deep human place we all have, to our inner fire that feels obscured at the moment.

So why not try that with making some food? Sometimes it helps to just focus on the creation part of cooking. Don't even worry about eating it. One. Step. At. A. Time. Just make it first, and then decide later. I don't usually have much of an appetite when I'm feeling big stuff, so it can help to take the pressure off the idea of actually eating. I know I *should* eat, but doing a *should* for yourself

when you are shut down or feeling a lot is near impossible. Chances are you'll take a bite or two.

Sometimes making something for someone I love can be easier than making something for myself. It can feel like borrowing a little of their life force. If I can make something that makes someone else feel loved, then a little warmth comes back to me. But it's not about pleasing others; it's about the act of kindness and creativity. It is not about erasing yourself; it is about building a healthy connection from one whole person to another. Making things—instead of only consuming them, watching them, judging them—is so healing. It's strange if you haven't noticed it before, but using your energy to make something can actually bring more energy, rather than draining it. Until you experience it, it is hard to trust. Even though I have experienced it many times, I still find it hard to trust. But it's true: Creating makes me feel stronger. And that is so mind-blowing because the kind of pain I'm talking about is the kind that tells you that you are nothing, that you are worthless and powerless and cannot accomplish anything. But creating is powerful and you can do it in the tiniest way. You make the smallest thing, and in the making of that thing, it is like you are given the gift of life. A deep true breath.

No matter what you choose to make, or how, or for whom, or how small, an act of creation is a direct counterattack to the belief that your life is passing you by and you aren't really living. (Stay with me here, because I know this seems a little woo-woo.) Fears fester when we sit and lurk and don't get involved, when we don't let ourselves do what we truly want to do. I did that for so many years. I defined myself as the kind of person who wants to sit on the sidelines and support others and help others achieve things. And I did like helping others, but it left me empty. I wasn't really creating anything for me, and I wasn't taking any of the risks required for true connection. I was afraid to show who I really was. Fear of that feeling haunts me when I begin to feel stuck—I am afraid I will revert to hiding and ignoring myself and simply following what others want.

We all want to live meaningful lives. But it's even simpler than that. We want to live *our* lives. Unfortunately, that is scary. Really scary. If we own up to what we want and try it and it doesn't go perfectly (which it won't), then we will feel pain. So instead, we try just existing. Floating through the world, not taking the risks a real choice requires. It feels like a great way to avoid the pain of loss and rejection. But over time, the loss and rejection come anyway, because when you never try, you are rejecting yourself, telling yourself you aren't worth trying for. So creating, even in the smallest way, builds self-trust. Anytime you create—even if it's "just" a plate of cheese and crackers or a shadow puppet or an outfit—you are living *your* life.

Being Your Own Best Parent

We have a lot of art and stories and culture about growing up, transitioning from child to adult, and leaving home. It can be painful; it's hard for both parents and children to change long-held roles of relating. But I wish we would say that the process of becoming an adult is more like realizing that you are the best parent to yourself. Though we may no longer need our parents, we will always need parenting, in the sense that we will need love and nurturing. Who does that loving and nurturing, and in what way, must shift as we grow into new phases of our lives.

> I have found it transformative to notice that there are parts of myself that need support and care and parts that can actually do that supporting and caring.

Let me be clear: I'm not saying that it's not okay to go to your parents for a warm meal, for childcare support, to ask for advice, to get sent home with a twelve-pack of toilet paper, or to devolve into a child version of yourself around them. No. Have the relationship with your parents that works for you. Have the relationship with your children that works for you. I'm talking about your internal world. I have found it transformative to notice that there are parts of myself that need support and care and parts that can actually do that supporting and caring. We can do more than one thing at a time. We can feel more than one thing at a time. And in my life, the ability to accept complex, ambiguous, and conflicting experiences has been *the* thing that has allowed me to feel safe and solid in the world.

We all need to be actively loved and cared for. While we can and should pursue that love and care from partners, friends, and relatives, other people cannot be as steady and reliable as we might wish. You know yourself best, you are with yourself at all times, and you can tend to your innermost needs quickly and easily, even if it's as simple as putting a hand on your heart. So if we can parent ourselves from the inside out, not minimize, dismiss, or explain away our emotions, but simply attend to our own needs with kind, calm attention, we can be free to thrive.

Healing Activities

Here are a few simple activities that have helped me when I get overwhelmed with feelings or circumstances. Take what works and leave the rest!

1. **Cooking and baking.** I go one of two routes: making something for someone I love that I know they love, or making something I remember enjoying in the past, even if it's hard to relate to the past me in my current state of mind.

2. **Reading a novel.** Watching a TV show or movie can sometimes work, but I find that reading is better because I have to be engaged in it to get immersed in the story. When the TV is on, I can sometimes drift off into thought or browse social media, and then I am missing out on the good stuff.

3. **Music.** Singing or humming to myself. Familiar music. Whatever I feel drawn to, happy, sad, or silly. And moving to it as much or as little as I want.

4. **Walking or running**, especially in nature, in a park, or on a quiet, tree-lined street.

5. **Drawing or writing** anything that comes to mind and feels good.

Safe Foods

Some might call these comfort foods, or lazy or sad or depressing, or whatever other judgmental words you use to describe the food you make for yourself when you really can't deal, but you are also genuinely hungry. For me, these toasts and sandwiches are safe foods; they taste good to me no matter what, even when I am physically sick. They are a first line of defense against any kind of struggle.

EGG SANDWICH ADDITIONS

- Cheese
- Hot sauce
- Bacon/sausage
- Sliced avocado
- Salsa (try Mango Salsa, page 115)
- Sweet and Spicy Chicken Dinner leftovers (page 108)
- Creamy Dill and Date Dressing (page 88) or the creamy cilantro dressing from the Smoky Honey Shrimp Tacos (page 266)
- Pickles
- Gruyère and ham
- Tomato and pepperoni
- British Beer Cheese, added to the eggs (page 173)
- Chile crisp (seriously, this is the most important one). This condiment with a cult following can be found online or in an Asian grocery store.

Cheese toast. Start with bread, whatever kind you have in the house. Rye bread is my favorite. Or sourdough. For the cheese, aged white cheddar is my go-to, but seriously, this is a very personal choice. Lay your cheese on your bread and heat until bubbly in a toaster oven, in a pan on the stove, or even in a microwave if you're in a pinch. If you need more, top with sliced pickled things, like olives, giardiniera, or jalapeños.

Avocado toast. Toast your bread of choice. While it toasts, cut an avocado in half and remove the pit. Smear half of the avocado on the toast, or neatly cut it into pieces or roses or whatever makes you happy. Sprinkle with salt and a squeeze of lemon or lime. Stop there or personalize with crushed red pepper flakes, more citrus juice, spice blends, tomato, onion . . . I could do this all day.

Egg sandwiches. I'll be honest and say that when I am feeling lousy, I am more likely to make cheese toast or avocado toast, if I have an avocado. The egg sandwich is something I often purchase for myself when I feel horrible, like when I'm hurrying to catch a plane at 3 a.m., stomach nauseous from stress. It always fills the void and helps me feel stable. But when I do make an egg sandwich at home, I never regret it—I just don't like washing the pan. So crack one or two eggs into a pan and fry, scramble, or cook in whatever way you like while your bread or bun or English muffin toasts. And since you are home, scour your fridge for the toppings you love and luxuriate in the comforting, creamy, salty bites. See the bullets at left for a decidedly nonexhaustive list of what you can add to your egg sandwich.

On Redefining Comfort Food

The foods in this chapter help me feel better when I'm struggling, but, of course, we are different and my foods may not feel the same for you. Nevertheless, I hope you can, through these examples, understand how they work for me so you might find your own. First we try safe foods, and then, when more of a meal begins to seem interesting, maybe we try something that might sound comforting. Take spaghetti and meatballs, for example, a dish that conjures up a strong image of comfort by dint of having been presented as a comfort food in practically every TV show, movie, and book consumed in Western culture for the last fifty years. But please don't take this as a suggestion without examining what image is comforting to *you* (not to others, and not in the traditional sense of the phrase). What I mean is: Take whatever dish has a strong comforting image for you, and make it a thing to look forward to. Comfort food doesn't have to be rich or heavy or storied or the work of a beloved grandmother. Instead, it should conjure up an image of comfort that you can hold in your mind as you engage your efforts to bring it forth into the world. An image that comforts with a thought long before it hits the plate. That lends you power. That supports you and cheerleads you through your efforts, like a friend.

Self-Love Potion

TL;DR: Simmer spices in water, then add oat milk and strain before serving.

Serves 1

½ cup water

1 tablespoon sugar or honey

1-inch piece of ginger, sliced

8 cardamom pods, crushed, or ½ teaspoon ground cardamom

Pinch of fine sea salt

1 cup oat milk

Being handed a mug of something hot feels like love to me. It's comforting, it's soothing, it's intimate. When I feel bad, whether physically or emotionally, it really can give a little boost of warmth and tend that little fire in my belly that might be lagging. In the spirit of that heat, the ginger here is important. It's not overpowering, like in ginger beer—it's mellowed by the oat milk—but it has that fiery, warming quality, and along with the aroma of cardamom and the sweetness and frothiness, it just . . . I close my eyes and I'm in a cabin in the woods and a magical old lady is handing me a mug of this and I trust her and I take a sip and the world shifts and it's scary for a second and then I'm warm and happy and I *know* I am loved. I love making this for myself and feeling like a magical witch powerful enough to bring that experience to reality.

1. Place the water, sugar, ginger, cardamom, and salt in a small pot and bring to a simmer over low heat. Stir to dissolve the sugar, then let the mixture simmer gently for 15 minutes.

2. Pour in the oat milk and let it heat through until a few bubbles form. Turn off the heat, put a lid on the pot, and let the potion steep for 10 minutes.

3. To serve, pour the potion through a sieve to catch the ginger and cardamom. To create a little frothiness, pour it into a favorite mug from high up. Enjoy immediately.

Steeping allows the flavors from the ginger and cardamom to infuse further and gives the feeling of letting the magic happen and also lets the potion cool just a bit so you can drink it right away.

Lime Tart Spritzer

TL;DR: *Whisk condensed milk with lime juice and zest.
Swirl syrup into seltzer and serve with ice.*

This is my hot-weather version of the Self-Love
Potion (page 132). A special drink makes me feel special. It is
pleasurable and healing in a way that feels different from a meal.
Sipping a drink, you sit and maybe look out the window and
appreciate the drink and let your thoughts flow. You are experiencing
something just for you, not because you have to, but because you can.
Because you are lucky and have a lot to be grateful for. This spritzer,
inspired by key lime pie, is a rich, creamy, and super tangy syrup
blended with bubbly seltzer. It's unusual enough to wake up your
senses and surprise you into the present moment.

1. Pour the condensed milk into a medium bowl. Zest each lime over
the bowl, using a Microplane.

2. Position a sieve over the bowl to catch any seeds or pulp. Slice the
limes in half and squeeze the lime juice out of them, using a citrus
reamer if you have one. Add the salt and whisk everything together.

3. To make a drink, measure out 2 to 3 tablespoons of syrup into a
glass. Add a splash of seltzer and stir, just to loosen the syrup so it can
fully incorporate into the drink. Top with ice and about 1 cup more
seltzer and stir. It will be foamy!

4. Taste and add more syrup to your liking. Serve with a lime wedge,
if desired. The syrup will last for a couple of weeks in a sealed jar in
the fridge.

*Makes about 2 cups of syrup,
enough for 10 to 16 spritzers*

**1 can (14 ounces) sweetened
condensed milk**

4 limes

Wee sprinkle of fine sea salt

Seltzer, for serving

Ice, for serving

**Lime wedge, for serving
(optional)**

Orange Cheesecake Brownies

TL;DR: *Make brownie batter and cheesecake batter separately, then layer them in a pan. Bake at 350°F for 40 to 50 minutes.*

Makes 8 large or 16 small brownies

BROWNIE LAYER

10 tablespoons (1 stick plus 2 tablespoons) unsalted butter, melted

1¼ cups sugar

Zest of ½ large navel orange

¾ cup unsweetened cocoa powder

½ teaspoon pure vanilla extract

¼ teaspoon fine sea salt

2 large eggs

½ cup all-purpose flour

CHEESECAKE LAYER

16 ounces (2 packages) cream cheese, at room temperature

½ cup sugar

2 large eggs

Zest of 1 large navel orange

¼ cup freshly squeezed orange juice

1 teaspoon pure vanilla extract

Orange and chocolate leave a strong impression on me. I think of a piece of orange rind twisting and releasing its oil, the air filling with the bright, sweet scent. I think of a block of dark chocolate breaking apart, the small crumbly bits melting and releasing their aroma under my hot fingertips. In my view, nothing complements chocolate so well as orange. It reminds me of warm, wintry experiences and Christmas and pleasure without guilt. For some reason, I quite often forget how much I like chocolate and orange together, but then I catch the scent of it somewhere, and it blasts into my consciousness and I feel so absurdly glad to be alive and able to taste and smell and eat.

1. Preheat the oven to 350°F. Butter an 8-inch square baking pan thoroughly or line it with parchment paper that comes up the sides and hangs over the edges, making a sling for removing the brownies from the pan.

2. Make the brownie layer: Place the melted butter and sugar in a medium bowl and whisk together. Add the orange zest, cocoa powder, vanilla, and salt and whisk to combine. Whisk in the eggs one at a time, being sure the first is fully incorporated before adding the second. Finally, gently fold in the flour until just combined. Pour the batter into the prepared pan and use a spatula to smooth its top.

3. Make the cheesecake layer: Place the cream cheese and sugar in the bowl of a stand mixer (in a pinch, mixing by hand is okay) and whisk until the cream cheese is a little lightened and smooth. Add the eggs and whisk, then add the zest, orange juice, and vanilla and whisk until smooth. Pour the cheesecake batter over the brownie batter in the pan and smooth it into an even layer.

4. Bake until a knife inserted into the center comes out clean (or with a little goo), 40 to 50 minutes. (If you like them gooey in the middle, go for 40; otherwise, they're more set after 50 minutes.) Let cool before slicing and serving. These brownies will keep, covered, in the fridge for up to a week.

Every Day Is Summer Berry Cookie Bars

TL;DR: *Make berry mixture. Make cookie bar layer and press into pan. Top with berries. Bake at 350°F for 50 minutes. Whip up topping and serve with cooled bars.*

When you are hurting, you need kindness, and yet it can feel like kind is the last thing you want to be to yourself. Berries are expensive and luxurious, and while I readily buy them and offer them to my daughter, some long-held habit keeps me from enjoying them myself as often as I could these days. So these berry-studded cookie bars are kind of a gentle challenge to the part of me that doesn't think I'm worth it. As they bake, the berry topping bubbles and melts into the cookie dough below to form a kind of cookie-pie-bar that feels celebratory. The moisture from the berries means that these bars have a long cooking time and a short fridge life, so enjoy the moment and eat them quickly.

1. Preheat the oven to 350°F. Line an 8-inch square baking pan with parchment paper that comes up the sides and hangs over the edges, making a sling for removing the bars from the pan.

2. Make the berry topping: Place the berries, sugar, cornstarch, and lemon zest in a medium bowl and gently mix together. Set aside.

3. Make the cookie layer: Place the melted butter, sugar, and vanilla in a medium bowl and whisk together. Add the egg and whisk until the mixture is smooth and a bit lighter.

4. Measure out the flour, baking soda, and salt into a small bowl and stir them together. Pour the flour mixture into the bowl with the liquid ingredients and use a wooden spoon to bring it all together. Press the dough into the prepared pan and top with the berry mixture.

5. Bake until a knife inserted into the center comes out clean, about 50 minutes. Let the bars cool to room temperature in the pan, then lift them out and cut them into 9 squares.

6. To make the whipped topping, place the heavy cream, sugar, and vanilla in a large bowl and beat with an electric mixer until soft peaks form, about 5 minutes. Serve the bars with a dollop of whipped cream.

Makes 9 cookie bars

BERRY TOPPING

4 cups mixed berries (blueberries, blackberries, raspberries; see note)

2 tablespoons sugar

1 tablespoon cornstarch

Zest of 1 lemon

COOKIE LAYER

½ cup (1 stick) unsalted butter, melted

¾ cup sugar

1 teaspoon pure vanilla extract

1 large egg

1 cup all-purpose flour

½ teaspoon baking soda

½ teaspoon fine sea salt

WHIPPED TOPPING (OPTIONAL)

1 cup heavy cream

2 tablespoons sugar

½ teaspoon pure vanilla extract

Note: I use fresh berries, but a 16-ounce bag of frozen mixed berries yields about 4 cups and works just fine.

Maple Chipotle "Campfire" Cornbread

TL;DR: *Mix dry ingredients and wet ingredients, then combine them. Fold in corn and pour batter into pan. Bake at 400°F for 25 minutes.*

Makes 8 pieces

4 tablespoons (½ stick) butter, melted, plus more butter for greasing the pan

1 cup all-purpose flour

1 cup medium- or coarse-grind cornmeal

1 tablespoon baking powder

1 teaspoon fine sea salt

2 large eggs

1 cup whole milk

¼ cup plus 1 tablespoon maple syrup

1 chipotle in adobo sauce, finely chopped

1 cup corn (fresh, canned, or frozen and thawed)

1 teaspoon adobo sauce (from the can of chipotles in adobo)

Making bread gives me a rush of good feelings. The flour and water becoming a smooth and stretchy dough, the yeast doing its magic, the wait for a rise, and then the final transformation in the oven—it's a miraculous process. But when I feel truly lousy, it can seem daunting, and the payoff too distant. Cornbread, though, all mixed up in one bowl, poured into a pan, and baked immediately—that feels attainable. This cornbread is sweet and smoky and extra corny. It reminds me of the scent of a campfire clinging to my hair and clothes and of communing with people I love in nature. And you'll have it ready in under an hour.

1. Preheat the oven to 400°F. Butter an 8-inch square baking pan.

2. Place the flour, cornmeal, baking powder, and salt in a large bowl and whisk just to combine.

3. Crack the eggs into a medium bowl and add the melted butter. Whisk to combine, then pour in the milk and whisk until smooth. Whisk in ¼ cup of the maple syrup and the chopped chipotle. Pour the wet ingredients into the dry ingredients and gently mix together with a spatula until smooth. Gently fold in the corn.

4. Pour the cornbread batter into the prepared pan. Bake until a knife inserted into the center comes out clean, about 25 minutes.

5. While the cornbread is in the oven, place the remaining 1 tablespoon of maple syrup and the 1 teaspoon of adobo sauce in a small bowl and stir to combine. When the cornbread comes out of the oven, baste it with the maple syrup–adobo topping. Let cool before cutting and serving.

Here and Now Jalapeño and Honey Biscuits

TL;DR: *Grate frozen butter into dry ingredients, then add wet ingredients and mix into a shaggy dough. Refrigerate for 20 minutes. Roll out and cut into 8 triangles. Glaze and bake at 375°F for 20 to 25 minutes.*

Biscuits tend to bring out a lot of opinions in people. *They aren't as flaky as my great aunt's! They have to be round! They have to be square! That's a scone, not a biscuit!* So they can feel a little risky to make. I will be the first to admit that these biscuits rarely come out perfect. I often don't let the dough rest long enough, or I cut them in a way that breaks the layers and I end up with a smaller rise and sides that are a little bloopy. But honestly, it doesn't bother me anymore. Sometimes fussing and perfecting is fun and worthwhile, but when you're making these, just with yourself, be kind and relaxed, and enjoy the way the dough feels on your fingers and the aroma and sight of your little browned beauties when they come out of the oven. You made them yourself and they are definitely good enough.

1. Place the butter in the freezer to chill for at least 20 minutes.

2. While the butter gets cold, combine the flour, baking powder, baking soda, and salt in a large bowl and whisk together. Combine the milk, yogurt, and honey in a liquid measuring cup and whisk together.

3. Use a box grater to grate the frozen butter into the flour mixture. Add the chopped jalapeño and the liquid ingredients and gently bring everything together with your hands. Knead gently and firmly until the dough just comes together into a lump with lots of visible butter flakes. It will be a fairly wet dough. Cover with plastic wrap and put the dough in the fridge to chill for 20 minutes.

4. While the dough chills, preheat the oven to 375°F. Line a sheet pan with parchment paper or a silicone baking mat.

5. When the 20 minutes are up, flour a counter generously. Gently but confidently shape the dough into a 6-inch square. Using a sharp serrated knife and a sawing motion, cut the biscuits into 4 equal

Makes 8 triangular biscuits

¾ cup (1½ sticks) unsalted butter

2½ cups all-purpose flour, plus more for dusting the counter

1 tablespoon baking powder

1 teaspoon baking soda

1 teaspoon fine sea salt

½ cup whole milk, plus 2 teaspoons for glazing (see note)

½ cup plain yogurt (see note)

¼ cup honey, plus 2 teaspoons for glazing and more for drizzling

1 jalapeño, stemmed, seeded (for less heat, if desired), and chopped

Flaky sea salt, to finish (optional)

Note: You can substitute 1 cup of buttermilk for the milk and yogurt.

squares. Then cut each square in half diagonally to create 8 small triangles.

6. Place the biscuits 1 inch apart on the prepared sheet pan. Mix the remaining 2 teaspoons of milk and 2 teaspoons of honey in a small bowl and brush the glaze over the tops of the biscuits.

7. Bake until the biscuits are puffed and golden, 20 to 25 minutes. Remove them from the oven, drizzle with a little more honey, and sprinkle with a little flaky salt, if you like. Store them in a sealed container at room temperature for up to 4 days.

I Spell Love Q-U-E-S-O

TL;DR: *Char poblanos. Sauté scallions and peppers, then beans. Turn down heat and pour in milk and sour cream, then cheese, and stir until smooth.*

There are days when I feel pretty awful about myself. Sometimes it's because a particular incident or conversation is on replay in my head. Other times it's because my internal critic is particularly loud and confusing. And still other times it's for no discernible reason beyond the fact that some days just seem hopeless. When I feel bad about myself, I am the last person I want to help. That's when a little ritual can be helpful. In a state of low self-esteem, I don't find my eccentricities charming. But, of course they still are! Even if I am not in a place to see them. So if I can, I like to make myself a meal that is particularly rooted in my individual taste. Working on something that is really just for me makes me feel a little special. Sure, I might wish that a partner, parent, or friend would make something special just for me and therefore give me that sense of being valued from the outside. Seems easier. But when the root of the problem is how you see yourself, and you spend some time acting like you value yourself, well, sometimes you can shift yourself into the reality that you are, in fact, worthy and lovable just as you are. And the pleasure of eating a fun thing just for you definitely helps, too.

In short, act like you care about yourself and you might catch some of the caring. And if not, you still have a meal. In my case, I think about my particular favorite flavor. What is the potato chip I will always choose, the taco I will always order, the aroma that causes immediate salivation? Green chile and cheese! And the pinnacle of this combination is the poblano pepper. This dark green, mild pepper has an incredibly special fresh chile flavor, and enough heat to be on the radar but not so much that you can't eat a lot. So I make this dip for myself because it simply brings me pleasure.

1. Set the oven to broil. Place the poblanos in a cast-iron skillet, set the skillet in the oven, and let them char on one side, about 5 minutes. Using tongs, flip the poblanos and broil until the skin on all sides is blistered and blackened, 5 to 15 minutes more.

Makes 4 cups

3 poblano peppers

2 tablespoons butter

1 tablespoon all-purpose flour

3 scallions, finely chopped

1 can (15½ ounces) black beans, drained and rinsed

½ cup whole milk

½ cup sour cream or yogurt

8 ounces sharp white cheddar and/or jack cheese, shredded (about 2 cups)

Fine sea salt, if needed

Cilantro, for serving (optional)

Tortillas, tortilla chips, or various cut-up vegetables, for serving

2. Transfer the blackened peppers to a metal bowl and cover with a dish towel to let them sit in their sweat and cool for 10 minutes.

3. Once the poblanos are cool enough to touch, gently peel off the skins, cut each poblano in half, and remove and discard the membranes, seeds, and stems. Chop the pepper flesh into small pieces and set aside.

4. Put the same cast-iron pan over medium heat and melt the butter. Add the flour and stir until it is no longer grainy. Sprinkle in most of the chopped scallions and all of the chopped poblanos and stir. Cook until the mixture smells great, about 1 minute, then add the beans and stir just to mix. Reduce the heat to low, pour in the milk and sour cream, and stir. Let the mixture just come to a boil and thicken slightly.

5. Turn off the heat, add all the shredded cheese, and stir until it melts into a smooth, thick cheese sauce. Taste and add a bit of salt if you think it needs it—but because of the salty cheese, I find it usually doesn't. Garnish with the reserved scallions and cilantro, if desired.

6. Serve the queso with tortillas, tortilla chips, and/or various cut-up vegetables. Extra queso can be stored in a sealed container in the fridge for 3 to 5 days.

Extra Elotes Bowl

TL;DR: *Shuck corn, broil it, and cut kernels off cob. Add beans, tomatoes, cilantro, cheese, and dressing and mix well.*

Serves 4 as a side dish or 2 as lunch

4 ears corn (see note)

2 cans (15½ ounces each) black or pinto beans, drained and rinsed

2 cups chopped tomatoes

½ cup chopped fresh cilantro

½ cup crumbled cotija or feta cheese, or grated parmesan

Juice of 1 lime

2 tablespoons mayonnaise

1 tablespoon adobo sauce (from a can of chipotles in adobo)

Note: If it's not corn season but you still want to make this dish, you can use about 3 cups canned or frozen corn. Instead of broiling the kernels, just toast them in a skillet with a little olive oil until they get a bit of color and come alive, about 5 minutes.

Mexican elote, grilled corn slathered in mayo, cheese, hot pepper, and lime juice, is an explosively delicious bite of sweet, spicy, tangy, and salty. When I feel down and nothing sounds appealing, it helps to simply trust that my mouth will send all that goodness to my heart. This bowl makes the brilliance of elote into a meal by adding beans, chopped tomatoes, and cilantro, and it substitutes for the incredible char flavor that comes from cooking corn on an open flame with the smokiness of adobo sauce. When I'm struggling, it's usually hard to summon the will to cook regularly, so making a large batch of something that lasts a while but still feels fresh, like this bowl, is a real gift. It lasts for three days or so in the fridge, but if you aren't going to eat it right away, consider leaving the tomatoes on the side so that it won't get too watery.

1. Set the oven to broil.

2. Shuck the ears of corn, making sure to get rid of all the stringy bits. Place the cobs on a sheet pan and broil them for 5 to 10 minutes. Check on them often, and turn them every couple of minutes so that they cook evenly and get a few brown spots all over. Leave the cobs longer if you like more charred flavor.

3. Once the corn is cooked and cooled enough to touch, cut the kernels off the cobs: Hold each cob by the green knob at the end and point it down over a large bowl. Cut down the side of the cob with your knife, letting the kernels fall into the bowl, and turning occasionally to get all of them.

4. Add the beans, tomatoes, cilantro, and cheese to the bowl and mix.

5. Place the lime juice, mayonnaise, and adobo sauce in a small bowl and stir to mix. Taste and adjust the dressing, adding more mayo if you want it creamier, more adobo if you want it spicier, or more lime juice if you want it tangier.

6. Pour the dressing over the salad, toss to combine, and serve.

Surprisingly Awesome Quesadillas

TL;DR: *Cook chorizo and zucchini. Top each tortilla with the filling and cheese and fold it over. Cook in a pan until brown on both sides. Repeat.*

Quesadillas are very much in the "I feel awful" rotation, along with cheese toast and company. They get the job done and taste good. This version is a little more than a plain cheese quesadilla—which can help the old self-esteem. You've got vegetables in there, and so much flavor, even with just a few ingredients. The zucchini has a great texture here, and the chorizo flavor soaks into it, and the cheese clings to everything. Every time I make these, I'm baffled by how they can be as flavorful as they are. It makes me feel clever and accomplished to be so efficient. Make a big batch and you can keep them to toast up for another meal.

1. To chop the zucchini, cut off the top and the bottom. Cut each zucchini in half lengthwise, then halve lengthwise again. Chop the quartered zucchini into thin slices.

2. Heat the oil in a large skillet over medium-high heat. Squeeze the chorizo from its casing and crumble it into the pan. Break up the sausage with a wooden spoon, then add the zucchini, sprinkle with salt, and stir. Cook, stirring every 5 minutes or so, until the chorizo is cooked (that will happen quickly) and the zucchini is softened, about 15 minutes. Remove from the heat.

3. Spread shredded cheese all over one side of a tortilla, and top it with the chorizo-zucchini mixture. Fold it over to create a half-moon. Repeat with the rest of the tortillas.

4. Heat a heavy pan over medium-high heat. Transfer as many quesadillas as you can to the pan—I find that I can do only 2 at once. Toast on each side until golden brown, about 3 minutes for the first side and 2 minutes more for the second. Covering the pan with a lid can help melt the cheese, but it's not essential. Repeat for the remaining quesadillas.

5. Serve the quesadillas with salsa and sour cream.

Makes 8 quesadillas

- 2 medium zucchini
- 1 tablespoon extra-virgin olive oil
- 10 to 12 ounces fresh chorizo (about 3 links)
- ½ teaspoon fine sea salt
- 4 to 6 ounces monterey jack or cheddar cheese, shredded (1 to 1½ cups)
- 8 tortillas
- Salsa, for serving
- Sour cream, for serving

Enlivening Green Soup

TL;DR: *Cook onions and garlic in butter, then add frozen spinach, water, and lemon zest. Bring to a boil. Melt cream cheese and add it to the soup, with herbs. Blend and serve.*

Serves 4

2 tablespoons butter

2 medium red onions, chopped

Fine sea salt

4 cloves garlic, chopped

2 tablespoons all-purpose flour

1 pound frozen chopped spinach

Zest and juice of 1 large lemon

2 ounces (¼ package) cream cheese

½ bunch fresh cilantro, roughly chopped

½ bunch fresh mint, roughly chopped

Note: Cooked spinach can turn a browny green sometimes. Don't worry, it will still taste good.

Strange to say, because I wouldn't usually associate this quality with soup, but this soup is refreshing and exciting and makes me feel more alive. On days when I feel happy and lively, I reach for flavors like bright lemon and refreshing mint and cilantro, and I want to eat lots of vegetables and rejuvenate my body. This soup brings those qualities together and feels like it's singing a healing song in my mouth. I love it. So on days when I do *not* feel happy and bright, if I can manage to find the energy to make this simple, quick soup, often by the end of the bowl I am remembering that bright, happy person who is still inside me and will be back soon.

1. Melt the butter in a medium pot over medium heat. Tumble the chopped onions into the pan, stir briefly to coat with the butter, sprinkle with a bit of salt, then leave it. Once the onions are translucent, about 5 minutes, add the garlic and stir until you can smell it, another minute or so. Finally, sprinkle the flour all over the vegetables and stir until the flour toasts a bit and everything looks starchy and thick.

2. Add the frozen chopped spinach to the pan, along with the lemon zest, and stir. Leave it, stirring occasionally, until the spinach is no longer frozen and has become soft enough to mix around easily, about 5 minutes. Add 3 cups of water and bring to a boil, then turn the heat down to low. Add 1 tablespoon of salt to the water and stir.

3. Place the cream cheese and 1 tablespoon or so of water in a small microwave-safe bowl. Microwave for 15-second intervals, whisking every so often, until the cream cheese melts just a bit, so that it can incorporate into the soup without clumping. Whisk it into the soup. (You can also melt the cream cheese in a small pot over low heat.)

4. Add the chopped cilantro and mint to the soup and cook until the herbs wilt just a little, about 1 minute.

5. Take the soup off the heat and carefully use an immersion blender to puree it directly in the pot. Taste and add more salt if you think it needs it. Drizzle a bit of the lemon juice over the soup to serve.

Make this soup in the same week as Herby Fish Cakes (page 176), Turkey Falafel Balls (page 268), or Saucy Spiced Chicken (page 102); all of these recipes use lots of mint and cilantro.

Citrus Refresher Pasta

TL;DR: *Zest and juice citrus. Mix with basil, olive oil, salt, and cheese. Cook pasta and toss with citrus sauce. Top with romano, basil, and cracked black pepper.*

This recipe came to me during a particularly brutal yoga class that I took over a lunch hour one day. I had gone to exercise in the hope of jogging myself out of an anxious and distracted state of mind. Near the end of the class, I asked myself, "What do I want to focus on this afternoon?" And the thought of this pasta tumbled neatly into my mind. So often, I've found that when I'm struggling to do one thing and it's just not coming, it helps to take a break from it and do whatever is flowing more easily. It's not giving up, it's putting the task aside to process in the background while I do something else. When I trust myself enough to follow this instinct, beautiful things can happen. Like this dish, which is so zingy, bright, sweet, salty, fun, and unexpected in your mouth. Winter can be heavy in terms of food, atmosphere, *darkness*. The brightness of citrus can interrupt dark thoughts. It won't cure them, but it can be a good reminder. In fact, citrus sauce works very hard for you, so here you will make more than you need so you can use it again over a few days.

1. Put a large pot of water on to boil for the pasta. Generously salt the water so your pasta will get seasoned while it's cooking.

2. Meanwhile, zest the lemon, lime, and orange with a Microplane into a medium bowl. Place a strainer over the bowl. Cut the lemon, lime, and orange in half and use a citrus reamer, if you have one, to squeeze the juice out of them, allowing the juice and bits of citrus flesh to rain down into the strainer, which you can trust to catch the fleshy bits.

Note: Although the amount of juice varies, usually you will end up with a bit less than 1 cup of juice. If you think your citrus is not juicy enough, add a bit more, if you have it, so you have somewhere near ¾ cup of juice total.

3. Add the basil, olive oil, romano, and 1 teaspoon of salt to the bowl and mix it all vigorously with a fork. Taste it and add more salt, citrus if you have it, or romano as you see fit. The sauce should taste really sharp and salty and make you salivate strongly.

Serves 4

Fine sea salt

1 lemon

1 lime

1 large navel orange

½ cup finely chopped fresh basil, plus more for serving

1 cup extra-virgin olive oil

1 ounce romano cheese, finely grated, plus extra as needed

1 pound spaghetti

Freshly cracked black pepper (optional)

FEELING ADVENTUROUS?

- Toss finely chopped dinosaur kale or another hearty green with the cooked pasta and sauce in Step 4 until the greens wilt.

- Top each pasta bowl with a fried egg.

- Add chunks of fresh mozzarella to top each pasta bowl.

4. Once the water is boiling, cook the spaghetti according to the package instructions until the pasta is al dente. Once it's cooked, quickly drain the water and transfer the pasta to a large metal bowl. Add about 1 cup of the sauce and toss thoroughly with tongs, coating every strand. Add a bit more sauce if the pasta seems too dry or if you want it slooshier. Serve in bowls, topped with more romano, basil, and a healthy grind of black pepper, if you like.

Note: *Like the other triple citrus recipes, this one makes more sauce than you'll probably need for the pasta. For more ideas on using up the leftover sauce, see page 285.*

Salty, Spicy, and Bright Brussels Sprouts Pasta

TL;DR: *Boil pasta. Sauté veggies. Add pasta to the veggie pan, along with pasta cooking water and romano. Toss and cook until coated.*

I made this one rainy afternoon when I was suffering from a sinus infection, my kid had just started at a new school and had her last day of day care, and there were so many things to think about, and feel, but little time and even less energy. I didn't really want to eat—no, I wanted to tackle the next thing on my to-do list. Instead, I took a moment to remind myself that food is vital, even when the body's signals are a little out of whack, and that if I slowed down to take care of myself for a few minutes, I would not lose track of everything. Even if it meant not getting to one of those tasks, attending to my own needs really should be on that list. So I took some deep breaths, grabbed my knife, and finely chopped some brussels sprouts while I waited for water to boil, and I treated myself to a quiet moment and a plate of comforting pasta that was JUST for me. I even had leftovers for my kid and babysitter.

1. Put a large pot of water on to boil for the pasta. Generously salt the water so your pasta will get seasoned while it's cooking.

2. Meanwhile, chop the brussels sprouts into ribbons. Tumble the shredded sprouts into a bowl and set aside. Slice the garlic and the shallot, if using, into half-moons.

3. Once the pasta water is boiling, add the orecchiette and give it a quick stir. Cook according to the package instructions until the pasta is al dente.

4. Warm the olive oil and melt the butter in a large pan over medium heat. Add the sliced garlic and shallot and sauté until fragrant, about 1 minute. Add the brussels sprouts and stir to coat them with oil and butter, and evenly distribute the shallot and garlic. Sprinkle with ½ teaspoon of salt, or to taste. Cover the pan with a lid and let everything cook for 5 minutes.

Serves 2 or more

Fine sea salt

8 to 12 ounces brussels sprouts (depending on how much you like brussels sprouts!)

5 cloves garlic

1 shallot (optional)

8 ounces orecchiette pasta

1 tablespoon extra-virgin olive oil

1 tablespoon butter

Zest of 1 lemon

½ teaspoon crushed red pepper flakes

1 cup grated romano cheese (see note)

Note: The sauce for this recipe works best if the romano is grated with the pointy, stabby part of a box grater, so that you end up with crumbly pieces of cheese. However, if you've bought your romano already grated, that will work fine, too.

5. Remove the lid and stir the vegetables—you should see some browning, and the brussels sprouts should be bright green and just tender. Reduce the heat to low, add the lemon zest and red pepper flakes, stir, and let the mixture cook until the pasta is done, another 3 to 4 minutes.

6. Once the pasta is cooked, use a strainer or slotted spoon to transfer the cooked pasta directly into the pan with the vegetables. Give everything a quick stir, then add ½ cup of the grated romano and ½ cup or so of the pasta cooking water. Stir briskly, adding more of the romano and loosening with more pasta water, if needed, up to ¾ cup, until the pasta is loose and swooshy.

Note: Don't worry if water pools in the orecchiette's little cups. You want pasta water here.

7. Taste and adjust with more lemon zest, red pepper flakes, or romano. Top with a bit more romano, serve, and enjoy!

Salmon Dinner Pie

TL;DR: *Thaw and refrigerate puff pastry. Sweat veggies in butter, sprinkle with flour, then add salmon and remaining ingredients. Pour into pie pan and top with puff pastry. Bake at 375°F for 35 to 40 minutes.*

Serves 6 to 8

2 tablespoons butter

1 medium onion, finely chopped

1 carrot, finely chopped

1 rib celery, finely chopped

1 pound russet or yellow potatoes, diced

1 lemon, zested and reserved

2 teaspoons fine sea salt

2 tablespoons all-purpose flour

1 teaspoon ground smoked paprika

12 ounces frozen salmon, thawed and cut into 1-inch pieces

1 cup whole milk

¼ cup sour cream

1 tablespoon dijon or grainy mustard

¼ cup chopped fresh dill

3 scallions, finely chopped

Freshly cracked black pepper

1 sheet frozen puff pastry, thawed (see note, page 162)

1 large egg, lightly beaten

Perfectionism says that comfort food is for the weak. It's numbing. It's wrong. It's ruining your life! And yeah, sure, it's not ideal to soothe yourself with food and food alone. Or to eat so compulsively that you make yourself ill. But comforting yourself with food is profoundly human and okay. It's in our deepest wiring to associate food with love and warmth because we (hopefully) experienced being fed snugly in the arms of our caregiver as a baby. It's okay to comfort yourself with food. I find that my comfort food needs change with the seasons and my moods, and this salmon pie is for the kind of drizzly, gloomy day that matches my drizzly, gloomy feelings. It has a buttery puff pastry crust that breaks open to reveal a steaming hot, creamy mixture of salmon, vegetables, and mustardy, lemony, dilly cream sauce. It's like chicken pot pie, but way better.

1. Preheat the oven to 375°F.

2. Melt the butter in a large pan or Dutch oven over medium heat. Add the onion, carrot, celery, potatoes, lemon zest, and 1 teaspoon of the salt, cover, and cook, stirring occasionally, until all the vegetables are translucent and the potatoes are soft, 15 to 20 minutes.

3. Sprinkle the flour and smoked paprika over the vegetables and stir until everything is coated and looking a little claggy and starchy. Add the salmon and the remaining 1 teaspoon of salt and stir. Finally, pour in the milk, sour cream, and mustard and stir. Once the mixture begins to bubble and thicken, turn off the heat. Stir in the dill and scallions. Add lots of fresh pepper. Taste and add more salt if needed. Scoop the contents of the pan into a 9-inch pie plate.

4. Remove the puff pastry from the fridge and, depending on its size and shape, roll it out or trim it to fit the pie plate with a little overhang. Place the puff pastry on top of the salmon filling. Roll the edges and crimp them a bit or simply tuck them under and squish them along the edge of the pie plate. Cut a couple of slits in the pastry or carve a

Note: Take the puff pastry out of the freezer ahead of time, ideally the morning you plan to cook. Once the pastry defrosts, keep it in the fridge and as cold as possible until you trim it, place it on the pie, and put it in the oven.

shape—like the moon pictured here!—to let out the steam from the pie. Brush the lightly beaten egg all over the pastry. Place the pie on a sheet pan to catch any juices or butter that might leak out while it's baking.

5. Bake until the crust is golden and puffed, 35 to 40 minutes. Check the crust halfway through—if it's getting too dark, cover the top with foil to prevent burning.

6. When the pie is done baking, remove it from the oven. Cut it into wedges and serve with fresh lemon juice squeezed over the top of each slice, as desired.

CHAPTER 6

Good Enough Fun

Having a Baby Is Like
the Movie *Speed*

"You will never know a love so great until you have a baby!" "You won't believe the love until you experience it!" "The way you love your child is just so different—you can't understand it until you have one of your own." Ugh. I used to get so irritated when people said things like this. First, it felt insulting. I understand love! I get that you love your kid, geez, I'm not a monster. Then it felt cliché—yeah, yeah, yeah, everyone says that. Then just needlessly vague. If it's so different, can't you just try to describe it?

But at least now I understand the feeling of being at the limits of communication with this particular experience. It's still annoying, and a little insulting, and needlessly vague. And I wish it didn't make parenthood sound even more exclusive than it already can. But sometimes a feeling is so challenging to capture in words, even if you have gone through it. The only response is to explain around it, zeroing in on the feeling and punctuating all your sentences with "You know what I mean?" as you go.

I won't pretend to know what all those other people who have had babies mean when they say loving a baby is *wild*. But here is what I mean: Having a baby is like the 1994 movie *Speed*. Remember that one? With Sandra Bullock and Keanu Reeves? When you have a baby, what was just a normal bus ride turns into the craziest day of your life, and in the process, you discover strength you never knew you had and you end up falling in love.

I was sick—throwing up daily—for my whole pregnancy, and toward the end, the misery ramped up. I was *so* ready to not be pregnant. But my due date came and went. I was pissed. It was the strangest kind of living in limbo. I wanted to enjoy my last few days baby-free, but nothing about my pregnancy had been enjoyable, so I mostly just stewed in frustration and discomfort.

At 3 a.m. one Friday night, I started having contractions. I was excited at first. This was finally going to be over! Over the next twenty-four hours, the pain steadily increased. By the time I lurched out of the Uber, having growl-screamed on my hands and knees in the back for the entire ride from Brooklyn to midtown Manhattan, I felt like I was on another planet. You know when a movie cuts to a person's point of view when they are getting shocking news or about to pass out, and you see that their vision gets blurry around the edges, everything is moving in slow motion, and people are talking in that low, distorted, underwater sort of voice? It was like that. There were heroes! There were definitely villains. And there was a lot of blood.

Then, at 10 a.m. on Sunday, our Io was born. The slow-mo trauma-vision abruptly shifted to that rom-com, glowy heart-eyes lens filter as my body was suddenly freed of pain.

I loved her instantly. And that is a big deal. I had never experienced that before. I've loved many people in my life. I know that feeling. But loving new people always happened slowly, over time, as my feelings grew and I made room for them in my life and heart. This happened instantly. This love just yelled, "I'm coming in!" It burst in with a huge grin and made itself very comfortable.

The other thing that makes this sort of love different from any other you have ever felt is that this tiny love of your life is terrifyingly delicate and completely dependent on you. You love this person, and it's on you for them to survive. All in all, the whole experience is a lot of pressure for the nervous system. First you feel so much pain and fear, then the kind of satisfaction that comes from digging into your fear and driving through it—resilience and awe at your human ability. Then comes relief and dizziness and the intensity of love. Then fear. Joy and fear, bouncing back and forth, giving you whiplash. But it's a new kind of fear that is enveloped on all sides by love and a kind of strange deep-down sense that you have got this. You've got this at this minute, at least, and you'll figure out the next minute when you get there.

I'd Rather Have the Joy, *or* The Oddly Terrifying Part of Happiness

A year and a bit after Io was born, on a bright Sunday morning, my husband, Dan, and I went for a run in the park with Io in the running stroller. It's something we try to do on Sundays, though it happens rarely.

Before I became pregnant, I was an avid runner. Running had come to me unexpectedly after years of believing there was no more unpleasant form of exercise and no more cultlike and annoying group of people than runners. But suddenly I loved it. Running made me feel alive. It was hard and painful, and often boring, and yet it made me feel so grateful for my body, and I was constantly amazed that I could do it. The sense of exhausted well-being I had after a long, hot run was deeply motivating. I trained for my first marathon while on tour with my last book, and while I was out running, I saw a sunset on the water in almost every city I visited.

Because of my difficult pregnancy, I had not kept up my running, and since I'd had Io, running had not felt the same. But this morning was different. Not the same as it had been, but there was a spark. The rush of blood pumping in my legs contrasted with the cold from the wind on my skin, and the momentum of my body felt glorious. I was happy. I remembered all the late-night runs Dan and I used to do, reconnecting after long days spent apart.

As we rounded the last bend to leave the park and jog the final three blocks to our house, I was hit by such a strong feeling of joy that it brought tears to my eyes. I loved Dan so much and was so grateful to be with him. I loved Io so much and was so happy she was with us. The two people I love most were there with me sharing my delight in being alive. And then, just as suddenly, another image blasted its way into my mind. Dan was just ahead of me and I imagined a truck barreling into the parkway and smashing into Dan and Io in the stroller, killing them both instantly.

I was shocked by the violence of the image, and my heart, already pumping from exertion, began pumping faster. The thought of losing them was impossible to me. Too horrible to contemplate. I wondered why my brain would send that image right then. And in that moment, rather than getting lost in the pain, some wise part of me remembered the vulnerability of joy and recalled how a strong surge of it can scare our lizard brain and make it think it needs to do something to keep us safe. Joy means leaving yourself open—having something to lose. And in that moment I realized that this fearful image arose because I had so much love in my life. I had a lot to lose. My body was trying to defend me from how scary that felt, screaming to me, "Vigilance!"

Rather than getting lost in horrible thoughts of loss and anxiety, I greeted the fear and the image, and I said, "Yes, I do have something to lose. I am so incredibly grateful for my life." And I heard my internal voices telling me that this joy was too much, and not appropriate, and that I looked like an emotional wild woman—but I turned away from them and back to the wild and raw and beautiful feeling of joy. I let myself well up and feel just how lucky I am.

Permission Slip for Excitement and Joy

Joy and excitement can be remarkably hard emotions to embrace. That's counterintuitive because we think we want them. But think about it—there is often no space for those feelings in your daily life. Excitement can feel childish, like when you want to scream with excitement that your best friend is coming to town, or your local store started carrying your favorite European chocolate bar. It's not very grown up. But the reason many of us think that is not because there is anything wrong with those feelings, but because childhood was the last time we made real space for joy. Many of us are taught that to be accepted, we have to appear calm, reasonable, and controlled—the cornerstones of adult behavior. But the urges that overtake our body when we feel joy and excitement are kind of unhinged, and they can feel threatening to that veneer of acceptability we fear we have to maintain.

Joy is sticking your head out of the car window and feeling the breeze. Excitement is squeezing something so hard you almost break it. It's laughing so hard you snort and cry.

It makes us want to:

Tell everyone the news! Scream Jump Smile Squeal High-five Laugh Dance Hug and Kiss and Stomp Cry

In some situations, these impulses are labeled as inappropriate. Whether as a child or later in life, we all have had our joy and excitement rejected and judged.

Maybe it's someone saying our favorite hobby is nerdy, or someone telling us to quiet down or stop interrupting, or any kind of glare, stare, or eye roll. It can be subtle, but we know when our joy is not welcome. So we squash it down. And the sad thing is that we often squash it down with really harsh thoughts full of shame, anxiety, anger, and fear. If we are told enough times in childhood that our joy is not welcome, then later, when we feel joyful, we will also feel anxious and overwhelmed. Our joy has become tangled up with shame and anxiety, and we may not know how to express all that. But just like sadness or anger, joy is not a choice. We need to feel it or it can get stuck and become unhealthy.

And yes, of course, some of the impulses of joy are not appropriate for every moment. Just as we learn to go punch a pillow rather than our sister when we are angry, we might take the impulse to scream and stomp with joy and let that flow instead into a giant face-splitting smile and maybe a little shimmy. But it's important to honor our joy and excitement and let it loose when it is the right time. You can share your wild expressions of joy with people who do welcome it . . . or, you know, just shout it out anyway.

We might not feel comfortable enough to tap-dance down the aisle of the grocery store because we are feeling so good—although if you do, I would be immensely delighted—but we don't want to squash those emotions. We want to find ways to feel them fully. Our adult world may not create enough space for them, but we can find ways to feel our joy and excitement safely, connect with what we love most, and tap into that beautiful energy. Joy in the face of oppression is a powerful form of protest. We get one life to live here, and we must not let our joy be stolen. It is brave to let your joy flow freely.

When we have the courage to share our joy, it almost always becomes a memorable moment. When I got my nails done with bright pink and yellow to delight my toddler, the slightly stifled grin on the aesthetician's face added to the sweetness of the moment. When tears sprang to my eyes as I got news of a friend's baby being born, I felt the person next to me noticing my reaction and I shared the news. That connection, even if it was brief, left us both lighter. And when we share our joy, we

ground it and set it free so others can benefit, and in the process we can calm ourselves a bit. Because joy is a little intense, and experiencing it alone can be scary. Sometimes you will share it and people will not get it or be ready for it, but that doesn't make the joy wrong—and there are other

We get one life to live here, and we must not let our joy be stolen. It is brave to let your joy flow freely.

ways to connect with joy and let it loose, safely, with yourself. As examples, the recipes in this chapter are all connected to joy and excitement for me personally. I hope that in showing how that works for me, it might spark something for you.

Rainy Day Focaccia

TL;DR: *Make dough and give it 2 hours of shaping and rest time as you prepare toppings. Bake at 425°F for 25 to 30 minutes.*

When I was growing up, my mum always wished that our oven had an oven light. She deeply wanted to give my sisters and me the experience of peering into an oven to watch batter turn into fluffy, craggy-topped mountains, so that we could see the magic happen. And so that we could feel the accomplishment and engage with what we made. Much of the pleasure of cooking comes from letting yourself be fully present with it—feeling the dough become smooth in your hands. I often multitask while cooking, and while there is nothing wrong with that, I do try to remember to allow myself the pleasure of focusing on making food and making food alone. It satisfies some primal part of me. The transformation. The power! I like to think Mum taught me to value those moments all those years ago. It's easy to miss them when I'm also vacuuming the living room or browsing Instagram or listening to NPR. So a rainy day always feels like the universe reminding me it's okay to bake something and really enjoy it.

1. Place the flour and yeast in a large bowl and stir them together. Add the salt and stir again. (It's best not to put the salt and yeast in together as the salt will impede the growth of the yeast.) Pour the water into the flour and gently mix it together with well-oiled hands until the dough just comes together and there are no clumps. This is basically a no-knead technique, so don't try to get a smooth dough.

2. Remove the dough, grease the bottom of the bowl, and put the dough back in. Cover the bowl with plastic wrap or a moist towel and let the dough rise in a warm spot until it has doubled in size, approximately 1½ hours. It can take more or less time depending on humidity and heat levels. The hotter and more humid, the faster it grows.

3. Line a sheet pan with parchment paper or a silicone baking mat. Generously drizzle olive oil over it.

4. Once the dough has doubled in size, upend the bowl and let the dough plop out onto the prepared sheet pan. Pour 1 tablespoon or so

Makes 1 flatbread about the size of a sheet pan

- 4 cups all-purpose flour
- 1 teaspoon instant yeast
- 2 teaspoons fine sea salt
- 2 cups water, at room temperature
- Extra-virgin olive oil, as needed

TOPPINGS

- 2 tablespoons shelled and chopped pistachios
- 2 cloves garlic, sliced
- 2 ounces melty cheese, such as provolone or white cheddar, diced (½ cup)
- 1 ounce hard cheese, such as romano, grated (¼ cup)
- Freshly cracked black pepper
- 2 tablespoons honey (optional)

FEELING ADVENTUROUS?

The toppings listed above come together to make my favorite kind of off-brand focaccia, but I tend to make it a little differently every time. Think about your favorite cheese platter (or the one you created on page 229) for inspiration, aiming for whatever combination suits you.

of olive oil over the top and gently smear it all over, pulling the dough a bit to stretch it. Once it starts to resist the stretch, leave it alone for about 30 minutes.

5. Meanwhile, move an oven rack to the lowest shelf and preheat the oven to 425°F.

6. Once the dough has been sitting in its second rise for 30 minutes or so, it should be easier to work with. Gently stretch it to fill the sheet pan. Dot the dough everywhere with your fingertips to get the classic focaccia nooks and crannies. Sprinkle the top with the chopped pistachios, garlic, cheeses, and pepper to taste.

7. Bake the focaccia on the lowest oven rack until it has risen and is golden brown on top and underneath, 25 to 30 minutes. Check it after 25 minutes—if it's browning unevenly, rotate the pan and let it bake for another 5 minutes.

8. Remove the focaccia from the oven and, if desired, drizzle the honey over it. Be sparing—you want just a few small strands of honey glistening over the top for the occasional sweet bite. Let it cool to room temperature and then cut it into long pieces for dunking or into squares for making sandwiches. If you don't plan to eat it all in the first couple of days, wrap it up and freeze it; it will keep, frozen, for up to a month.

British Beer Cheese

TL;DR: *Make roux, then add beer, mustard, and cheese, while whisking, until everything is melted together. Serve with roasted broccoli.*

As I've grown up, I have found myself drawn to British recipes because they connect me to the comforting, fantastic worlds in the British fantasy books I adore. Especially on a rainy day, there is nothing I want more than fish and chips or shepherd's pie and sticky toffee pudding. Eating them, I can imagine sitting in a wingback chair by a fire in a dim yet well-kept pub, waiting for a mysterious stranger to come sit with me and tell me I'm secretly a descendant of a line of ancient wizards. And this beer cheese, known across the British Isles as Welsh rarebit, is the ultimate example. It is so *not* what I thought when I first saw mention of it in a book years ago. It has nothing to do with rabbits and everything to do with sharp, beery, salty, cheesy sauce. And it doesn't even require more than a brief turn by the stove to achieve this symbol of the cozy pub experience at home! Sit by the window and imagine what could happen next, or curl up with a good book and be carried away. Serve it over toast, as is traditional, or with roasted broccoli—or both, as is my preference.

Makes about 2 cups

2 tablespoons butter

2 tablespoons all-purpose flour

½ teaspoon ground cayenne pepper or a squirt of hot sauce, plus extra as needed

1 cup dark beer, such as an amber ale or porter

1 tablespoon dijon mustard, plus extra as needed

Splash of Worcestershire sauce, plus extra as needed

½ pound cheddar cheese, shredded (about 2 cups)

Roasted Broccoli, for serving (page 175)

Toasted bread, for serving (optional)

1. Melt the butter in a small saucepan over medium heat, then add the flour and cayenne and whisk to form a smooth paste (if you're using hot sauce, add it in Step 2). Keep whisking until the flour just begins to turn golden, 2 to 3 minutes.

2. Add the beer in a slow stream, continuing to whisk. The mixture will thicken and bubble. Add the mustard and Worcestershire sauce (and the hot sauce, if using) and stir to make sure there are no lumps.

3. Once the mixture is bubbling again (it should be fairly thick), add the shredded cheddar a handful at a time, letting it melt smoothly into the mixture with each addition. Once all of the cheese is in and the mixture is smooth and creamy, turn off the heat. Taste and adjust

with more mustard, cayenne, or Worcestershire, as desired. The beer cheese should be rich and cheesy, but also zingy, with a savory, beery taste that cuts through the cheddar. So delicious.

4. Pour the warm beer cheese into a bowl and place it at the center of a large plate or serving platter. Pile roasted broccoli all around it. Serve with toasted bread, if desired, and dip!

Roasted Broccoli

TL;DR: *Chop broccoli and roast until tender. If serving with beer cheese, make dip as broccoli roasts. Serve warm.*

1. Preheat the oven to 425°F.

2. Place the broccoli in a roasting pan or on a sheet pan and toss it with the olive oil and generous sprinklings of salt and pepper. Roast the broccoli for 10 to 15 minutes. I like to do 10 minutes in the summer when I want a bit of crispy bite to it, and 15 minutes in the winter when I want it to be tender with a bit of char.

Serves 4 as a side dish

2 heads broccoli, chopped into bite-size (or larger) pieces

1 tablespoon extra-virgin olive oil

Fine sea salt and freshly cracked black pepper

Herby Fish Cakes
with Chipotle Mayo

TL;DR: *Pulse fish cake ingredients in food processor, form 8 patties, and fry them. Serve with chipotle mayo.*

Makes 8 fish cakes

1 shallot, roughly chopped, or ½ cup chopped red onion

2 scallions, chopped

¼ cup chopped fresh cilantro

¼ cup chopped fresh mint

2 garlic scapes (optional)

1 pound cod or other white fish, thawed if frozen, roughly chopped

¼ cup breadcrumbs

1 tablespoon mayonnaise

1 teaspoon fine sea salt

2 tablespoons vegetable oil

1 tablespoon butter (see note)

CHIPOTLE MAYO, FOR SERVING

¼ cup mayonnaise

1 tablespoon adobo sauce (from a can of chipotles in adobo)

1 teaspoon freshly squeezed lemon juice

Lemon wedges, for garnish

Note: I like frying these fish cakes in oil with a bit of butter for the flavor, but not all butter so the cakes don't burn.

I feel playful making these herb-packed, flavorful fish cakes. Simplicity is great, and drives the vast majority of cooking at home, but sometimes something with a few more steps feels like play. Here, that takes the form of whizzing the herbs and onion into a bright green paste, using your hands to shape the fish into little patties, and then frying it all up until the fish cakes smell fragrant and savory. These cakes aren't difficult, but they have just enough process and transformation that you can feel proud when you are nestling them onto a plate with a big leafy salad, pea tendrils, or a potato salad, and garnishing with a lemon wedge.

1. Place the shallot, scallions, cilantro, mint, and garlic scapes, if using, in a food processor and blitz until you have a fairly fine paste. Add the cod, breadcrumbs, mayonnaise, and salt and pulse a few times until the fish is broken up and smooth, but not a complete paste. You want the patties to have some texture.

2. Scoop the mixture into a large bowl and mix everything together with your hands to evenly distribute the components. Divide the mixture into 8 equal clumps and form each clump into a small patty.

Note: You can do Steps 1 and 2 in advance. Cover the uncooked fish cakes in plastic wrap and store them in the fridge for a few hours or overnight.

3. Heat 1 tablespoon of the oil and the butter in a large nonstick or cast-iron pan over medium heat. Add half of the fish cakes, or as many as comfortably fit, to the pan and cook until golden brown, 2 to 4 minutes per side. Remove the fish cakes from the pan and set aside. Add the remaining 1 tablespoon of oil and repeat until all of the cakes have been cooked.

4. Make the chipotle mayo: Place the mayonnaise, adobo sauce, and lemon juice in a small bowl and mix well. Serve the fish cakes with a squeeze of lemon over the top, alongside the bowl of chipotle mayo.

Samosa Puffs

TL;DR: *Defrost puff pastry. Boil potatoes. Sauté remaining filling and mix. Roll pastry, fill, and fold, then bake puffs at 400°F for 25 to 30 minutes.*

Makes approximately 32 puffs

1 pound potatoes

1 medium to large red onion, chopped

2 cloves garlic, minced

1 tablespoon butter

2 teaspoons cumin seeds

1 teaspoon coriander seeds

1 teaspoon ground turmeric

½ teaspoon ground cayenne pepper

1 tablespoon fine sea salt, plus extra as needed

1 cup frozen peas

¼ cup chopped fresh cilantro (optional)

1 pound ground chicken

2 sheets (usually 16 to 20 ounces total) frozen puff pastry, thawed (see note, page 180)

All-purpose flour, for rolling out the dough

1 or 2 large eggs, for brushing the pastry

Sesame seeds, for sprinkling (optional)

Green chutney, sweet chili sauce, or your favorite dipping sauce (see note, page 180)

Samosas, the greatest Indian street food—my favorite street food and, in my opinion, what should replace every hot dog cart in NYC—are also the perfect party food and late-night snack. I can't improve on them and won't try, but when I don't feel like deep-frying and still want a crispy pastry filled with potato and cumin, coriander, and other aromatic spices, this is a fun alternative. Don't make them when you are in a rush. This recipe is all about relaxing with a glass of wine, some good music, and the part of you that enjoys folding origami, building LEGO houses, or making Pinterest boards. You make a delicious filling and then cut out a bunch of puff pastry and fold each one into a little package. I love to make a big batch, eat enough to satisfy, and freeze the rest for another time. Being able to pull these out on a busy weeknight is another kind of joy.

1. Scrub the potatoes and cut them into chunks. Place them in a medium pot and cover with water. Bring to a boil over medium heat, then reduce the heat to low and let simmer until the potatoes are soft enough that a knife can easily pierce through, 15 to 20 minutes.

2. While the potatoes are cooking, melt the butter in a small pan over medium heat, then add the onion. Let it cook until it begins to brown, about 5 minutes. Add the garlic, cumin seeds, and coriander seeds and stir until it all smells amazing, about 1 minute. Add the turmeric, cayenne, salt, peas, and a little water—about ¼ cup—and scrub the pan with your spoon to lift the spices and browned bits from the bottom. Cook, stirring occasionally, until the peas are cooked, about 2 minutes. Turn off the heat.

3. Drain the boiled potatoes and transfer them to a large mixing bowl. Add the spiced onion and peas along with the cilantro, if using, and stir everything together. Let the mixture cool enough to handle. Taste. It should be strongly flavorful and a bit too salty. You want it salty and strong, because not only do potatoes need a lot of spice, but you are

Note: Take the puff pastry out of the freezer ahead of time, leaving it in the fridge overnight or on the counter for a few hours. If you defrost the pastry on the counter, make sure it is fully thawed and then chill it in the fridge for about 30 minutes before you begin rolling it out in Step 5.

Note: Green chutney can be found in the hot sauce section of the grocery store, or wherever they keep jarred curry sauces. But it's very easy to make at home and so delicious. Simply blend equal parts of cilantro and mint with a jalapeño and lime juice until smooth. Tamarind sauce is traditional with samosas, so you can also serve them with that, or with a sweeter chili sauce of your choice.

about to add unseasoned meat to it. Add the ground chicken and mix it all together gently.

4. Preheat the oven to 400°F. Line 2 sheet pans with parchment paper or silicone baking mats.

5. Remove 1 sheet of thawed puff pastry from the fridge, sprinkle the countertop with flour, and roll it out until it is about ⅛ inch thick. Cut the pastry into 16 or 18 squares, depending on the shape of your pastry (square or rectangular!).

6. Divide half of the filling among your 16 or 18 pastry squares. Then fold the edges of the pastry around your filling. Some bits of filling will show, and that's as it should be. You are not trying to encase it like a dumpling, just folding the pastry around it. Gently move the puffs to one of the prepared sheet pans.

7. Repeat Steps 5 and 6 with the second pastry sheet and the rest of the filling.

8. Crack 1 egg into a small bowl and whisk it. Using a pastry brush, gently brush the egg wash over the top of each puff. Use the second egg if you run out of wash, but I typically need just one. Sprinkle the puffs with sesame seeds, if desired.

9. Bake the puffs until the tops are golden and the bottoms are a little brown, 25 to 30 minutes.

10. Serve hot, with green chutney, sweet chili sauce, or your favorite dipping sauce. If you want to freeze any of the leftovers, cool them to room temperature, tumble them into a freezer bag, and pull them out to bake (at 400°F for 15 minutes) when you want them. They will keep for up to a month in the freezer.

Cozy Cold-Weather Bolognese

TL;DR: *Brown beef and pork, combine with chopped vegetables, and cook for 20 minutes. Deglaze pan, add remaining sauce ingredients, and cook for 45 minutes more. As the sauce cooks, boil pasta, grate cheese, and chop parsley for serving.*

When I broke my fifteen-plus years of vegetarianism, this bolognese was one of the dishes I was most excited to enjoy again. I don't have an Italian grandmother or any particular memory of it, but the experience of this kind of sauce is everything that makes cooking feel like magic. As the meat browns and begins to go from soft and pink to dark brown and crispy, the air is full of savory, buttery smells. You add the vegetables and the aroma becomes more complex, then suddenly a rush of steam and a burst of bright sweetness hit you as the wine deglazes the pan. Then the tomato paste mixes with the fats, and suddenly it looks like sauce and smells almost illegally savory. Finally, the tomato and milk and parmesan simmer, and you take off the lid and it's gone from soupy to a thick, red, oily sauce that smells like everything you could ever want. It's not fast, but this is Potions Class and you are making magic.

1. Melt the butter in a Dutch oven or a large heavy-bottomed pot over medium heat. If it begins to brown, that is just fine, but make sure it doesn't burn. Add the beef, pork, and 1 teaspoon of salt and break up the meat with a wooden spoon. Let the meat cook, stirring occasionally, until it is no longer pink and has plenty of dark brown bits, 15 to 20 minutes.

2. Add the onions, carrot, celery, and bell pepper to the browned meat and stir. Place a tight lid on top and let the vegetables sweat, stirring occasionally, until they cook down about halfway in volume and your kitchen smells incredibly savory, about 20 minutes.

3. At this point you will probably have some dark brown sticky bits on the bottom of the pan. This is good! Pour in the white wine and stir to gently lift the brown bits off the bottom of the pan. Cook until the mixture dries out a bit, a few minutes more.

Note: *The white wine deglazes the pan, meaning it gets the delicious brown bits into the sauce instead of letting them burn.*

Serves 8 to 12

- 4 tablespoons (½ stick) butter
- 1 pound ground beef (preferably 80% lean, 20% fat; see note, page 183)
- 1 pound ground pork (preferably 80% lean, 20% fat; see note, page 183)
- 1 teaspoon fine sea salt, plus extra as needed
- 2 small red onions, diced
- 1 large carrot, diced
- 2 ribs celery, diced
- 1 bell pepper (any color), stemmed, seeded, and diced
- ½ cup dry white wine
- 6 tablespoons (3 ounces) tomato paste
- 1 can (28 ounces) crushed or diced tomatoes
- 1 cup whole milk
- 1 parmesan rind (see note, page 183)
- 1 pound pasta of your choice, such as tagliatelle (traditional) or orecchiette (pictured)
- Grated parmesan, for serving
- Chopped fresh flat-leaf parsley, for serving

4. Add the tomato paste, mix it up with everything, and leave it until it loses its bright red uncooked color, a couple of minutes. Then add the canned tomatoes, milk, and parmesan rind—which will add a lot of savory saltiness! Stir it all together and put the lid on, just a little askew so a small amount of steam can escape. Turn down the heat to low and gently simmer for about 45 minutes.

5. Cook the pasta in boiling salted water according to the package instructions, but take it off the heat a minute or so before it reaches al dente. That way the pasta will cook through in the sauce, drinking in a little more of the bolognese flavor. Drain the pasta and taste the sauce; add more salt, if needed. Add the pasta to the sauce and cook until it is al dente and totally covered in sauce, a minute or so.

6. Remove the parmesan rind and serve the pasta and sauce in bowls, topped with grated parmesan and chopped parsley. Any leftovers will keep in a sealed container for a week in the fridge.

Note: I make a lighter, warm-weather version of this by substituting finely chopped cauliflower for half the meat; I add the cauliflower with the other vegetables in Step 2. It is still lovely and hearty without sitting quite so heavily in your tummy.

Note: The parmesan rind adds salty richness to the sauce. If you don't have one, just add 1 extra teaspoon of salt in Step 4.

Curried Chickpeas and Spinach

TL;DR: *Cook rice, if using. Blend onions and garlic and cook together. Add rest of aromatic ingredients, tomatoes, chickpeas, and finally spinach. Serve chickpeas and spinach with cilantro and yogurt.*

Serves 6 to 8

2 medium red onions, quartered

4 large cloves garlic

3 tablespoons butter or ghee

1 teaspoon cumin seeds

2 teaspoons fine sea salt, plus extra as needed

1-inch piece of ginger, finely grated

1 green chile, finely chopped (optional)

2 teaspoons ground coriander

1 teaspoon ground smoked paprika

1 teaspoon ground turmeric

½ teaspoon ground cinnamon

½ teaspoon ground cloves (optional)

1 can (28 ounces) whole tomatoes

2 cans (15½ ounces each) chickpeas, drained and rinsed

1 package (16 ounces) frozen chopped spinach

Chopped fresh cilantro, for serving

Cooked brown rice, for serving (optional; see note)

Plain yogurt, for serving

I love this meal. It's nostalgic. It sends me back to my early twenties, when I finally learned to make really tasty vegetarian food that wasn't cheese toast. South Asian cooking was the biggest spark for me. How was it always so much more flavorful than the sum of its ingredients? I was lucky to be taken by the hand many times by generous women who showed me how to toast the spices, how to create a good onion gravy, and all kinds of subtleties that make vegetables sing, and showed me a new way to think about creating food. This meal feels like comfort food—the kind that is deeply nourishing and relaxing and fun to make when you have a fair bit of downtime and don't have to hurry. It also keeps really well and tastes delicious the next day, once the spices mellow and everything hangs out long enough to really get to know each other and become one delicious flavor. I recommend making this dish at the beginning of the week and keeping it as leftovers that get tastier and tastier.

1. Use a food processor or immersion blender to blitz the onion and garlic together.

Note: If you plan to serve this dish with the optional brown rice, get that going just when you start the curry. If you simmer the rice over low heat, with a pat of butter and a couple of teaspoons of salt, it will be fluffy and soft in about 45 minutes, roughly the same time the curry is ready.

2. Melt the butter in a large pot over medium heat. Add the cumin seeds and let them sizzle for 10 seconds before pouring in the onion-garlic mixture. Add 1 teaspoon of the salt and let cook, stirring occasionally, until the red onions go from bright purple to a medium brown, 10 to 15 minutes. As it cooks, if you find that the onion-garlic mixture is sticking, drying out, or getting super dark bits, add a bit of water to deglaze the pan.

3. Add the ginger and chile, if using, stir, and cook for 1 minute. Add the coriander, paprika, turmeric, cinnamon, cloves, and the remaining

1 teaspoon of salt and stir until the spices are thoroughly mixed and smelling super aromatic, about 1 minute more. The mixture will have an almost pastelike consistency.

4. Use a food processor or immersion blender to blitz the tomatoes, then add them to the pan along with the chickpeas, and stir. Let cook until the sauce thickens and a bit of the butter starts to separate from the vegetable mixture, about 10 minutes. Then add 1 cup of water and simmer to let the flavors meld, another 10 minutes.

5. Add the spinach, stir, and let it cook until it's incorporated, 3 to 5 minutes. Taste and adjust the salt to your preference. Sprinkle with chopped cilantro. Serve heaped over brown rice, if you like, with a dollop of yogurt.

Cinnamon and Spice Cream Cheese Rolls

TL;DR: *Make dough and let it rise for 2 to 2½ hours. Mix filling. Roll out dough and spread filling over it. Roll it up, slice, and let rise for 20 to 30 minutes. Bake at 375°F for 25 minutes.*

I am so proud of these rolls. They were good from the start, but I kept finding excuses to make them again and again because "that recipe needs testing" one more time. They are exactly what I like all at once, both as an end product and as an experience. Kneading the dough and watching it go from shaggy to silky smooth, letting it sit and rise, knowing something exciting is happening. Smooshing together the filling and smelling all the spices and sweetness come together. The shaping and rolling and cutting of the buns. The way they rise and get fluffy and soft and gooey in the oven. It is comfort on comfort on comfort. I can feel my deeper breaths returning as I describe them. These are like cinnamon rolls, but with the cream cheese frosting baked into them, there is even more goo and spice and no sad, dry part in the middle, only a sublime final bite.

1. Make the dough: Place the flour, salt, sugar, and yeast in a large bowl or the bowl of a stand mixer. Give it a quick stir.

2. Place the water, melted butter, and eggs in a medium bowl and whisk, breaking up the yolks, until the liquid becomes frothy and yellow, about 1 minute.

3. Add the wet ingredients to the dry ingredients:

With a stand mixer: Using the paddle attachment, turn the mixer to low and slowly pour the wet mixture into the flour mixture until it comes together into a shaggy dough, about 2 minutes. Switch to the dough hook and knead on a low-medium setting until the dough is smooth and elastic, about 5 minutes.

By hand: Lightly flour a clean countertop. Slowly pour the wet mixture into the flour mixture and, using your hands or a wooden spoon, mix everything together until a shaggy dough forms. Dump

Makes 12 rolls

DOUGH

3¼ cups all-purpose flour, plus extra to dust the countertop

1½ teaspoons fine sea salt (see note, page 189)

¼ cup sugar

1 package (2¼ teaspoons) instant yeast

¾ cup water, at room temperature

4 tablespoons (½ stick) unsalted butter, melted, plus more butter, at room temperature, for greasing the bowl

2 large eggs

FILLING

½ cup (1 stick) unsalted butter, at room temperature

4 ounces (½ package) cream cheese, at room temperature

1 cup packed light brown sugar

1 tablespoon ground cinnamon

1 teaspoon ground cardamom

½ teaspoon ground ginger

¼ teaspoon ground cloves

the dough onto the counter and knead until it is smooth and elastic, 7 to 10 minutes.

4. Grease a large bowl lightly with butter. Shape the dough into a ball, place it in the bowl, then turn it over so that every side of the ball is lightly greased and the dough is seam side down. Cover the bowl with plastic wrap or a moist towel and let the dough rise in a warm spot until it has doubled in size, 2 to 2½ hours. It can take more or less time depending on humidity and heat levels. The hotter and more humid, the faster it grows.

Note: *I like to prep this recipe in advance to make mornings a little easier. The dough can be made through Step 4, covered, and refrigerated. The next morning, put it on the counter, do your thing for 1 hour as it comes to room temperature, then make the filling and continue with the recipe.*

5. While you are waiting for the dough to rise, make the filling: Place the butter, cream cheese, brown sugar, cinnamon, cardamom, ginger, and cloves together in a bowl and cream together with a mixer or wooden spoon to form a smooth paste.

6. When the dough has risen, dust your countertop with flour. Punch down the dough and form it into a short log. Using a rolling pin, roll the dough into a rectangle about ¼ inch thick.

7. Using a spoon or palette knife for icing cakes, spread the filling evenly over the rectangle of dough. Roll it up lengthwise, like a carpet. Slice the log into 12 rolls as evenly as you can.

8. Place the 12 rolls into a glass baking dish with the swirl facing up. Cover the rolls with plastic wrap or a moist tea towel and let them rise until they have puffed up just a bit and are getting chummy with one another in the dish, 20 to 30 minutes.

9. Meanwhile, preheat the oven to 375°F.

10. Bake the rolls until the tops are golden brown and the bottoms are just golden, about 25 minutes. (You should be able to see the color of the bottoms through the glass baking dish.) You want them fully cooked, but not overcooked, or they won't be as gooey as you want. Serve them as soon as they are cool enough to handle and not burn anyone's tongue. They will keep, covered, in the fridge for a few days, or if you want to save some for later, wrap them up and freeze them for up to a couple of weeks.

Note: In the Rainy Day Focaccia (page 171), I add the salt separately to keep the yeast from losing its punch. It's not as crucial in this rich dough, but in Step 1, I typically add salt to the flour, give it a little whisk, and then add the rest of the ingredients.

Lemon Poppyseed Drizzle Cakes

TL;DR: *Mix cake batter in one bowl. Bake in muffin pan at 350°F for 25 to 30 minutes. Make drizzle. Poke holes in each cupcake and drizzle while still warm.*

Makes 12 cakes

LEMON POPPYSEED CAKES

¾ cup (1½ sticks) unsalted butter, at room temperature

1 cup sugar

Zest of 3 lemons

1 tablespoon poppyseeds

1 teaspoon pure vanilla extract

3 large eggs

1⅓ cups all-purpose flour

1½ teaspoons baking powder

½ teaspoon fine sea salt

LEMON DRIZZLE

2 tablespoons freshly squeezed lemon juice

¾ cup confectioners' sugar

When I was a kid, my mum was pretty strict about what we ate. We didn't get sugar; we had fructose. We didn't get chocolate; we had carob. But when I asked to bake something, she let me choose whatever I wanted to make. I remember making devil's food cake and peanut butter chocolate bars and these ridiculous Rice Krispies treat rolls with peanut butter and chocolate. All forbidden food was suddenly open to me. So I learned to love making desserts.

This recipe is an homage to my favorite comforting experiences, which include British stuff (lemon drizzle cake), the act of making dessert, and the use of additional flourishes (the poppyseeds and the cupcake form), all of which get my fires crackling.

1. Preheat the oven to 350°F. Line a 12-cup muffin pan with paper or silicone liners.

2. Make the cakes: Place the butter, sugar, and lemon zest in a medium bowl and cream them together with an electric mixer or wooden spoon until they're fluffy and lighter in color. (When you add the zest at this early stage, the lemon oils can really bond with the butter.) Add the poppyseeds, vanilla, and eggs and mix vigorously. Finally, scatter the flour, baking powder, and salt over the wet ingredients and gently stir until you have a loose batter free of any visible flour bits.

3. Distribute the batter among the prepared muffin cups, filling each about three-quarters or so full. Try to keep the amount of batter in each cup relatively even. I tend to underfill them to begin with and then slowly top them up. Bake the cakes until a knife inserted into the center comes out clean, 25 to 30 minutes.

4. Meanwhile, make the drizzle: Place the lemon juice and confectioners' sugar in a small bowl and whisk together.

5. As soon as the cakes come out of the oven, quickly poke them all over with a toothpick or skewer, making about 10 little holes in each one. Try to reach the skewer all the way down to the bottom of the cakes for maximum drizzle penetration. Carefully pour drizzle over each cake, a bit at a time, until you've used it all up.

Note: *Glazing can be tricky because the dome of the baked cakes makes the drizzle roll off the side. If you are troubled by this, use a pastry brush or spoon to gently moisten and glaze each cake.*

6. Let the cakes cool. The top will dry into a glaze and the center of the cakes will be nice and moist. Store the drizzle cakes, covered, at room temperature; they should keep for a few days.

Sticky Toffee Cookies

TL;DR: *Mix dry and wet ingredients, then combine and let chill. Bake cookies in batches at 350°F for 10 minutes.*

I first saw the words "sticky toffee pudding" in one of the many British children's books I read as a child. The thought of it became lodged in my mind: a mythically fantastic dessert dripping with ooey-gooey sweetness. I didn't have the chance to try the real thing for many years, and amazingly, it did not disappoint. The stickiness of sticky toffee pudding comes from a beautifully moist, brown sugar–rich date cake doused in toffee sauce. It's the perfect warming treat for a cold winter night. These cookies have the flavor and magic of sticky toffee pudding, but they come together quickly and are easy to store. They give me a little dose of childlike wonder.

1. Preheat the oven to 350°F. Line a sheet pan with parchment paper or a silicone baking mat.

2. Place the flour, baking soda, and salt in a medium bowl and stir to combine.

3. Place the butter and brown sugar in the bowl of a stand mixer and cream together until the mixture lightens in color, 2 to 4 minutes. Add the eggs one at a time, beating well with each addition. Add the vanilla and beat to combine.

4. Add the flour mixture all at once and gently stir the dough with a wooden spoon or spatula until there are no pockets of flour. Mix in the toffee bits and dates. Let the dough chill in the fridge for 10 to 20 minutes. At this point, you can freeze it to bake later (see note).

5. Spoon 6 cookies of equal size—about a heaping tablespoon each—onto the prepared sheet pan. Bake for 10 minutes. They will be quite flat and look a little gooey; let them rest on the pan for a few minutes to set up before removing them to a wire rack to cool.

6. Repeat Step 5 to bake the rest of the cookies. These cookies are at their gooey best in the first 2 to 3 days (stored in a sealed container at room temperature) and lose a little magic when they get stale.

Makes 30 to 36 cookies

2 cups all-purpose flour

1 teaspoon baking soda

1½ teaspoons fine sea salt

1 cup (2 sticks) unsalted butter, at room temperature

1½ cups packed dark brown sugar

2 large eggs

2 teaspoons pure vanilla extract

1 cup toffee bits (such as Heath bar pieces)

1½ cups chopped dates

Note: You can freeze the dough in a log to bake later. Just pull it out and thaw in the fridge.

Banana Bread

If I see a tray of forgotten raspberries blooming with mold in my refrigerator, I feel guilt and disappointment. If I lift up a bell pepper and it leaves its squishy skin behind, I am devastated. But when I see a sneaky banana, blackened beyond the bounds of a simple peel-and-eat, I feel . . . well, delighted! I wouldn't want to waste this banana, after all. So here are a loaf and a muffin for just that occasion.

My Favorite Banana Loaf

TL;DR: *Mix bread batter in one bowl, pour into loaf pan, and bake at 350°F for 65 to 75 minutes. Cool before eating.*

Makes 1 loaf

Butter, at room temperature, for greasing the pan (optional)

3 super ripe bananas (see note, page 195)

1 cup packed dark brown sugar

½ cup (1 stick) butter, melted and cooled

1 teaspoon pure vanilla extract

2 large eggs

1½ cups all-purpose flour

1 teaspoon baking soda

½ teaspoon salt

½ cup plain whole-milk yogurt

Note: If you use frozen bananas—I almost always do—let them defrost and come up to room temperature before mashing them. I often am too impatient to wait for that (it takes 30 to 60 minutes), but cold bananas can affect the baking time and rise. Although a consistent temperature for all ingredients is ideal, this

I wasn't planning to include this recipe in this book—banana bread is such well-trodden territory. Sure, I think the yogurt adds moisture and tang, and this loaf has just the right amount of sweetness and a great texture, but . . . what am I really adding to the world here? Then I kept making it with my daughter over and over again. It was such an easy way to connect with her and have fun together, making bread from the dregs of old bananas, with her two-year-old hands to help. Banana bread has brought delight and purpose to so many afternoons. It has helped us connect when we were listless or grouchy. And so, in the end, really, how could I not share it with you?

1. Preheat the oven to 350°F. Generously butter a standard metal loaf pan or line it with parchment paper that comes up the sides and hangs over the edges, making a sling for removing the bread.

2. Place the bananas in a large bowl and mash them with a fork until they are shiny and loose. Add the brown sugar, melted butter, and vanilla and whisk until smooth, about 1 minute. Add the eggs one at a time, beating well after each addition. If the bananas had been frozen and are still a bit too cold, the warm butter will get a little crystalized. Don't worry, the banana bread will be fine.

3. Sprinkle the flour, baking soda, and salt over the wet mixture and use a spoon or spatula to gently stir them in. Once the dry ingredients are mostly incorporated, fold in the yogurt and mix until the batter is smooth, without any pockets of flour.

4. Pour the batter into the prepared loaf pan and bake until a knife inserted into the center comes out clean, 65 to 75 minutes. It's a long bake time, but it's a very moist, dense bread and it takes time! A few gooey crumbs on the knife are okay, but it shouldn't seem wet.

5. Let the banana bread cool completely in the pan. Then remove it from the pan, either by lifting it out with the parchment sling or by cutting carefully around the edges, inverting it, and gently shaking to release the loaf. The bread will keep in a sealed container at room temperature, and it will stay lovely and moist for several days.

banana bread is very forgiving, so don't worry if your butter crystallizes a bit in Step 2.

Banana, Date, and Cashew Muffins

TL;DR: *Mix muffin batter in one bowl, pour into muffin pans, and bake at 375°F for 20 to 25 minutes. Cool before eating.*

Makes 15 to 18 muffins

Butter, at room temperature, for greasing the muffin pans (optional; see note)

3 super ripe bananas (see note, page 195)

⅔ cup packed dark brown sugar

½ cup (1 stick) unsalted butter, melted

1 teaspoon pure vanilla extract

2 large eggs

1½ cups all-purpose flour

1 teaspoon baking soda

1 teaspoon fine sea salt

½ cup plain whole-milk yogurt

6 dates, pitted and chopped

½ cup roughly chopped cashews

Note: There is usually enough butter left stuck to the wrapper to grease the muffin cups—a classic trick!

This is kind of a sticky toffee pudding/banana bread hybrid. The muffins are extra caramelly, rich, complex, and nutty. They feel like all the things I love about the winter. When I'm stuck being cold and the weather is windy or drizzly, I want to lean into it, and these muffins feel like they are here to warm and nourish a frostbitten body from the inside, like the Turkish delight that gets Edmund to betray his family in *The Lion, the Witch and the Wardrobe.* These are very White Witch, but without the nefarious intent.

1. Preheat the oven to 375°F. Line 18 muffin cups with paper or silicone liners or grease them with butter.

2. Place the bananas in a large bowl and mash them with a fork until they are shiny and loose. Add the brown sugar, melted butter, and vanilla and whisk until smooth, about 1 minute. Add the eggs one at a time, beating well after each addition.

3. Sprinkle the flour, baking soda, and salt over the wet mixture and use a spoon or spatula to gently stir them in. Once the dry ingredients are mostly incorporated, fold in the yogurt and mix until the batter is smooth, without any pockets of flour. Gently fold in the chopped dates and cashews until they are just incorporated.

4. Pour the batter into the prepared muffin cups, filling them about three-quarters full with batter, or about ¼ cup in each. Bake until a knife inserted into the center of one comes out clean, 20 to 25 minutes.

5. If you used liners, remove the muffins (with the liners) from the pan as soon as they are cool enough to touch. If you greased the pan, let the muffins cool to room temperature before you invert them to let them fall out. If they don't come out easily, use a small knife to cut around the edge and release them. These muffins will keep in a sealed container at room temperature for several days.

Lemon-Ginger Squares

TL;DR: *Make crust and bake at 350°F for 30 minutes. Juice lemons and ginger, then whisk filling together. Pour it over the cooled crust and chill in fridge for at least 4 hours.*

Makes 16 squares

CRUST

½ cup (1 stick) unsalted butter, at room temperature

⅓ cup sugar

1 teaspoon ground ginger

½ teaspoon fine sea salt

Zest of 1 lemon

1 cup all-purpose flour

FILLING

7 tablespoons freshly squeezed lemon juice

1 tablespoon fresh ginger juice (see note)

2 large eggs

2 large egg yolks

¾ cup sugar

⅛ teaspoon fine sea salt

4 tablespoons (½ stick) cold unsalted butter, cut into pieces

Note: To extract juice from ginger, finely grate about 1 inch of room-temperature ginger. Squeeze the grated ginger with your fingers to extract the juice. (You can use frozen ginger, too—and you can grate it much more quickly—but after you grate it, let it come to room temperature so that you can extract the juice more easily.) If you don't like the mess, gather the grated ginger into cheesecloth before squeezing out the juice.

My daughter's favorite color is yellow—just like these vibrant and delicious and exciting and bright Lemon-Ginger Squares. When it comes to dessert, I bounce between extremes, wanting rich and chocolatey or bright, zingy, and fruity. This powerfully gingery combination came from some fun experimentation on a few summer afternoons. It can also be made as a tart in an 8-inch tart pan.

1. Preheat the oven to 350°F. Line an 8-inch square pan with parchment paper that comes up the sides and hangs over the edges, making a sling for removing the squares from the pan.

2. Make the crust: Place the butter and sugar in a large bowl and cream together with a mixer or wooden spoon until smooth. Add the ground ginger, salt, and lemon zest and mix again. Finally, add the flour and stir until a crumbly dough forms.

3. Gently press the crumbly dough into the prepared pan to form an even, flat crust, but don't press it down too hard, just enough for it to be even. Bake until the crust is light brown, about 30 minutes. When it's done, let it cool to room temperature.

4. Meanwhile, make the filling: Fill a medium pan half full with water. Bring it to a boil over high heat, then turn the heat down to maintain a simmer.

5. Combine the lemon juice and the ginger juice in a cup or bowl that is easy to pour from.

6. Place the eggs, egg yolks, sugar, and salt in a wide bowl and whisk to combine. Place the bowl over the pan of simmering water for a minute or so, then add the lemon-ginger juice slowly and whisk continuously until the mixture thickens enough to coat the back of a spoon, 5 to 10 minutes. The mixture will foam a bit, and don't panic if it looks like it is separating or if it seems like it will never thicken. Just keep whisking and let it heat, because once it hits the right temperature, it will magically develop a smooth, custardy texture.

Note: *Using a metal bowl is fine, but those with extremely sensitive taste buds might detect a very slight metallic taste in the finished custard. If that's you, use a heatproof glass bowl.*

7. Take the bowl off the heat, add the butter, and whisk until the butter melts into the filling. Pour the filling over the cooled crust and let it set, covered, in the fridge for 4 hours or overnight.

8. Lift the whole thing out of the pan, using the parchment paper as a sling. Cut into 16 small squares and enjoy. Store in a sealed container in the fridge for up to 2 weeks.

Oops! I Made Them Again Chocolate Chip Cookies

TL;DR: *Beat wet ingredients, add dry ingredients, form into logs, and chill for at least 20 minutes. Bake at 350°F for 8 to 10 minutes.*

Makes 3 dozen(ish) cookies

2 cups all-purpose flour

1 teaspoon baking soda

1 teaspoon fine sea salt

1 cup (2 sticks) unsalted butter, melted

1½ cups sugar

3 tablespoons molasses

1 large egg

1 large egg yolk

2 teaspoons pure vanilla extract

2 cups chocolate chips (see note)

Flaky sea salt, for sprinkling

Note: For added fun, try using a variety of different cocoa percentages for the chocolate chips, or use different shapes, or chop the chocolate yourself from bars.

I am not a creature of habit in the kitchen. I rarely make the same thing twice, but these cookies are an exception. Once I came upon this recipe, I refined it slowly, and I've made it hundreds of times since. These are the best. They are thin, but not too thin, and crispy on the bottom but gooey in the middle. They are very dark-brown-sugary and caramelly from the molasses, and I would not change a thing. I always have the ingredients for these cookies available in case a craving strikes, and I could probably make them blindfolded—although please don't ask me to, that sounds horrible. Friends who never bake ask for the recipe. There is nothing better than a good chocolate chip cookie. I will not hear otherwise.

1. Measure the flour, baking soda, and salt into a medium bowl and whisk together.

2. Place the butter, sugar, and molasses in a large bowl or the bowl of a stand mixer and cream together at medium speed until the mixture gets lighter in color, 3 to 5 minutes. Add the egg, egg yolk, and vanilla, mixing a bit between each addition. Beat the mixture on medium speed until it lightens in color again, about 2 minutes.

3. Sprinkle the dry ingredients over the wet ingredients and use a wooden spoon or spatula to gently form a dough—you don't want to work it too much. Finally, pour in the chocolate chips and stir to combine.

4. Form the dough into two logs, wrap them in plastic, and chill them in the fridge for at least 20 minutes or up to a day.

5. When you're ready to bake, preheat the oven to 350°F. Line a sheet pan with parchment paper or a silicone baking mat.

6. While you wait for the oven to come to temperature, create golf ball–size cookies (about 18 from each log) and place them on the

prepared pan with lots of space in between them. I usually do just 6 per pan because they spread out a lot while they bake. Sprinkle a little flaky salt over them.

7. Bake the cookies for 8 to 10 minutes. You may want to experiment with the time to find your ideal amount of chewy outside and soft middle. Mine are perfect after 9 minutes. They will seem gooey when you remove them from the oven, but leave them on the sheet pan to solidify for 10 minutes, and they will be perfect. If you let them bake a little longer, they won't have as much chew, and what a shame that would be.

8. Once the cookies have solidified enough that you can safely move them, transfer them to a wire rack to cool completely. Continue baking in batches until you have run out of dough. They will keep, covered, at room temperature for 4 days.

Note: You can also freeze the dough. I like to freeze half of the batch— that's one of the logs from Step 4—so that I can bake fresh cookies another day. Like a love letter to my future self. The dough will keep in the freezer for up to a month.

Good Enough for You

Harry's Grilled Cheese

Normal looks different to everyone. When I was a teenager, I was always amazed by how different my friends' households were compared to mine—who was around, what they ate, the way it smelled and sounded. Being in someone else's home felt intimate, and as a self-conscious teenager dying to be liked, I found it uncomfortable until I could figure out how to fit in. I was always worried about doing the wrong thing. Visiting someone else's home felt like visiting another country. You might know your friend from school, but once in their home, there was a whole other world of information to process. It was an opportunity to see other ways to be a person. And I'll never forget Matt's dad's grilled cheese sandwich.

Matt is one of my dearest friends to this day. His house was calm, and his parents were often home, but usually off in other rooms doing their own thing. No pets. Sometimes you would hear classical music playing or TV sounds from another room. It made me feel at peace. Or at least as peaceful as a squirrelly kid like me, always worried about losing approval, could ever be.

One evening we were in the kitchen scrounging up some dinner when Matt's dad, Harry, came down the stairs. Now, I fully admit I was not paying much attention to what he was doing because I was too busy doing my usual self-conscious routine of trying to ignore him while trying not to do anything too weird in front of him. He started slowly and carefully taking out ingredients and utensils from the cupboard: a cheese grater, a wineglass, cheese, bread. When he finally caught my full attention, he was standing by a little pile of shredded cheese, with three or four little blocks out on the cutting board, bread slices buttered, holding a glass of red wine. He swirled the wine, sniffed it, and took a sip and a deep, contented breath. He was making a grilled cheese sandwich.

Surely this was not how you make a grilled cheese sandwich. Grilled cheese was something you made late at night when your parents had gone to bed. For grilled cheese, you slice the cheese or take it out of its plastic coating and simply drape it over bread in a hot pan. You get it done, so you can eat it. You don't pour yourself a glass of wine and have a good time!

Harry piled his buttered bread high with the shredded cheese blend. He slowly walked over to the stove and pressed the sandwich into a pan while taking another slow sip of wine, all the while chatting to us about the play we were ostensibly working on—you know, like a normal, pleasant person. I'm sure I hiccupped a few sentences out while trying to process the miracle that was occurring in front of me. I was hypnotized but unable to voice what felt so significant. Harry sliced his perfectly golden grilled cheese into triangles, gently nestled them onto his plate, and raised his glass of wine to us before heading back up the stairs. After he left, I turned to Matt and said, probably unable to keep the reverence out of my voice, "Wow, does your dad always make grilled cheese like that?" He replied with the indifference of familiarity: "Oh yeah, that's my dad."

It's the little things. He used more than one cheese. He *shredded* the cheese. Now I shred cheese for my grilled cheese every time. You get better cheese distribution that way, and if you use more than one cheese, you get a mixture in each bite. You can pile in more and mix scallions or bits of chile into it. That is what cooking is to me and why I love it. It's about engaging with our food joyfully to make it just right for you or the person you are making it for. It's all about attitude. You can have that gorgeous pleasure with even the most simple meals—like grilled cheese.

Silly as it may seem, that grilled cheese–making process spoke to me in a way that was deep and powerful. I needed it in my life. The idea that such a simple act could be done with such pleasure and joy and beauty spoke to my soul. In fact, Harry's example that day may have been what set me on the path that I'm on now. He gave me the power to notice how the simplest everyday meals can be made special and beautiful depending on how you engage with them.

One of the most common sentiments I hear is "I live alone so I don't cook" or "It's just me now so I don't bother cooking anymore." People say this to me like it's a simple fact, like they just told me they are lactose intolerant so they switched to oat milk. Basically, they're telling me that cooking is something you do only for other people. That it is a show to be put on. That if none of us had people to impress, we would simply eat crackers dipped in peanut butter for every meal, crumbs collecting on our chins and chests. Harry's example is exactly why this idea of cooking only for others has always felt off to me and why I think seeing Harry make that grilled cheese struck me with such force. He had to eat, and he chose to slow down and scrape every bit of pleasure he could out of the opportunity. Thank you, Harry.

Rest and Pleasure

I am a person. I love feeling good. I love resting. But letting myself rest when I am tired? Scheduling or prioritizing pleasurable activities? Um . . . no, I can't do that. A person can't just sit down or sleep later because they're tired! Resting makes me feel lazy, weak, entitled, unambitious, boring, lonely, and, well, sacrilegious (!?). If I check in with myself when I'm resting, I often find that I'm uneasy, which is, of course, why it's easier not to do it, or to "rest" by doing something distracting.

Letting myself rest, *truly* rest, has been a lifelong struggle, as I know it is for so many people in this culture. We are told that busyness is status and stillness is death, and of course we should be doing things to prove ourselves *at all times*. When I was very young, I didn't want to rest. Life was exciting and I didn't want to miss anything. That excitement later morphed into a pressure and a burdened sense of restlessness—if I rested, I might let someone down. That pressure then transformed into a habit of mind and body so powerful that I truly thought I was resting even when I definitely was not. I thought things like *I love having this dinner party where I feel responsible for making sure everyone feels perfectly loved and cared for and important and impressed all at once!* and *This is fun and totally not to prove my worth to myself and others!* I thought I could make that connected pleasurable feeling happen through my labor, without being honest about what I really needed, which was simply connection with loved ones. Instead, I was trying to force connection through effort and willpower, rather than letting it naturally occur through honest, vulnerable communication. *I will feel good after this party! I'll feel good when everyone else feels good!*

When I finally experienced genuine rest, it was shocking how foreign it felt, and the realization of how much rest I had denied myself struck me deeply. When I allowed others to take care of me, I felt uncomfortable and guilty instead of relaxed. I was living for others and took myself for granted. When I needed to be cared for, I would find some junk to do, believing that cultivation of my self-worth lay at the end of a to-do list. But it never came.

Rest and pleasure are basic needs, just like food, water, and safety. They are *not* a waste of time. The thing I have come to believe in my core is that resting—whether by sleeping, meditating, reflecting, reading, or sitting with a warm beverage staring at the world going by—might be the most important thing I do all day. When I'm resting, I try to just rest and allow thoughts to come and go, checking in with how my body feels. Ten minutes of sitting can feel like a lifetime, whereas forty-five minutes of scrolling on the smartphone can feel like two blinks. Resting helps me home in on how I really should be spending my time because I have a moment to figure it out rather than just anxious energy impulsively moving me from task to task. When I am rested, I worry *far* less about whether I am doing the right work. I have a sense of ease. Resting enough lets my unconscious mind process and then blast into my consciousness a beautiful idea that I am then rested enough to act on.

This statement feels subversive, but resting and enjoying your life *is* your life's purpose, and it is worthy in and of itself. If you are doing nothing more than caring sweetly and gently for yourself, that is a beautiful kindness you are sending into the world. You deserve to have pleasure and rest and to feel good. Everyone does. And you feeling good is putting good out into the world. Being miserable serves no one. It is not noble. We are all put into the world to love and care for ourselves, and the sooner we embrace that gorgeous duty, the sooner the rest of life begins.

Make Your *Own* Happy Hour

Happy hour is such a wonderfully inviting term. And, of course, the idea of connecting with friends and colleagues over drinks before dinner is great. But what if we took the concept and broadened it to be really about spending an hour—or whatever time you might have—doing something fun? Free, agendaless playing. It is just as good for you as it is for kids. The only thing you have to fear is your own judgment.

- You can go classic and make yourself a drink or a snack.

- Get an ice cream.

- Let yourself obsess over the indoor terrarium you've been dreaming of.

- Build with LEGO.

- Go on a bird-watching walk.

- Pet your dog.

- Ride your bicycle.

- Mix Mentos with Diet Coke (and stand back!).

- Draw something.

- Think about what your kid-self loved to do and then let yourself do that, without judgment.

How to Take a Break Like You Mean It

1. Decide to rest and for how long.

2. Breathe deeply for five breaths.

3. Notice. What are you trying to accomplish on this break? Refresh your energy? Get a glass of water or a cookie? Talk to someone? Do a chore? (Or don't!)

4. Pick one thing and do just that. Even if you have time for more, do just that one thing. You can try the other thing next time. It's an experiment.

5. Think about something that makes you feel good. If you are thinking about a friend and you start to worry about them, imagine them in a peaceful place with you.

6. Sit and let your thoughts come and go, breathing easily. Imagine your thoughts projected onto a movie screen. Enjoy the show. You don't have to act on any of them.

Vegetable Celebration

I'm not the best at celebrating myself. I always want someone else to do it for me! And while it's lovely when that works out, it can't always. Celebrating yourself is not self-important; rather, it can help you keep things in perspective.

Sure, you can be traditional and celebrate with cake when you can or want to, but I like to celebrate with vegetables because they are under-celebrated themselves! Some of what makes cake so festive (besides the butter and sugar) is that it is associated with special moments. Vegetables are something we are socialized to believe we "should" eat to be "good" and to "get our vitamins." But really, health feels good, when we take the time to notice. Health is not neutral. Not every day is our birthday, but there are many days when we exhibit bravery, and when we cherish those moments and celebrate them, rather than dismissing them, it is like vitamins for the soul.

Taking the time to stop and appreciate yourself today will help you live more fully in the truth. It is healthy to be proud of yourself for doing the things that are hard for *you* in your specific experience in your unique life. Often we stifle this healthy pride with embarrassment or even shame, believing that we are wrong for struggling to do what we perceive "everyone" can do easily. So celebrating yourself requires courage. The courage to own that it was hard for you to do something that many others think "shouldn't" be hard. Like going to a party, making it to a dance class, or calling a friend you haven't seen in a while. If it required courage from you, then you can be proud. It doesn't matter that it would be easy for someone else. That imaginary person has not lived your life. And there is no one or right way to be a person.

Everyday Celebrations

Here are some examples of everyday accomplishments. What has been hard for you that you got done anyway? What would your child or past self be amazed by that is routine for you now?

- You did your taxes and they were only a week late!

- You worked out.

- You are an adult.

- You are a parent.

- You have a big choice to make, and it's scary, but you have the choice.

- You got through that awful day.

- You went to couples therapy.

- You went to the dentist.

- You asked for a raise.

- You spoke up in class or a meeting.

- You said no.

- You said yes.

- You had that really hard talk.

- You started learning something new.

Honeyed, Cheesy Asparagus

TL;DR: *Roast asparagus at 400°F for 5 minutes. Sprinkle with shredded gruyère and roast again until the cheese is melty and crispy.*

Serves 4 as a side dish

- 1 bunch asparagus
- 1 tablespoon honey
- 1 teaspoon fine sea salt
- 2 teaspoons extra-virgin olive oil
- ½ cup shredded gruyère cheese

A sweet and salty, rich alternative to the usual (and excellent!) roasted asparagus with lemon. Like you would serve asparagus to ancient royalty.

1. Preheat the oven to 400°F. Line a sheet pan with parchment paper or a silicone baking mat.

2. Cut off and discard the woody end of each asparagus spear to prepare them for roasting.

3. Arrange the trimmed asparagus spears in a row on the prepared sheet pan. Drizzle them with the honey, salt, and olive oil. Get in there with your hands and rub the honey, oil, and salt all over the spears, then put them back into a neat(ish) row.

4. Roast until the asparagus is bright green, 5 minutes. Remove it from the oven and sprinkle the shredded gruyère over the top. Roast again until the asparagus is super bright green with some little dark bits at the top and the cheese is melty and bubbly, 5 minutes more. Serve immediately. I usually eat about half the spears directly off the pan, burning my fingers and tongue.

Roasted Smoky and Salty Sweet Potatoes

TL;DR: *Cube sweet potato, roast at 425°F for 20 to 25 minutes, and top with feta.*

For me, this recipe is like a game. Take a too-sweet vegetable and bring balance to it. Let it get crisp and develop a whisper of bitterness from roasting and from the smoked paprika, and enrich it with a heavy crumble of super salty feta. Finally, be satisfied or continue to add balanced complexity with bright herbs, lemon juice, or floral pistachio crumbles.

1. Preheat the oven to 425°F.

2. Dice the sweet potato into 1-inch chunks. Tumble them onto a sheet pan, drizzle them with the olive oil, and sprinkle with salt and paprika. Use your hands to toss it all together and coat evenly. Roast the sweet potato until you can easily pierce it with a fork, 20 to 25 minutes.

3. Crumble the feta over the warm sweet potato and toss to coat. Serve with a scattering of chopped cilantro or mint, a squeeze of lime juice, and chopped pistachios, if desired.

Serves 1 or 2 as a side dish

1 sweet potato

1 teaspoon extra-virgin olive oil

1 teaspoon fine sea salt

1 teaspoon ground smoked paprika

2 ounces feta cheese

Chopped fresh cilantro or mint, for serving (optional)

Squeeze of fresh lime juice, for serving (optional)

Finely chopped pistachios, for serving (optional)

Maple Soy Cashew Brussels Sprouts

TL;DR: *Cook halved brussels sprouts in butter, maple syrup, and soy sauce. Cook cashews in maple syrup until coated like candy, then top brussels sprouts with nuts.*

Serves 1 or 2 as a side dish

1 pound brussels sprouts, trimmed and halved

3 tablespoons maple syrup

1 teaspoon fine sea salt

2 tablespoons butter

1 teaspoon soy sauce

2 tablespoons chopped cashews

This is a very Thanksgiving-type brussels sprouts preparation. I adore brussels sprouts in almost any form, but it's fun to make them sweet and crispy, with a little chewy-ness from the caramelized maple syrup. The candied nuts are almost gilding the lily, but I think it makes the dish feel that much more celebratory.

1. Place the brussels sprouts in a large bowl with 1 tablespoon of the maple syrup and the salt. Mix with your hands to coat the brussels sprouts.

2. Melt the butter in a 10-inch (or larger) pan over high heat, then add 1 tablespoon of the maple syrup and the soy sauce. Swirl the pan to mix the two together, then tumble the brussels sprouts into the pan, flipping as many as possible flat side down so that they can caramelize. Let them sit untouched until you see bubbling, thickening, and, dare I say, "syrupification" happening, 8 to 10 minutes. Use a spatula to flip a brussels sprout and check how dark it is getting underneath. You want it nice and dark. Stop when the brussels sprouts are bright green and soft enough to be easily pierced with a fork, but don't cook beyond that or they get mushy and horrible.

3. Take the brussels sprouts off the heat and scoop them into a serving dish. Refill the pan with the last 1 tablespoon of maple syrup and the cashews, turn the heat to medium, and cook until the cashews are coated and the syrup thickens just slightly, 1 to 3 minutes. Pour the candied cashews over the brussels sprouts and serve.

Maple Soy Cashew
Brussels Sprouts,
opposite page

Pickle-y
Sausage
Caulifower,
page 218

Mouthwatering
Miso Roasted
Broccoli and
Shallots, page 219

Pickle-y Sausage Cauliflower

TL;DR: *Roast cauliflower and sausage at 450°F for 40 to 45 minutes and top with dill pickle slices.*

Serves 2 or 3 as a side dish

1 large head cauliflower

2 tablespoons extra-virgin olive oil

1 teaspoon fine sea salt

Zest of 1 lemon (optional)

1 link spicy Italian sausage

Sliced dill pickles (see note)

FEELING ADVENTUROUS?

- Pile shredded cheese, like aged cheddar or gruyère, on top
- Drizzle with hot sauce

Note: I like spicy dill pickles, but bread and butter pickles, or whatever you like best, would work well. The pickles add a hit of salty brightness that brings everything together.

This makes a dynamite pizza topping, or you can toss it with non-noodle pasta, like shells or rigatoni (just leave the pickles off until after it's baked, please).

1. Preheat the oven to 450°F.

2. Chop the cauliflower into small florets. I like them to be bite-size because they are easier to eat and have more surface area to get brown and crispy.

3. Place the cauliflower on a large sheet pan and add the olive oil, salt, and lemon zest, if using. Squeeze the Italian sausage out of its casing and dot the bits of meat around the pan, in maybe 20 or so small clumps.

Note: *It's important to use a sheet pan here rather than a baking dish with sides. You want all the cauliflower to have enough room to breathe (rather than being piled in) so it doesn't end up steaming and getting mushy from sitting in the liquids of its brethren.*

4. Roast the cauliflower and sausage for 20 to 25 minutes, then remove from the oven and use a spatula to flip the cauliflower florets over and generally just toss and disturb everything. Roast again until the cauliflower is dark golden, another 20 minutes.

5. Toss everything together to get the sausage juices all over the cauliflower. Serve with slices of pickle on top, to your taste.

Mouthwatering Miso Roasted Broccoli and Shallots

TL;DR: *Roast broccoli at 425°F for 15 minutes. Make dressing. Cook shallots until crispy and sweet. Toss broccoli and dressing and top with shallots.*

This is a "What is this, and why is it so good?" kind of recipe. Broccoli is bitter and powerful (in addition to being impossible to spell, amirite?) and can totally hang with other strong flavors. This dish is like an amazing ensemble cast with fantastic chemistry, where everyone gets better just by being part of the team.

1. Preheat the oven to 425°F.

2. Cut the broccoli into florets and spread the florets out on a sheet pan. Toss the florets with 1 tablespoon of the olive oil and the salt. Roast until there are some dark brown crispy bits, about 15 minutes.

3. Place the white miso, peanut butter, honey, lemon juice, soy sauce, and water in a bowl and whisk together to make the dressing.

4. Warm the remaining 1 teaspoon of olive oil in a small pan over medium-high heat. Add the shallot and cook until it is frizzled, about 5 minutes.

5. Toss the broccoli with the miso dressing while it's still hot. Top with the shallots and serve immediately.

Serves 2 to 4 as a side dish

1 head broccoli

1 tablespoon plus 1 teaspoon extra-virgin olive oil

1 teaspoon fine sea salt

1 tablespoon white miso

1 tablespoon peanut butter

2 teaspoons honey

1 tablespoon freshly squeezed lemon juice

1 teaspoon soy sauce

2 teaspoons water

1 shallot, halved lengthwise and thinly sliced

Sour Cream and Onion Potatoes

TL;DR: *Roast potatoes at 425°F for 40 minutes and toss with onion dip.*

The best potato chip flavor made into a hot dish? Need I say more? Only that these potatoes are sweet and creamy and salty and tangy, and that this dish is so absurdly good that I don't know why it took me so long to think of it.

1. Preheat the oven to 425°F.

2. Tumble the whole potatoes onto a sheet pan. Drizzle them with the olive oil and sprinkle with salt. Toss it all together with your hands to evenly coat the potatoes.

3. Roast the potatoes until a fork inserted into the center meets no resistance and the skins are crispy and browned, about 40 minutes.

4. Scoop the Caramelized Onion Dip into a large bowl. Use tongs to toss the still-warm roasted potatoes with the onion dip until they are evenly coated. Serve immediately.

Serves 2 as a side dish

1 pound baby potatoes (any color will do)

1 tablespoon extra-virgin olive oil

1½ teaspoons fine sea salt

½ cup Caramelized Onion Dip (page 261)

Macadamia-Crusted Delicata Squash
with Maple Mustard Tahini Dressing

TL;DR: *Roast squash at 400°F for 35 to 40 minutes. Toast macadamia nuts. Mix dressing. Toss nuts and squash together and drizzle with dressing.*

Serves 2 as a side dish

1 small to medium delicata squash, seeded and sliced into thin half-moons

1 tablespoon extra-virgin olive oil

1 teaspoon fine sea salt

10 macadamia nuts, crushed (see note)

MAPLE MUSTARD TAHINI DRESSING

1 tablespoon freshly squeezed lemon juice

1 tablespoon maple syrup

1 tablespoon tahini

1 teaspoon dijon mustard

Pinch of fine sea salt

Note: Crush the macadamia nuts with the side of a knife, or finely chop them. You want their texture to be like breadcrumbs.

Enjoy this dish as is or use it as a star element of the Best Friend Salad (page 77). Better yet, make a double recipe; eat some now and use the rest in a salad later in the week. Any leftover dressing is amazing tossed with sliced cucumber and sesame seeds.

1. Preheat the oven to 400°F. Line a sheet pan with parchment paper or a silicone baking mat.

2. Dump the squash slices onto the sheet pan and drizzle them with the olive oil and salt. Toss it all together with your hands to evenly coat the slices. Arrange them on the pan so that they are evenly spaced; having a bit of space between them is good, but a little overlap is not a big deal.

3. Roast the squash until it is brown around the edges and can be easily pierced with a fork, about 30 minutes. Flip and roast until the slices are lightly browned all over, 5 to 10 minutes more.

4. Place the crushed nuts in a dry pan over medium-high heat and toast them, shaking the pan occasionally, until they are medium brown, about 5 minutes. Stay close—they go from light to dark in a flash. Once they have darkened, take the pan off the heat immediately.

5. Make the dressing: Place the lemon juice, maple syrup, tahini, mustard, and a pinch of salt in a small jar with a lid. Put the lid on and shake until all the ingredients come together.

6. Transfer the warm squash to a metal bowl, add the macadamia nuts and a drizzle of the dressing, and toss to combine. Pile the mixture high on the center of a serving plate and drizzle with a bit more dressing. The squash is best the first day or two after you've made it but will keep in a sealed container in the fridge for 3 to 5 days.

Pesto Corn

TL;DR: *Boil corn, cut kernels off cob, and toss with pesto.*

Yes, this dish is technically just two ingredients. Except, of course, that pesto is a magical sauce made from just a few super flavorful elements: herby and pungent basil leaves, rich and nutty parmesan and pine nuts, powerful garlic, and sharp and silky olive oil. It's so perfectly savory and yet bright. The only thing missing is some form of sweetness—and in walks fresh summer corn and we're done, folks! Sometimes life is good and it's just that easy.

1. Peel the green parts and all the stringy silk off the corn. Relax and take your time—rushing will not help. You have to zone in on your obsessive side to get all those little silky bits off, and you can't hurry it.

2. Place the corn in a pot big enough for the cobs to lie flat and cover them with water. Bring to a boil over medium heat. You can either continue to boil, with the lid off, until the corn is cooked through, 5 minutes, or, if you are not in a hurry and are preparing other things, you can simply put a lid on the pot once it comes to a boil and turn off the heat. The corn will sit in the hot water and cook through, staying nice and hot for whenever you're ready to take them out of the hot water bath.

3. Remove the corn from the hot water with tongs. Once it has cooled enough to touch, cut the kernels off the cobs into a large bowl. Then get in there with your hands and break up all the kernels to your satisfaction.

4. Add the pesto and stir to coat. That's it! Enjoy!

Serves 4 as a side dish

4 ears corn
¼ cup prepared pesto

Bacon and Mint Snap Peas

TL;DR: *Cook bacon until crispy. Crumble bacon and mix it with snap peas, mint, and dressing.*

Serves 1 as a meal or 2 as a side dish

2 strips bacon (see note)

8 ounces snap peas, trimmed or sliced as desired (see note)

10 kalamata olives, pitted and finely chopped (optional)

4 stalks fresh mint

Zest and juice of ½ lemon, plus more juice to taste

1 tablespoon extra-virgin olive oil

1 tablespoon finely grated romano cheese, plus more as needed

½ teaspoon fine sea salt

Freshly cracked black pepper

Note: Leave out the bacon and make sure to include the optional olives to make a delicious vegetarian version.

Note: I cut the snap peas diagonally into 4 to 6 pieces. But if you're not much for chopping, you could simply trim the woody ends and leave it at that.

This dish is like a meditation for me because the chopping feels sort of unnecessary and fun. Do it slowly and lovingly while listening to soft jazz. The resulting pile of finely chopped snap peas shot through with mint and lemon is crisp and refreshing, but with a delicious hit of salt. With its plentitude of fiber, this meal makes my heart and body feel good. It's great with a glass of crisp white. My kind of meal for myself. The bacon cooks on low heat so you can even go take a (quick) shower or relax while that happens. But I understand if you feel like you need to try it once before you leave the room. I have trust issues, too.

1. Line a plate with paper towels. Place the bacon in a cast-iron or heavy-bottomed pan over low heat and cook, flipping it once or twice to check it, until it's crispy and most of the fat has rendered out, about 20 minutes. Remove the bacon to the towel-lined plate to soak up the grease.

2. Tumble the snap peas into a medium serving bowl. Add the olives, if using, and crumble in the bacon. Pick the leaves off the stalks of mint and quickly run your knife through them to roughly chop. Add them to the bowl, along with the zest, lemon juice, olive oil, romano, salt, and pepper to taste.

3. Mix it all up with your hands. Taste and adjust the amount of romano if you like it saltier, or squeeze some more lemon juice if it needs brightening.

Create Your Own Cheese Platter

When a friend visits or my daughter's little friends come over, I love setting out a cheese platter. Let your right brain take over for a bit. Everyone can grab what they like, it looks pretty, and it's kind of like a little art project. Even better, I don't have to worry about timing for serving it hot. But I cherish it even more when I have a night to myself and I make a board of all my favorite little treats just for me. Paired with a glass of wine and something to watch that makes me giggle, it feels like I have taken myself on a date and it is going *very* well.

- Craft a cheese-heavy board with a bit of honey and jam.
- Douse a big ball of mozzarella in pesto, and arrange spears of bell pepper and other vegetables on the sides.
- Arrange hard cheeses and soppressata with honey, apple slices, and crackers.
- Make one big, round brie-type cheese the focal point, surrounded by a pile of fruit and crackers.
- Build small mountains of fresh berries.
- Pair brightly colored, sharp, pickled vegetables with crumbly aged cheeses.
- Let yourself play with coordinating or complementary colors to create an edible art project—for example, purply red salami next to light yellow cheese, with green herb accents.
- Drizzle olive oil, honey, or even a smear of hot sauce on the cheese platter.
- Get inspiration from the seasons—both natural and human-made.
- Channel your inner child and create something to delight your younger self.

Emily's Pizza Salad

TL;DR: *Make dressing. Make croutons. Crisp soppressata at 400°F in oven and drizzle with honey. Assemble mozzarella, lettuce, basil, and croutons, toss with dressing, and add soppressata and cheese.*

Serves 4

DRESSING

½ cup extra-virgin olive oil

3 cloves garlic, sliced

1 canned tomato, finely chopped, or 1 tablespoon tomato paste

Zest and juice of 2 lemons

CROUTONS

2 tablespoons extra-virgin olive oil

3 cups cubed or torn bread

SALAD

30 thin slices soppressata or pepperoni

2 tablespoons honey

6 cups baby lettuces

1 cup fresh basil

6 ounces fresh mozzarella, cubed or torn into small pieces

Freshly grated parmesan or romano cheese

Note: This makes more dressing than you need for one salad, so store leftovers in an airtight container in the fridge and enjoy again sometime within a week.

My sister Emily is my North Star when I'm developing recipes. My first foray into cookbooking was making her a personal cookbook as a gift. She has always been discerning, and making food I think she will like has always been a fun challenge. I still consult with her all the time about the food I make and share with people. She reminds me of my past triumphs and reels in my harebrained ideas. She loves pizza more than most people, which is saying a lot. Despite that, ordering pizza can remind her of times when pizza was the only good thing in the day. Of course, we should all order pizza when we want it. But there's also a place for this special salad, with all the flavors of pizza and some extra self-love in the making.

1. Preheat the oven to 400°F. Line a sheet pan with aluminum foil or a silicone baking mat.

2. Make the dressing: Warm the ½ cup of olive oil in a small pot over low heat. Add the garlic, tomato, and lemon zest and cook, swirling the mixture occasionally to help the flavors infuse, about 5 minutes. Remove from the heat, add the lemon juice, stir, and set aside.

Note: *If you're using tomato paste instead of chopped tomato, whisk briefly after adding the paste to incorporate it.*

3. Make the croutons: Warm the 2 tablespoons of olive oil in a large pan over medium heat. Scoop the bread cubes into the pan. Cook, tossing occasionally, until the bread cubes are browned and crispy, about 10 minutes. Remove them from the pan and set aside.

4. Place the slices of soppressata on the prepared sheet pan. Bake until they are just crispy, about 5 minutes. Immediately drizzle them with honey to your taste, up to 2 tablespoons.

5. Assemble the salad: Pour half the dressing into a large bowl and add the lettuce, basil, mozzarella, and croutons. Tear the soppressata in half, shower everything with parmesan, and mix well. Drizzle with more dressing if the coverage is not satisfactory.

My Spicy Umami Pasta

TL;DR: *Cook pasta. Make sauce. Pour pasta into sauce and cook.*
Sprinkle with cheese and scallions and serve.

Serves 1

Fine sea salt

4 ounces rigatoni, shells, or orecchiette-style pasta

2 tablespoons butter

1 clove garlic, chopped

1 shallot, chopped

1 tablespoon (or more!) sambal oelek or chile paste of your choice

1 tablespoon tomato paste (see note)

1 teaspoon honey

¼ cup white wine or pasta water

4 kalamata olives, pitted and chopped

Grated parmesan or romano cheese

1 scallion, chopped

Note: I like the tomato paste that comes packaged in a tube. You can keep it in your fridge and it lasts for ages!

Making an amazing dish out of whatever bits you have lying around feels so heroic, and this version of that experience happens to be just to my odd taste. It is all the things I love together, and honestly, it's so incredible that I really struggle not to make myself a second bowl after I finish the first. It's a strange hybrid of nations and flavors, but it is so spicy and umami and sweet and savory that I just can't stop eating it. It's my kind of pantry pasta, using all the things I always have left over, like half or less of a box of pasta, some butter and garlic and chile paste and honey, and usually a partially finished bottle of wine. I wish I could help you all develop your own version of pantry pasta, but here is mine to get the creative juices flowing.

1. Bring a large pot of salted water to a boil. Cook the pasta according to the package instructions for al dente, but take it off the heat and drain it 1 minute early.

2. As soon as you get your pasta in the boiling water, start the sauce. It comes together very quickly. Melt the butter in a small saucepan over medium heat. Add the garlic and shallot and sauté, stirring or swirling occasionally, until aromatic, about 2 minutes. Then add the sambal oelek, tomato paste, and honey and cook for another minute, stirring and squishing the sauce to mix it thoroughly—it will be bubbling and seem kinda weird because the tomato paste and chile paste are a bit thick, but don't worry. Add the white wine and chopped olives, stir, and let everything cook for a minute or so. The sauce should look like a sauce now.

3. Add the slightly undercooked pasta to the sauce. Cook, tossing to coat, until the sauce is thick and every noodle is coated, about 3 minutes. Add more liquid if the sauce becomes too thick at any point.

4. Sprinkle parmesan over the pasta and toss one more time. Taste the pasta to make sure it is cooked enough and add salt if you need it. Remove the pan from the heat, sprinkle with chopped scallions and a little more cheese, and serve.

Extra Crunchy Jalapeño Cheddar Snack

TL;DR: *Toast tortilla with cheddar and jalapeño in skillet until crunchy. Top with lettuce, tomato, and sour cream.*

Jalapeño and cheddar has to be my favorite flavor. I mean, I have a lot of favorite flavors, but this one is always on the list. I like the spiciness and cheesiness, but especially that special, grassy, bright flavor of a fresh jalapeño. Oh man, it's like my particular body chemistry is perfectly designed to be attracted to it; my senses get all tingly and happy. I will never in my life turn down a jalapeño and cheddar potato chip. So, when I am wanting that hit of yum I might get from eating a whole bag of jalapeño and cheddar chips, but the grown-up in me wants to head off to bed without a bellyache and dehydration, I make myself this simple, spectacular treat. It's like a giant tortilla chip covered with molten cheddar, studded with spicy jalapeños, topped with crunchy lettuce and acidic tomato, drizzled with sour cream, and crammed into my mouth.

Serves 1

1 flour tortilla

Shredded cheddar cheese (enough to generously cover the tortilla)

1 fresh jalapeño, stemmed, seeded (for less heat, if desired), and finely sliced

Shredded crunchy lettuce, like romaine or butter lettuce

Diced tomato

Sour cream

1. Place the tortilla in a dry nonstick skillet and cover with shredded cheddar right up to the edges. Artfully arrange thin slices of jalapeño all over the cheese and then sprinkle on a bit more cheese. The cheese should be a little excessive. Turn the heat to medium-high and cover with a lid so the cheese melts. Leave it until the cheese is melted but the bottom isn't toooo dark, 3 to 5 minutes. I love when the cheese melts off the side a bit and gets crunchy.

2. With a spatula, scoop the jalapeño cheese snack onto a plate and top with shredded lettuce, diced tomato, and a drizzle of sour cream. Fold it over and eat it!

Better-than-a-Milkshake Mango Lassis

TL;DR: *Peel mango, then blend with yogurt, salt, and vanilla until smooth.*

Serves 2

1 large mango or 2 small mangoes

1 cup plain yogurt

Pinch of fine sea salt

Splash of pure vanilla extract

Drizzle of honey (optional)

Mango lassis are deeply comforting. They remind me of my teenage years, when I was an avid vegetarian and became obsessed with South Asian cuisine. I also made them almost every day for weeks after Io was born. My local market was selling these amazing little Haitian mangoes, and I just kept buying them, and Dan and I would have lassis every day. Though I always think I will need honey to sweeten them, I rarely do because ripe mangoes are perfectly sweet just as they are. You can use frozen mango to make a lassi, but let's be real, frozen mango is never ripe! And the mangoes need to be ripe for a lassi to be what it should.

1. Peel the mango and cut off as much of the flesh from the pit as humanly possible. You are going to blend it so you don't need to be pretty about it.

2. Drop the pieces into a blender along with the yogurt and a wee pinch of salt. Blitz everything until it is smooth and a little foamy. Taste and add a splash of vanilla, plus a drizzle of honey if it's not sweet enough. Blitz one more time and then pour into cups to enjoy.

Cheesecake Pots

These luxurious single-serving desserts feel so special and fancy, while requiring no baking and very little fuss. I couldn't stop at one recipe. Serve them in cute little bowls or cups with long-handled spoons.

Orange and Chocolate Cheesecake Pots

TL;DR: *Whip cheesecake together. Layer chocolate cookie crumbles, cheesecake, and orange segments.*

Serves 4

1 cup (8 ounces) mascarpone cheese

¾ cup (6 ounces) heavy whipping cream

3 tablespoons sugar

1 teaspoon pure vanilla extract

4 mandarin oranges

1 cup Oreo or other chocolate cookie crumbles, or as desired (see note)

Note: Crumble the cookies in whatever way you find most convenient—blitz them in a food processor, crush them in a mortar and pestle (my choice!), or put them in a tea towel or plastic bag and smash them with a rolling pin.

Serious Creamsicle vibes here. The contrasting colors—bright orange citrus, dark brown cookie, and bright white cheesecake—are super elegant. And the dish is fast and fun but still feels special.

1. Place the mascarpone, whipping cream, sugar, and vanilla in a large bowl and whip, using an electric mixer, until stiff peaks form, 2 to 3 minutes. If you prefer to mix by hand, whisk the mascarpone and sugar together for about 30 seconds and then slowly pour in the whipping cream and vanilla, continuing to whisk to keep lumps from forming.

2. Peel the oranges, removing as much of the pith as possible and breaking up all the sections. For a more elegant look, supreme the oranges: Slice off the top and bottom of each mandarin orange and set it flat on a cutting board. Use a very sharp knife to slice off the peel and pith. You should now see the membranes that divide the sections. Cut out each section, carefully slicing just inside the membranes, so that you're left with sections of the bright orange inner flesh.

3. To assemble, layer about ¼ cup of chocolate cookie crumbles at the bottom of 4 small bowls or glass cups. Then layer the cheesecake mixture evenly into each vessel and top with the orange slices. Sprinkle with a few more cookie crumbles, if you like.

Peach Mascarpone Cheesecake Pots

TL;DR: *Blend peaches until smooth. Whip cheesecake together, then fold in peach puree. Layer graham cracker crumbles, cheesecake, and peach slices.*

This dish is the perfect peak-summer treat when the peaches or nectarines are so juicy and fragrant and you want to try something besides just eating them out of hand—or, as is often the case for me, you bought too many and don't want them to go bad. It comes together with no fuss or baking and has a kind of "cheesecake meets ice cream meets peaches" vibe that is both indulgent and beautiful.

1. Peel 2 of the peaches, halve them, and remove the pit. Blend the peach flesh in a blender until smooth.

2. Place the mascarpone, whipping cream, sugar, and vanilla in a large bowl and whip, using an electric mixer, until stiff peaks form, 2 to 3 minutes. If you prefer to mix by hand, whisk the mascarpone and sugar together for about 30 seconds and then slowly pour in the whipping cream and vanilla, continuing to whisk to keep lumps from forming.

3. Use a spatula to fold in the pureed peaches. You can mix them in fully or leave ribbons of brighter yellow in the cream—your choice. Taste and add more sugar if you prefer it sweeter.

4. Slice the other 2 peaches into 8 or 12 slices each.

5. To assemble, layer about ¼ cup of graham cracker crumbles at the bottom of 4 small bowls or glass cups. Then layer the peach cheesecake evenly into each vessel and top with the peach slices. Sprinkle with a few more graham cracker crumbles, if you like.

Note: For the graham cracker crumbles, aim for the thickness of a layer of a crumb crust in a tart or pie. It's just for a little crunch and sweetness, so use as much or as little as you like—it's not important to be exacting.

Serves 4

4 peaches (see note)

1 cup (8 ounces) mascarpone cheese

¾ cup (6 ounces) heavy whipping cream

¼ cup sugar or 2 tablespoons honey, plus more to taste

1 teaspoon pure vanilla extract

1 cup graham cracker crumbles, or as desired (see note)

FEELING ADVENTUROUS?

- Garnish with lemon, thyme, or mint leaves
- Drizzle honey on top for extra fanciness

Note: If you use nectarines instead of peaches, you can leave the skin on in Step 1.

Note: Crumble the graham crackers in whatever way you find most convenient—blitz them in a food processor, crush them in a mortar and pestle (my choice!), or put them in a tea towel or plastic bag and smash them with a rolling pin.

Triple Citrus Custard Cream
with (or without) Meringue

TL;DR: *Bring custard together in double boiler, then add butter off heat. Let set in 4 bowls in fridge until cold, 1 hour. Whip meringue and dollop on top.*

Makes 4 small bowls

1 lemon

1 lime

1 navel orange

⅔ cup sugar

2 large eggs

2 large egg yolks (see note)

Teeny pinch of fine sea salt

4 tablespoons (½ stick) unsalted butter, cold

Graham cracker crumbs or a shortbread cookie, for serving (optional)

Note: You can use the whites from these eggs to make the meringue topping.

I am a huge proponent of citrus and use citrus zest and juice constantly to bring out flavor and add depth or brightness to dishes, but something really exciting happens when you blend lemon, lime, and orange. The sweetness of the orange is enhanced by the zing from the lemon and lime, while the lemon and lime are mellowed by the orange, and it all becomes just a big wow in your mouth. This is a lovely little dessert to end a meal with or to stir into yogurt and granola (see page 52). If you are into gilding lilies, like I am, make the meringue topping as well! It's a nice use for the egg whites you have left over from making the custard cream, and meringue makes the whole thing seem a little fancier. And if you ever have leftovers of the citrus blend, put it to good use in Triple Citrus Dressing (page 88) or Citrus Refresher Pasta (page 155)!

1. Set a strainer over a small bowl. Juice the lemon, lime, and orange over the strainer to catch any flesh or seeds. Measure out ½ cup of the citrus juice blend and save the rest for another use.

2. Fill a medium pot half full with water. Bring it to a boil over high heat, then turn the heat down to maintain a simmer.

3. Place the sugar, eggs, egg yolks, and salt in a large, wide metal bowl that will fit snugly into the pot without touching the simmering water. Place the bowl over the pot and whisk until you have a bright yellow, thick liquid. As it heats, it will begin to thin out—keep whisking so the egg doesn't curdle and so the sugar melts and gets smooth instead of grainy.

4. After a few minutes of whisking, add a splash of the citrus juice and whisk it in. The mixture will begin to get frothy. Continue to add the juice a little at a time until you've added the entire ½ cup. Keep

whisking until the mixture thickens enough to coat the back of a spoon.

5. Once the custard has thickened, remove it from the heat. Cut the cold butter into small pieces and add it to the custard, whisking it to incorporate.

6. Pour the custard into 4 small bowls, cover them, and let set in the fridge for an hour or so. Serve with meringue topping, if desired, and graham cracker crumbs or a shortbread cookie for crunch. Or you can pour it into a jar and keep it to mix with yogurt and/or granola at breakfast. You can even spread it on toast like lemon curd.

Meringue Topping

TL;DR: *Whip egg whites over boiling water until marshmallowy, 5 to 10 minutes.*

Makes about 1 cup

2 large egg whites (see note)
½ cup sugar
½ teaspoon pure vanilla extract

Note: Use the egg whites left over from the custard to make the topping.

1. Fill a medium pot half full with water. Bring it to a boil over high heat, then turn the heat down to maintain a simmer.

2. Add the egg whites to a large, wide metal bowl that will fit snugly into the pot without touching the simmering water—you can use the same one you just used to make the custard, thoroughly washed and dried. Add the sugar and whisk continuously until the mixture is frothy and light, a minute or so. Then place the metal bowl over the pot of hot water. Continue to whisk until the mixture begins to lighten and thicken and becomes marshmallowy, 5 to 10 minutes. The meringue will be thick and glossy. Be sure to keep the water at a gentle simmer; you want a gentle heat to slowly cook the eggs and melt the sugar, but you don't want scrambled egg.

3. Once you have the thick, marshmallowy consistency, take the meringue off the heat, add the vanilla extract, and whisk.

4. Dollop equal heaps of meringue onto each custard and chill in the fridge until you're ready to eat.

Good Enough
for Others

The Myth of Effortless Entertaining

I've said it hundreds of times: "Oh, it's nothing" … "I was cooking any-way" … "Oh, it's so much fun for me, it's no big deal" … "We'll just have a few snacks." When I say these things, in reality, I've often been cooking and planning for days. I got up early, arranged childcare, went to four stores, and gave up all kinds of other activities in pursuit of making food and caring for my guests. When they walk into my home and smell the garlic cooking, see the homemade pie on the counter, and accept from me a freshly made cocktail, the truth is undeniable: I care. I've been caught red-handed caring. A true nightmare.

Backing up a moment, in case you missed it, cooking and making food is how I express my love. It's how I connect—with myself, with those I love, and with the wider world. My daughter is a huge fan of the TV series *Daniel Tiger's Neighborhood*, and while many of the episodes inexplicably make me cry, I will never forget when Daniel and Dad Tiger made banana bread for Mom Tiger and sang, "Making something is one way to say I love you." I wept. "It is, it is," I gulped and sniffled, trying to calm my extreme reaction.

Making something is one way to say "I love you." We know this is true. We feel it. But yikes, it is embarrassing! I feel reduced to the age of five, giving the kids in my class Valentine's Day cards, compelled to participate, excited and brimming with love to share, yet hideously afraid to stand out and be seen. Would my valentine be too much? Would they realize I like them more than they like me?

However, it is undeniable that I am now a grown-up. I need to let myself express my excitement and joy and love and delight in my friends and family without down-playing any of it. I deserve that. They deserve that.

We downplay to minimize our own discomfort, but when we brush aside our friends' sincere thanks for our efforts, it is unkind. That's the last thing I want to be to my loved ones. What helped me shift and stop waving off my effort was thinking about it from the other person's perspective. My friend walks in and sees what I have done. They express their sincere delight in my efforts. "Wow! Look at this! I can see how much effort this must have been, and I am humbled and grateful for it. Wow, you must care about me." A warm, glowing smile radiates from their whole being. And then what do I say? "Oh, it's nothing." Smile turns to a grimace, warmth becomes strained incredulity. How do they feel now? Confused? Check. Rejected? Probably! Uncomfortable because I am expecting them to help maintain the obvi-ous fantasy that this is no big deal? It's like that feeling when you think someone is waving at you, so you wave and smile back, and then it turns out they were waving at their friends behind you.

No. No, I don't want to do that to my friends. That is the opposite of why I invited them over! I want to strengthen our bond, not strain it.

The myth of effortlessness is pure self-sabotage because it's all about avoiding vulnerability. It stops the vulnerability (that despicably embarrassing moment!) that leads to the intimate, warm, connected together time that you are craving and that you are trying to create with your efforts. Don't lose your nerve! You are so close to your goal. You can do this. Let them know you care! Jump off the cliff—you came all this way to do it! The embarrassing moment is the leap of faith.

Saying you care is jumping off the cliff. That's why you can actually have a super warm and intimate evening over a bag of chips from the corner store . . . the secret ingredient is emotional vulnerability. So often these hostings can be the most fun because the veneer of formality is gone and intimacy flourishes. For me, it's important to do both. To show people you want to be with them for popcorn on a difficult Wednesday, or fully going for it for Sunday brunch.

I want to own that the people I invite into my home are people I love. I love them whether or not they equally return my level of love. Sometimes that means I will have to deal with mild discomfort. Maybe they are a little distracted or disengaged. Maybe they find it hard to accept my love because it makes them feel insecure about their own abilities or circumstances. Maybe it's just as hard for them to accept my love as it is for me to receive thanks. That is not about me. But most of the time, none of it is the big cliff you imagine. It's just a tiny step over a crack in the sidewalk. The risk is not so great. The people you are inviting into your home are, for the most part, established friends who, more often than not, are going to be seriously touched by your efforts because they love you and will be delighted to see that you love them, too.

This chapter appears last in the book because it is the culmination of all the effort embodied by the previous chapters. I think we all want to skip to the end. To be the radiant cook at the center of a beautiful meal. But to really own that place, you have to take care of yourself. To live that image, not just as an actor but as your reality, you have to build up the stamina and courage to love openly and fully. It is a lifelong practice.

Social Anxiety and Loneliness

When someone first asked me why I cook and write cookbooks and do what I do, I felt awful because I didn't know. Sure, "I like it" and "it's an honor" were true, but not real. I couldn't think of anything to say that would honor the depth of feeling I have for what I do. When I really think about why I do what I do, it usually brings tears to my eyes. A feeling of love wells up in my chest and it's a little hard to bear, and some tears slip out. I cook to express love. Since cooking for everyone is impossible, I make cookbooks. I need to express my love because it is a fire burning inside me and I have to let it out somehow. This is the way I know how.

I was a lonely kid who became a lonely adult. But I didn't realize I was lonely until the isolation of new motherhood jolted me into realizing that the loneliness I was feeling was not the new and awful thing I thought it was but an old, familiar pain. I am grateful for that realization because it was that unconscious loneliness that motivated my earliest explorations in the kitchen. I cook from the youngest, most earnest part of myself, because when I am expressing love I am connected and protected from loneliness. Expressing love feels so good, and cooking is the way I managed to do it in a world where loving others sometimes feels vulnerable and frightening. Cooking is the place where I have allowed myself (and I say "allowed myself" because I have not allowed myself much) to take up space. To be me. To love purely as myself. The kitchen is the place where I can be my authentic self. Somehow, because cooking is practical and has to be done anyway, it slipped past my perfectionist radar and I got to express and practice and grow more powerful. I do not ask permission in the kitchen. I *have* permission. I ask for help and I ask for inspiration. But the decisions are *mine*, and the best meals come from my mind and creativity—and so do the flops. There is almost nothing else in my life like this, nothing else where I feel that ease and right to be there and total comfort with taking up space. In the kitchen, and nowhere else, I have the confidence to move with the knowledge that I can do this.

So for me, the cooking part is pretty easy now. It's the connecting-with-those-I-love part that I need help with. I definitely don't find connecting with others to be effortless. For some of us, it can be an immense struggle. Social anxiety can be incapacitating, and no one chooses it. But food can help us connect, and I'm here to try to remove the barriers we put up so we can get a little closer to that connection we crave.

A Menu for Doing Enough

Pick One Thing

Think about one thing you want to make for your guests, like a pie or homemade buns or biryani—or Smoky Honey Shrimp Tacos with Spicy Fennel Slaw (page 266). Build the meal around that one dish, keeping the rest simple.

Ask for What You Need

Ask people to bring a contribution to the meal. You can learn to be comfortable with asking for help at the last minute, or if you are organized, you can share the menu in advance and ask them to bring something specific or something that fits, making it clear you trust them with the choice.

Ground Yourself

If you get nervous and want to do too much, think about the person who makes you feel most accepted and make what you would make for them.

Create Structure

Pick an event or some activity you and your guests can do together to relieve the pressure on the food and entertaining. Like a birthday party or a movie night or a holiday—the objective is clear!

Do a Spread

Cheese plates, cut fruit, dips, breads, and finger foods are fun to chat and share over.

Show Up

Make an effort to be fully present when you greet your guests and let them know you are happy they are there. I am so bad at this one. I wimp out and do a quick wave from the kitchen while I pretend that what I'm doing has to be done now.

Summer Produce Glory

Effortless entertaining. It's what we think we want—to look amazing and receive all kinds of praise while also not doing too much. I think that, at some level, at least in my own addled mind, the ideal version of this fantasy is that you call up a couple of your friends and say, "Hey, want to come over this afternoon?" and they say, "Sure!" When they arrive, they find an incredible spread of drinks and food that delight and amaze. Foods you know they love. And you just happen to have been able to throw it together from what you had lying around. Some part of the fantasy is being the kind of person who lives a lavish and extraordinary lifestyle—to act as though you always have an amazing spread every afternoon. You are simply inviting them into that. But that is dishonest (though benignly dishonest), and it creates a barrier to intimacy.

How can we be honest and have fun while also not burdening ourselves or making ourselves stressed out? Well, the best time to create a lavish spread genuinely easily is during peak summer produce season. There is little to do besides sit back and say, "Yes, thank you, thank you, I did invent corn." "Watermelon and mint? I birthed this from my loins." (I kid, I kid.) The point is that summer produce allows you to experience and share the pleasure of refreshing, delicious food with minimal stress, worry, and planning and still have the kind of open, loving experience that makes long summer evenings so memorable years later.

Make any of these the stars:

- Sliced watermelon
- Corn with butter and/or cheese and spices
- Water with herbs in it
- Cucumbers, radishes, or tomatoes with salt and olive oil
- Peach and Burrata Beauty (page 262)
- Tomatoes, mozzarella, and basil with salt and pepper
- Stone fruits or berries and cream

Serve with:

- Dips with cut veggies and chips
- Bread and butter
- Hot dogs or veggie dogs
- Burgers
- Snacks from Assembly Only (page 24)

Sunday Morning Pancakes
with Coffee Syrup

TL;DR: *Mix batter, let sit for 10 minutes, then cook pancakes in hot pan.*

Makes 8 to 10 small pancakes, enough for 2 adults and a small person

1 cup all-purpose flour

1 tablespoon baking powder

1 tablespoon sugar (brown or white)

1 teaspoon fine sea salt

2 large eggs, at room temperature

½ cup (1 stick) unsalted butter, plus more for the pan

1 tablespoon apple cider vinegar or distilled white vinegar

Scant ½ cup plain yogurt

Scant ½ cup whole milk

Coffee Syrup (recipe follows) or your favorite syrup, for serving

Fresh fruit, for serving

Note: These are ostensibly buttermilk pancakes, but I never have buttermilk; I always just use milk, yogurt, and vinegar as a substitute and don't miss the real thing. If you have buttermilk around, by all means, simply substitute 1 cup of it for the milk, yogurt, and vinegar.

One day I decided to stop trying to make pancakes healthy, and that was the time my husband said, with eyes wide, "Wow, sometimes I forget how good a cook you are, and then this happens." So now, of course, I make them this way all the time. I am as vulnerable to flattery as the next person. These pancakes are rich, pillowy, buttery, and really quite cakey, but without the sweetness. They leave the job of sweetness for the syrup, and for their part they will soak that syrup up expertly.

You can easily add berries, banana slices, or chocolate chips to these pancakes. Simply sprinkle them on top of the pancakes after you have them in the pan, but before the flip to the second side. This works much better than trying to add the mix-ins to the batter itself.

1. Measure the flour, baking powder, sugar, and salt into a small bowl and give it a quick whisk so that all the ingredients are reasonably distributed.

2. Crack the eggs into a large bowl and whisk them. Melt the butter in the microwave or on the stovetop and, whisking continuously, pour it into the egg mixture slowly, to prevent scrambling the eggs. Whisk until you have a smooth, thick, yellow liquid that looks kind of like hollandaise.

3. Pour the vinegar into a liquid measuring cup, then add the yogurt and milk and stir. You should have 1 cup total. Let the mixture sit for a couple of minutes. Then, whisking continuously, slowly pour it into the egg mixture.

4. Sprinkle the flour mixture over the wet mixture and gently mix it with a wooden spoon until most of the dry ingredients are incorporated. It's okay to leave the batter a little lumpy because the lumps will cook themselves out. It's much better to undermix than to overmix and have tough, chewy pancakes. Let the batter sit for 10 minutes.

5. Preheat the oven to 150°F or the warm setting. Place an oven-safe plate or baking sheet in the oven—that's where you'll leave finished pancakes to keep warm while you make the rest.

6. Place a cast-iron skillet over medium-low heat. Add a pat of butter to the pan and gently swirl it to coat. Use a ladle to pour a dollop of pancake batter into the buttered pan. It should become reasonably round naturally. It looks messy but will seize up and start cooking

soon, so don't panic. I usually do two pancakes at a time in our pan, but you can do more if your pan is bigger or if you are braver.

7. Let the pancakes cook until bubbles begin to form not just around the edges but all the way through to the middle and they begin to look a little dry at the edges, 2 to 3 minutes. Then use a spatula to flip them over with confidence. Cook until they are just lightly browned on the bottom, another minute or so. The second side is always faster. Remove the pancakes from the pan and place them on the warming plate in the oven.

Note: The truly perfect time to flip is just before the edges begin to dry out. You'll get the hang of it with practice.

8. Repeat until you are finished with the pancake batter, adding more butter to the pan in between each batch.

9. Serve the pancakes warm with Coffee Syrup (or your favorite syrup), fresh fruit, and whatever else you like!

Coffee Syrup

TL;DR: *Bring leftover coffee and sugar to a boil, thicken into a syrup, and add vanilla.*

Makes 1 cup

1¼ cups brewed coffee

1 cup sugar

½ teaspoon pure vanilla extract

In our house, we often make slightly more coffee than we can drink before it gets cold. Sometimes, by the time we get done running around after a small person, what's left in the pot isn't that appealing. So one day, when we had run out of maple syrup, I thought I should take that unappealing cold coffee and add sugar and heat. The result is surprisingly dark and complex, without being too in your face about its coffee-ness. Pouring this syrup over your pancakes creates the feeling of a great diner experience, where the smell of coffee is always in the background.

1. Pour the coffee and sugar into a small saucepan. Bring to a boil over medium heat, then turn the heat down to medium-low and simmer until the liquid thickens into a syrup, about 20 minutes.

2. Remove the pan from the heat, add the vanilla, and stir.

3. Use the syrup immediately over pancakes, plain oatmeal, yogurt, ice cream, coffee cake, and so on. Or let the syrup cool and store it in an airtight canning jar or bottle in the fridge for up to a month.

Corn Chowder Quiche

TL;DR: *Freeze butter for 20 minutes. Make dough and chill for 20 minutes. Roll out dough; press into a pie plate. Mix corn, cheese, and scallions. Spoon into crust and pour egg mixture on top. Bake at 375°F for 1 hour. Cool.*

When I have people over for brunch, I always try to make everything in advance because mornings are not my best time. Making this flavorful quiche the day before and simply popping it out of the fridge to serve feels great. You get to lovingly make a quiche for your guests, but at your own pace, and you can fully enjoy being with them without fumbling around in the kitchen at the last minute. Serve the quiche with a fruit salad, yogurt, toast, or whatever simple brunchy things you (or your guests) want to add to the table.

1. Make the crust: Place the butter in the freezer for at least 20 minutes and up to 1 hour. Place the flour and salt in a medium bowl and stir a couple of times to combine.

2. Take the butter out of the freezer and, using the large holes on a box grater, grate it into the bowl with the flour. Crumble up the mixture with your fingers, working it for just 15 to 20 seconds. Add 3 tablespoons of the cold water and mix it quickly with your hands. Add 2 more tablespoons and mix again, then immediately and confidently bring the dough together into a ball.

3. Once the dough forms a lump (it does not need to be perfect), dump it onto the counter. Add the remaining 1 tablespoon of water if the dough is still too crumbly. Quickly shape the dough into a disk, put it back in the bowl, cover with plastic wrap or a moist towel, and place it in the fridge to chill for 20 minutes.

Note: Grate the butter as quickly as you can because your hands give off heat and you want the butter to melt as little as possible.

4. Sprinkle a clean, dry surface with flour and place the chilled dough in the center. Roll it out with a rolling pin a few times, then turn it 90 degrees, flip it over, and roll again, sprinkling it with some more flour if it sticks. Continue rolling, turning, and flipping the dough until it forms a circle about 12 inches in diameter.

Serves 6 to 8

CRUST

½ cup (1 stick) unsalted butter

1¼ cups all-purpose flour, plus extra for rolling out the dough

½ teaspoon fine sea salt

5 to 6 tablespoons cold water

FILLING

2 cups corn (fresh, canned, or frozen and thawed)

4 to 6 ounces sharp cheddar cheese, shredded (1 to 1½ cups)

1 bunch scallions, chopped

6 large eggs

1 cup heavy whipping cream (see note)

1 cup whole milk

1 teaspoon fine sea salt

Freshly cracked black pepper

Note: You can substitute plain whole-milk yogurt or sour cream for the heavy whipping cream.

5. Transfer the dough to a 9-inch glass pie plate, pressing it onto the bottom. Trim away any excess dough until you have ½ inch of pastry hanging all the way around the rim. Roll up the overhanging edge of the dough and pinch it to create a rim on the lip of the pie plate. Use your fingers or the tines of a fork to crimp the edge. Place the finished crust in the fridge to chill while you make the filling.

6. Preheat the oven to 375°F. Move an oven rack to the lowest position.

7. Make the filling: Place the corn and cheddar in a large bowl. Add the scallions, reserving a small handful for garnish, if desired, and mix well. Place the eggs, whipping cream, milk, salt, and a generous sprinkling of pepper in a medium bowl and whisk to combine.

8. Take the crust out of the fridge and pour the corn mixture into the crust, spreading it evenly. It will look like a lot, but don't worry, the egg mixture will fill in the cracks. Pour the egg mixture on top and gently stir it with a spoon to disperse the ingredients evenly. Place the pie on a baking sheet to catch any errant drips.

9. Bake the quiche on the lowest oven rack (or even the bottom of the oven) until the center of the quiche is set but still a bit wobbly, and a knife inserted into the center comes out dry, about 1 hour. The filling should be browned all the way to the center.

10. Let the quiche cool to room temperature before serving, garnished with the reserved scallions, if desired. If you like your quiche chilled, let it cool in the fridge for a few hours. It will keep, covered, for up to a week in the fridge.

Brunch Gnocchi

TL;DR: *Cook bacon and then gnocchi while you scramble eggs.*
Add crumbled bacon and greens to gnocchi. Serve with eggs.

Serves 4

6 strips bacon

4 large eggs

Fine sea salt and freshly
  cracked black pepper

2 scallions, finely chopped
  (optional)

2 tablespoons butter

1 package (16 ounces)
  gnocchi

½ bunch kale, chard, or
  spinach, stems removed,
  roughly chopped (about 1
  cup)

Freshly squeezed lemon juice
  or hot sauce, to finish (a
  vinegar-based sauce, like
  Tabasco, works best)

This is a weekend idea, and before you think "No thanks, that will take way too long," I would like to point out that gnocchi are basically potatoes that are already cooked and cut up for you. Our favorite neighborhood joint does gnocchi for brunch, and it is just so clearly brilliant. This is a good dish to make for guests since it's impressive but relatively easy.

1. Line a plate with paper towels. Place the bacon in a cast-iron or heavy-bottomed pan over low heat and cook, flipping it once or twice to check it, until it's crispy and most of the fat has rendered out, about 20 minutes. Remove the bacon to the towel-lined plate to soak up the grease.

2. While the bacon cooks, break the eggs into a bowl, sprinkle with salt and pepper, and add the chopped scallions, if using. Whisk the eggs with a fork.

3. When the bacon is done and cooling on a plate, pour off most of the fat from the pan. Set the pan over medium heat and drop in 1 tablespoon of the butter. Once the butter is melted, tumble the gnocchi in and let them cook until they are light golden on one side, about 5 minutes. With a wooden spoon or spatula, move the gnocchi around the pan so they can brown on all sides, about 3 minutes more per side. Pour in 1 tablespoon or so of water to deglaze the pan and keep the gnocchi from sticking.

Note: When you are draining bacon fat from a pan, pour it into a jar and save it for later or throw it away. Never dump it into your drain.

4. While the gnocchi cook, melt the remaining 1 tablespoon of butter in a small nonstick skillet over low heat. Add the eggs. Because the heat is low you will not need to monitor them too closely (see Creamy Hands-Off Scrambled Eggs on page 40 for more on this technique). Occasionally use a spatula to disturb the eggs and gently fold them over. They should cook at about the same rate as the gnocchi. If they seem to be cooking too fast, pull them off the heat or finish them and set them aside. Cook until you have loose curds of just-cooked egg, about 20 minutes. They should be creamy and a little runny.

5. Once the gnocchi are browned on both sides, add the chopped kale and crumble the cooked bacon into the pan. Stir until the greens are wilted, 1 to 2 minutes. Taste and season with salt and pepper to your liking.

6. Pull the gnocchi and the eggs from the heat and plate them together. To serve, squeeze lemon juice or sprinkle hot sauce all over. Please don't skip this step—the dish needs a touch of acidity and sharpness to really make it sing!

Caramelized Onion Dip

TL;DR: *Caramelize onions in butter for 30 to 45 minutes; mix with sour cream.*

I serve this dip at almost every party I have, and I always expect that this time people will ignore it and go for the other dishes that took so much more effort, but every time, the onion dip is gone first and everyone asks me how I make it. "It's just caramelized onions mixed with sour cream," I tell them. Then they give me the obnoxious "you're lying to me to keep your little chef secret" eyebrows. But it's this easy! It really is! Not everything in this world has to be difficult to be fantastic. If by some miracle you have leftover dip because you are sick or your friends are all lactose intolerant, toss it with roasted potatoes (see page 221).

1. Melt the butter in a medium pan over low heat. Add the onion, sprinkle with ½ teaspoon or more of salt, and stir to coat. Leave the onion to turn golden and darker brown, disturbing it only when the onion is getting stuck to the pan and looking like it could burn. (In that case, add a little water and stir until the sticky onion bits lift up and glaze the onion.) It will continue to get darker and stickier and silkier until the onion is truly dark and caramelized, after 30 to 45 minutes. Remove the onion from the heat and let cool to room temperature.

2. Mix the caramelized onion with the sour cream, sprinkle with chopped scallions (if you like), and serve with your favorite potato chips or whatever else you like to dip.

Makes about 2 cups

2 tablespoons butter

1 red onion, finely chopped (see note)

Fine sea salt

1 cup (8 ounces) sour cream

Chopped scallions, for garnish (optional)

Potato chips or other dippers, for serving

Note: Cut the onion in half through the root and place each half flat on your cutting board. Cut the ratty top end off but keep the root for now, just to help hold the onion together while you slice it. Peel off the crispy, dry outer layers. Slice each onion half into thin half-moons, then discard the root. Roughly chop the half-moons into smaller pieces. It's harder to eat the dip if there are huge, drippy pieces of onion.

Peach and Burrata Beauty

TL;DR: *Arrange sliced peaches and tomatoes on platter with burrata, gently torn apart, nestled in center. Garnish with mint, salt, pepper, and olive oil.*

Serves 4 as an appetizer or side dish

4 ripe peaches, halved and pitted

20 cherry tomatoes, halved

1 large ball burrata (see note)

Extra-virgin olive oil

1 teaspoon fine sea salt

Freshly cracked black pepper

Fresh mint or basil leaves

Note: Burrata needs to be fresh and ideally made in-house. Try an Italian market, cheese store, or high-end grocery store. It will be in the fridge, packaged with its brine to keep it fresh. Use it as soon as you can.

This simple dish feels like luxury to me, in part because burrata is such a treat and (rightfully so) on the costly side. But it's also because the platter, as a whole, looks so beautiful, summery, pleasurable, and impressive. When made during the height of summer peach and tomato season—which is really the *only* time it should be made—it actually lives up to the hype, taste-wise. It's a great dish for hosting friends because you can put it together while talking, amaze and delight them with the prettiness, and then sit, chill, and be present with them while you all appreciate the deliciousness. It's *stunning*. And it took you 5 minutes.

1. Cut each peach half into 6 to 8 slices. Artfully arrange them on a big platter. Scatter the cherry tomatoes among the peaches.

2. Gently rest the burrata in the middle of the platter and carefully pull it apart, letting the gooey center ooze out a bit. Finish with a drizzle of olive oil, a sprinkling of salt and pepper everywhere, and a scattering of a few mint or basil leaves.

You want the craggy bits; they get crispy. If they stick to your smashing object, just scrape them off.

Garlic and Lemon Butter Smashed Potatoes

TL;DR: *Boil potatoes, smash them, and slather them with garlic and lemon butter. Roast at 450°F for 30 minutes and top with herbs, sour cream, and lemon juice.*

There is a measure of confidence required when deciding what to serve to guests. Dishes like this one are confident enough for you. Whoever first thought of smashing a potato to create more crispy-crunchy bits really did us all a service. These have a zillion craggy little browned edges, and the center is so fluffy. And it's all so salty and buttery, and then you get hit with the garlic and lemon.

1. Preheat the oven to 450°F.

2. Tumble the potatoes into a large pot, cover them with water, and add 2 tablespoons of the salt. Bring to a boil over medium-high heat, then lower the heat and let simmer for 10 to 15 minutes. When you can easily pierce them with a fork, they are done. Drain the potatoes and let them cool.

3. Zest the lemon into a small bowl. Add the melted butter, olive oil, and garlic and mix well.

4. Line two sheet pans with aluminum foil or silicone baking mats. Put half the potatoes on each pan. Using another baking tray or any wide, flat object—my favorite is my cast-iron skillet—smash the potatoes. It will be messy! That is good.

5. Sprinkle the potatoes with the remaining tablespoon of salt and fresh black pepper to taste, and then coat them evenly with the melted butter mixture.

6. Roast the smashed potatoes until lots of crisp, dark brown bits appear, about 30 minutes. Remove them from the oven and sprinkle them with whatever herbs you have around, a squeeze of lemon juice from the lemon you zested, and a plop of sour cream. Serve warm.

Serves 4 to 6 as a side dish

2 pounds Yukon Gold potatoes, chopped into bite-size pieces (see note)

3 tablespoons fine sea salt, plus extra as needed

1 lemon

2 tablespoons butter, melted

2 tablespoons extra-virgin olive oil

3 cloves garlic, finely chopped or pressed

Freshly ground black pepper

Chopped fresh dill, cilantro, parsley, basil, or any herb you have, for serving

Sour cream or yogurt, for serving

Note: If you're using baby potatoes, there's no need to chop them.

Note: This is a few more steps than an average side dish—boil, smash, roast—so if you serve it as part of a full meal, balance it with something easy like Pesto Corn (page 225) or burgers. These will be the star anyway.

Smoky Honey Shrimp Tacos
with Spicy Fennel Slaw

TL;DR: *Thaw shrimp and chop slaw. Blend dressing.*
Cook shrimp and toast tortillas. Assemble tacos!

Serves 4

2 pounds small (41 to 50 per pound) frozen shrimp, thawed, peeled, tails off, and deveined (see note)

¼ cup honey

2 teaspoons ground smoked paprika

2 cloves garlic, grated

1½ teaspoons fine sea salt, plus extra as needed

1 cup (8 ounces) sour cream

1 jalapeño, stemmed, seeded (for less heat, if desired), and roughly chopped

¼ cup roughly chopped fresh cilantro

Juice of 1 lime, plus extra as needed

1 medium fennel bulb, very thinly sliced (see note, page 267)

1 cup chopped mango

2 tablespoons extra-virgin olive oil

12 corn tortillas

Note: To thaw the frozen shrimp, place them in a sieve and submerge it in a bowl filled with cold water. The shrimp should thaw in 20 to 30 minutes. If you are in a hurry, you can run the cold water through the sieve to make it go faster.

I love serving my guests food that is slightly messy. It forces us to be a bit more intimate because we can't pretend that we are all perfectly dignified—and it feels like family that way. I also like to keep the meal on the light side so we can enjoy each other and not feel like we need to take a nap afterward. Plus it leaves room for dessert. These tacos might seem complicated on the surface, but it's a matter of chopping the slaw, whizzing up a dressing, then cooking the shrimp in a pan. The most tedious part is toasting the tortillas and keeping them warm, but that's not so bad, is it?

1. Pat the shrimp dry. Place the shrimp in a medium bowl with the honey, smoked paprika, grated garlic, and 1 teaspoon of the salt. Mix it all together.

2. Make the dressing: Place the sour cream, jalapeño, cilantro, lime juice, and ½ teaspoon of the salt in a blender or food processor. Blend until the jalapeño and cilantro are well mixed and the dressing is a very light green. Taste and add more salt or lime juice as desired.

3. Toss the fennel and mango together in a bowl with the dressing. Start with 2 tablespoons and add more, if necessary, up to ¼ cup. The amount will depend on how big your fennel bulb was and how juicy you like your slaw!

4. Heat the olive oil in a large pan over medium heat. When the oil is warm, add the shrimp with all their marinade and cook, stirring occasionally, until the shrimp are pink and cooked through, about 5 minutes.

5. Meanwhile, place another large pan over medium-high heat and warm the corn tortillas for about 30 seconds per side.

6. To serve the tacos, pile each tortilla with fennel slaw, top with shrimp, and drizzle with a bit more dressing, as desired.

You'll use the fennel to make slaw, so slice it as thinly as you can manage without being ridiculous. If your fennel bulb came with its fluffy green tops still on it, and they look fresh and vibrant, add them to the slaw as well.

Turkey Falafel Balls
with Tangy Tomato Sauce

TL;DR: *Process chickpeas and spices, mix with ground turkey, and form into balls. Bake at 425°F for 25 minutes. Make sauce. Add balls to sauce and warm through.*

Serves 8

TURKEY FALAFEL BALLS

1 can (15½ ounces) chickpeas, drained and rinsed

¼ cup roughly chopped fresh cilantro

¼ cup roughly chopped fresh mint

¼ cup roughly chopped fresh parsley

1 scallion, roughly chopped

1 teaspoon ground cumin

1½ teaspoons fine sea salt

1 pound ground turkey

Extra-virgin olive oil, for the pan and your hands

TANGY TOMATO SAUCE

1 tablespoon extra-virgin olive oil

1 medium onion, chopped

4 cloves garlic, sliced

½ teaspoon crushed red pepper flakes

Zest of 1 lemon

Pinch of fine sea salt, plus extra as needed

1 can (28 ounces) crushed tomatoes

When company's coming, it's great to serve a meal you can make in advance and leave simmering on the stove. Then you can welcome your guests with both heavenly aromas and your own presence, since you're not stuck cooking in the kitchen. It's also fun to serve food that's both interesting yet crowd pleasing. Turkey Falafel Balls have the comforting pleasure of meatballs with the flavor and surprise of falafel. Serve this dish with pasta (I like big shells best), couscous, or polenta—whatever suits you and your guests.

1. Preheat the oven to 425°F.

2. Make the turkey falafel balls: Place the chickpeas, cilantro, mint, parsley, scallion, cumin, and salt in a food processor and blitz to form a fine paste. Add a tablespoon or so of water if you need to get the mixture moving.

3. Use a spatula to scrape the bright green paste into a big mixing bowl. Add the ground turkey. Using clean hands, gently mix the turkey with the paste until the mixture is relatively uniform.

4. Pour enough oil into a 10- or 12-inch oven-safe skillet (preferably cast iron) to coat the bottom. Oil your hands well (and keep the oil nearby!) and then form the turkey-chickpea mixture into 30 small balls, oiling your hands again when the mixture starts to stick to you. I find I can do 4 or 5 balls before I need to re-oil. Nestle the turkey falafel balls into the oiled pan.

5. When all the turkey falafel balls are in the pan, set it in the oven and bake until they are browned, about 25 minutes.

6. Meanwhile, make the sauce: Warm the olive oil in a large pot or Dutch oven over medium heat. Add the onion and cook, stirring occasionally, until it's translucent, about 5 minutes. Add the garlic, crushed red pepper flakes, lemon zest, and a pinch of salt and cook until it smells wonderful, another 2 minutes. Pour in the crushed tomatoes and 1 cup of water and bring to a boil, then lower the heat and let the sauce simmer, with a lid on and slightly askew to let steam escape, until the turkey falafel balls come out of the oven.

7. When the turkey falafel balls are ready, use tongs or a spoon to transfer them to the pot of simmering sauce. Taste the sauce and add more salt as needed. Let the balls simmer until the sauce has thickened a bit, about 10 minutes.

8. To serve, spoon the sauce over cooked pasta, or the starch of your choice, top with a few turkey falafel balls, and garnish with chopped mint, parsley, and cilantro and a generous dollop of plain yogurt.

Spicy Ginger-Honey Blondies

TL;DR: *Mix batter and pour into pan. Swirl spicy honey into batter and bake at 350°F for 35 to 40 minutes.*

The intense, almost sharp sweetness of honey, cut by the spiciness of ground and fresh ginger, amplified by the slightest hint of cayenne, against a background of gooey brown-butter blondies is quite the experience. I love making desserts because it really feels like play. With savory foods, I always feel like nature is the true cook. A basil omelet, for example, is the product of the chickens and the earth and gentle tending from the farmer. Desserts, though, are somehow authentic to the baker—a treat crafted for a highly specific experience, with sugar carrying that chosen flavor and presenting it to your tongue like a slap on the back. Desserts feel both human and reverent, like art.

1. Preheat the oven to 350°F. Generously butter an 8-inch square baking pan.

2. Melt the butter in a small pot over medium heat. Take it off the heat and let it cool for 5 to 10 minutes.

3. Meanwhile, place the sugar, 1 tablespoon of the ground ginger, the grated ginger, the salt, and ½ teaspoon of the cayenne in a large bowl and whisk to combine.

4. Gently pour the slightly cooled butter into the bowl with the sugar and whisk to combine. Add the eggs one at a time, mixing well after each addition, and then whisk the mixture until it looks like a smooth caramel, 1 to 2 minutes. Add the vanilla and whisk to incorporate it.

5. Sprinkle the flour over the top of the caramel-colored batter and whisk until no floury pockets remain.

6. Oil a glass measuring cup, if desired (see note), and add to it the remaining 1 teaspoon of ground ginger and a pinch of cayenne. Add the honey and gently stir to mix it with the ginger and cayenne.

Note: Oiling the measuring cup is optional, but it really helps the honey slide out of the cup easily, and you won't lose a lot of honey sticking to the cup.

Makes 16 blondies

1 cup (2 sticks) unsalted butter, plus more for greasing the pan

1½ cups sugar

1 tablespoon plus 1 teaspoon ground ginger

1 heaping tablespoon grated fresh ginger

1 teaspoon fine sea salt

½ teaspoon plus a pinch of ground cayenne pepper

2 large eggs, at room temperature

2 teaspoons pure vanilla extract

2 cups all-purpose flour

Vegetable oil, for oiling the measuring cup (optional; see note)

½ cup honey

Flaky sea salt, for the top

7. Pour the blondie batter into the prepared pan and smooth it to fill the pan evenly, all the way to the edges. Drizzle the honey mixture over the top and use a butter knife to gently swirl the honey into the batter in long ripples. Bang the pan gently on the counter to even out the batter. Sprinkle the top with flaky sea salt, as desired.

8. Bake until a knife inserted into the center comes out with just a few little bits of batter on it, 35 to 40 minutes. You want the blondies a little underdone and moist, so you don't want a perfectly clean knife here. Let the blondies cool to room temperature, then cut them into squares and enjoy. They keep for a week or so in a sealed container at room temperature (although you will probably have eaten them or given them away by then!).

Brian's Peanut Butter and Honey Cupcakes

TL;DR: Mix batter and bake at 350°F for 15 to 18 minutes. Brush on diluted honey. Make frosting, then pipe it over cooled cupcakes. Make peanut brittle, let cool, break it up, and decorate with it.

My friend Brian has pushed me to be honest about how I feel with greater success than anyone I know. He is a Jedi of knowing when I'm full of nonsense. My usual Olympic-caliber ability to hide my messier feelings or to appear calm and cool when I'm not are, to him, little more than an elementary-school talent show performance, and not a winning one. But he has the grace not to call me out in the moment—he is always gentle and kind in his noticing. He makes me feel safe. And in return, I love him with my whole heart. He's really into peanut butter and honey sandwiches, so these cupcakes are just for him.

1. Preheat the oven to 350°F. Line 10 muffin cups with paper or silicone liners.

2. Make the honey cupcakes: Place the flour, baking soda, and salt in a medium bowl and stir together.

3. Crack the eggs into a large bowl. Add the honey and sugar. (When adding the honey, grease the measuring cup with a bit of butter or oil to make the honey come out smoothly.) Beat with an electric mixer or whisk until the mixture is lighter in color and about doubled in volume, about 2 minutes. Gently stir the melted butter into the egg mixture. Sprinkle in half of the flour mixture, then the sour cream, and then the rest of the flour mixture, mixing a bit with each addition. Stir just until the batter is smooth and golden. Be careful not to overmix.

4. Fill each muffin cup about three-quarters full with batter. As a general guideline, I slightly underfill a quarter-cup measuring cup. Bake the honey cupcakes until they are light brown and puffed up, 15 to 18 minutes. They change from golden to light brown quite quickly just at the end, so watch for it.

5. While the cupcakes are baking, make the cupcake soak: Place the honey and water in a small bowl and whisk them together. As soon as

---

Makes 10 cupcakes

HONEY CUPCAKES

1 cup all-purpose flour

½ teaspoon baking soda

½ teaspoon fine sea salt

2 large eggs

¼ cup dark, flavorful honey (see note, page 275)

¼ cup sugar

4 tablespoons (½ stick) butter, melted

¼ cup sour cream

CUPCAKE SOAK

2 tablespoons honey

2 tablespoons water

PEANUT BUTTER FROSTING

4 ounces (½ package) cream cheese, at room temperature

1 cup creamy peanut butter

1 teaspoon pure vanilla extract

⅓ cup heavy whipping cream

1 cup confectioners' sugar

PEANUT BRITTLE

1 cup unsalted peanuts

¼ cup honey

½ teaspoon fine sea salt

you take the cupcakes out of the oven, poke each one all over with a skewer, then use a pastry brush to brush the diluted honey over the top of the cupcakes until you have used it all up. Let the cupcakes cool to room temperature.

6. As the cupcakes cool, make the peanut butter frosting: Place the cream cheese, peanut butter, and vanilla in a large bowl and whip them together with the mixer. Pour in the whipping cream and mix, starting out slowly so it doesn't splatter everywhere. Once the mixture has come together into a smooth consistency, add the confectioners' sugar, just a bit at a time so you don't puff it everywhere. Mix until the frosting is thick and light, 2 to 3 minutes. Cover the frosting and let it rest in the fridge until you're ready to use it.

7. Make the peanut brittle: Line a sheet pan with parchment paper or a silicone baking mat. Pour the peanuts, honey, and sea salt into a nonstick pan over medium-high heat and cook, stirring occasionally, until the edges of the honey begin to darken, about 5 minutes. Stir to coat the peanuts, then take the pan off the heat and continue stirring until the peanuts are coated with caramelized honey. The honey will continue to darken and caramelize as it cools. Pour the brittle onto the prepared pan and let it cool until hard. Then break it up into small chunks with clean hands.

8. When the cupcakes are fully cooled, pipe or spread the peanut butter frosting on each cupcake, and decorate with the peanut brittle. Serve immediately or keep in a sealed container in the fridge for up to a week.

Note: These cupcakes are generously frosted in the "piled high" style, so if you aren't into that, simply halve the frosting recipe.

Note: The darkest, most flavorful honey will come across best in this cake. The consistency needs to be quite liquid, so make sure it's runny or thin it by warming the honey in a microwave.

Dan's Birthday Carrot Cake

TL;DR: *Mix cake batter and bake at 350°F for 40 minutes, then let cool. Make frosting. Layer cooled cakes with frosting in between, on the sides, and on top, and decorate as desired.*

Makes a two-layer 9-inch cake

CARROT CAKE

Butter or oil, for greasing the cake pans

2 cups packed dark brown sugar

1 cup vegetable oil

4 large eggs

½ cup sour cream

1 teaspoon pure vanilla extract

2 cups grated carrots

1 cup chopped and drained canned pineapple

2 cups all-purpose flour

2 teaspoons baking soda

2 teaspoons ground cinnamon

1 teaspoon fine sea salt

FROSTING

16 ounces (2 packages) cream cheese, at room temperature

1 cup (2 sticks) unsalted butter, at room temperature

2 teaspoons pure vanilla extract

3 cups confectioners' sugar

½ teaspoon ground cinnamon

FOR SERVING

Chopped pineapple (optional)

Sprinkles (optional)

I like to make birthday cakes. If you tell me when your birthday is and what kind of cake you like, I will make you one. I think that making a personalized cake is the epitome of fun. It's difficult yet doable, and fussy yet messy enough to feel really satisfying, and it always looks impressive. So, for many years, when my husband said he wanted carrot cake for his birthday, I would say "Okay!" with a smile on my face while being secretly disappointed that I couldn't do something more interesting. I mean, I could make you salted caramel yuzu cake! Come on! But year after year, this is what he wants, and year after year, we serve it to guests and they absolutely rave about it. The pineapple is not a strong flavor in the cake, but my theory is that the citric acid really brings all the other flavors forward. It's a great cake, and I now accept that it's traditional, but not boring.

1. Preheat the oven to 350°F. Line the bottoms of two 9-inch round cake pans (see note) with parchment paper—yes, you have to cut it to fit (ugh). Grease the sides of the pans.

Note: *If you only have one round cake pan, not two, just use it to bake the first cake, then wash it and bake in it again. That's how I do it.*

2. Make the cake: Place the brown sugar and oil in a large bowl and whisk vigorously by hand or with an electric mixer until the mixture is slightly lightened in color, about 2 minutes. Add the eggs, one at a time, mixing after each addition, and whisk until the batter is smooth and light, about 2 minutes more. Add the sour cream and vanilla and whisk again. Finally, add the carrots and pineapple and mix gently with a wooden spoon.

3. Place the flour, baking soda, cinnamon, and salt in a medium bowl and whisk a couple of times just to blend.

4. Shake the flour mixture on top of the wet mixture and gently stir to form a loose, wet batter free of any floury pockets. Pour it into the prepared pans.

5. Bake the cakes until a knife inserted into the center comes out clean, about 40 minutes. Remove from the oven and let cool.

6. While the cakes cool, make the frosting: Place the cream cheese, butter, and vanilla in a large bowl or the bowl of a stand mixer, and beat until the mixture is smooth and light, about 2 minutes. Carefully pour in the confectioners' sugar and cinnamon, just a bit at a time, continuing to beat with each addition. Adding the sugar slowly will keep it from puffing up and making a mess. Beat the frosting until it is light and fluffy, another 5 minutes.

7. Once the carrot cakes have completely cooled, remove them from the pans. Place a sheet of parchment paper on the plate or stand you want to serve the cake on. Place one cake on top of it. With a serrated knife, cut off the domed top of the cake to make it as flat as possible. Add one-third of the frosting to the top of the cake and spread it into an even layer, leaving about ½ inch of space from the edge.

8. Place the second cake on top of the frosted bottom cake. Now comes a matter of taste: For the most professional look, cut off the domed top of this cake, too, or set it upside down so that its flat bottom becomes the top of the cake. But if you like the dome on top, simply leave it as is. Add another third of the frosting to the top and the remaining third to the sides of the cake. Use a butter knife or a flat spatula to spread the frosting smoothly. Swirls and imperfections look great, so don't worry about making it perfect.

9. When you're done spreading frosting, carefully pull out the parchment from beneath the cake. Decorate the cake with some cut pineapple chunks, sprinkles, or nothing at all. Serve at room temperature. The cake will keep, covered, in the fridge for 5 days or more—but let your slice warm up to room temperature (set it on the counter for 30 minutes or so) before you plan to eat it.

After the Meal

A Tale of Two Leftovers

In my quest to uncover the full experience of feeding ourselves, I did not want to forget about the end-of-life cycle. Not all food that is chosen, cherished, and cooked can be eaten—at least not immediately. Some will end up . . . elsewhere. Leftovers.

Death is a difficult topic. Waste and garbage are a difficult topic. We have a very human tendency to avoid difficult topics if we can. It's my belief that leftovers and the uncooked food in our homes can take on the same emotional weight as these topics, when, in reality, they are little more than fridge management problems.

Our natural discomfort with waste is a good thing. It's our ancestors speaking to us through the generations. Those ancestors knew that as we take from the earth to live, we must give back enough so we can keep going. Being out of sync, and taking too much, feels wrong because it can hurt our future selves and our community.

That's why it's important to me to practice ingenuity, throw out as little as I can, and generally be efficient and organized in the kitchen. But I can't always live up to my standards, and managing the food intake of my family occasionally gets the better of me. I have felt an inordinate sense of guilt about my imperfections here, to the point where I would be ashamed to admit I threw out some old sauce.

At the same time, leftovers seem so unappealing, all cold and claggy in the fridge. I always say I'm not a big fan of them, but really there are tons of leftover foods that I love. It's just that when I love them, I don't think of them as leftovers. I think of them as treats and bonuses.

So here I attempt an experiment and play anthropologist with myself to try to understand why I struggle with leftovers and waste. I list my good and bad leftovers and analyze what is driving these categorizations. From those observations I offer some advice and ways to reframe the problem of leftovers, so it can be less fraught and more fun.

Leftovers Cycle of Shame

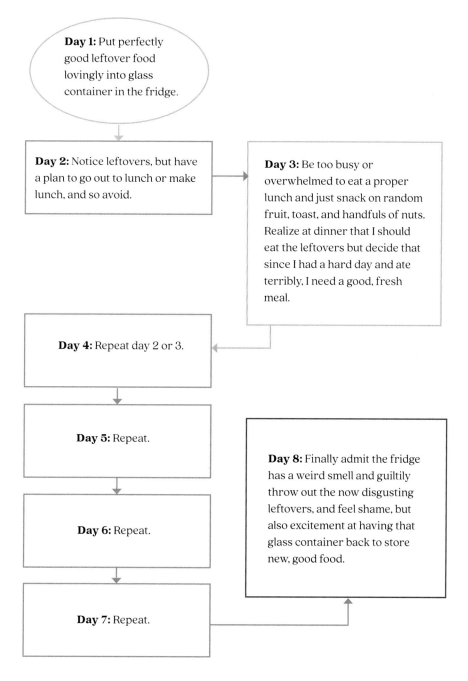

Day 1: Put perfectly good leftover food lovingly into glass container in the fridge.

Day 2: Notice leftovers, but have a plan to go out to lunch or make lunch, and so avoid.

Day 3: Be too busy or overwhelmed to eat a proper lunch and just snack on random fruit, toast, and handfuls of nuts. Realize at dinner that I should eat the leftovers but decide that since I had a hard day and ate terribly, I need a good, fresh meal.

Day 4: Repeat day 2 or 3.

Day 5: Repeat.

Day 6: Repeat.

Day 7: Repeat.

Day 8: Finally admit the fridge has a weird smell and guiltily throw out the now disgusting leftovers, and feel shame, but also excitement at having that glass container back to store new, good food.

THE GOOD LEFTOVERS

Pizza
Can be eaten hot or cold and I always want pizza.

Cake or desserts of any kind
I mean . . .

Thai leftovers
Warm up well and look appetizing even when cold.

Asian noodle dishes
Keep well and retain their shape and integrity when cold.

Chickpea salads or undressed green salads
A love letter to my future self.

Roasted vegetables
Healthful when eaten for lunch, but also great topped with melted cheese or wrapped up in a warmed tortilla, and super easy to eat.

THE BAD LEFTOVERS

Soup
It seems boring and unappetizing when cold. But my husband likes it, and it makes good baby food.

Pasta
Pasta loses its bite and the sauce usually sinks into it, making it soggy and not as flavorful. It's okay, but not great.

Mac and cheese
Same as above, but in a big chunk. And the cheese separates.

Chili
Similar to soup, but also I just don't need to eat chili that often. When I crave it, I crave it for one day only! (Maybe I should freeze it after day one and pull it out two weeks later, when it can be exciting again?)

Roasted meat and mashed potatoes (a.k.a. Thanksgiving)
The consistency is horrible, I'm sick of smelling them, and it feels like I have to do a lot to eat them again.

Dressed salad
Wilts so fast!

Take-out rice
Gets stuck together in a hard mass, and I have to do something to it to make it tasty.

Precooked fish
Smells weird. Not appetizing when cold.

Initial Observations

All the bad leftovers have in common several factors: They don't keep well for more than a few hours or a day, they don't retain their desired consistency in the fridge, and/or I just find them to look unappetizing when they're not hot or when they're sitting in containers in the fridge.

So "the bad" is really more of a perception issue. I need to eat the food that becomes unappetizing when I first make it or very soon after, and if I'm going to have leftovers, I need to ensure they're the kind that actually keep well. And if I have too much food stocked away to eat within the next few days or I know I will be away, I should immediately put the leftovers in the freezer, not the fridge. Seems simple, but this is something to practice and work on and not beat myself up about. Now, how can I put that into practice?

Takeaways

1. In terms of keeping food appetizing, putting my leftovers in glass or see-through containers makes a big difference.

2. Make the fridge more user-friendly. Keep all the food that's ready to eat on one shelf and the jars of jam, pickles, and the like on another, so it's not confusing. That helps for sure. (I have never kept this up for more than a few days, but they are such great days!)

3. Stop avoiding the leftovers and make a decision! Do this before going to the grocery store. Take them out of the fridge, look at them, and decide whether they're going to taste good as is or not. If they will, eat them. If you aren't sure, think about how you could transform the leftovers into something that does appeal (ideas on page 284) or if they should be thrown away or composted. Be gentle; this will take time to become a habit.

4. Take a "reduce" approach to anything that doesn't keep well. Only make enough fish, for example, for one night.

5. Tell anyone else in your household about leftovers that they might like—even going so far as to keep an updated whiteboard on the fridge. (Who am I kidding? This is a pipe dream!)

Leftovers Refresh

Given the observations of the last few pages, these are the recipes that I have identified to be potentially tricky leftovers. If eating them again just as they are does not wholly appeal, I offer some alternatives. Let's set an intention to minimize penance eating (eating the leftovers you don't want out of guilt), and maximize the leftovers that feel like treasures to be eaten as is or refreshed.

Creamy Dill and Date Dressing (page 88).

- Toss with any kind of salad, particularly a Greek salad, or raw veggie combination.
- Use as a sauce for a bowl with protein, veggies, and carbs, such as grilled chicken with rice or farro or a beef and broccoli bowl.
- Serve it with a veggie tray as dip, or mix it with hummus to stretch it even further—it would be especially good over raw or roasted bell peppers.
- Swap it in as an alternative dressing for the Days and Days Salad (page 78).

Triple Citrus Dressing (page 88).

- Add white beans or chickpeas to a bowl of triple citrus dressing; serve with bread, for soaking, and snow peas.
- Squash 1 tablespoon of dressing with 1 avocado for a zingtastic guacamole or toast topping.
- Pour it onto a plate and dip your bread in it—a perfect meal for a night to yourself.
- Pour it over fresh mozzarella and greens for a simple, elegant salad.
- Weird, but hear me out: Slosh it over your yogurt in the morning.
- Eat it with crudités like you would bagna cauda (a traditional Italian garlic and anchovy dip for fresh vegetables).

Fast White Bean, Chorizo, and Hearty Greens Stew (page 97). Cook off some of the liquid to make a burrito filling. Serve over mashed potatoes or roasted vegetables.

Saucy Spiced Chicken with Tomato, Goat Cheese, and Mint (page 102). Serve over farro or pasta bowl, or use as a taco filling.

Chile, Garlic, and Date Butterflied Roasted Chicken (page 111). Add it to a noodle or tortilla soup or simple green salad.

Sambal Shrimp Lettuce Wraps (page 120). Serve extra Sambal Shrimp in a rice bowl with pickled veggies and kimchi.

Salty, Spicy, and Bright Brussels Sprouts Pasta (page 157). Put an egg on it.

Samosa Puffs (page 178). If you made more filling than you have puff pastry, cook just the filling on its own—throw it back in the pan after Step 3 and let the chicken cook all the way through. Bake it under mashed potatoes to make an Indian-inspired shepherd's pie dish or a variation of Midwestern hot dish with tater tots on top.

Curried Chickpeas and Spinach (page 184). This dish becomes thicker after some time in the fridge and is great in a pita or tortilla.

Anything from the Vegetable Celebration (pages 210–227). Bulk it out by adding to a bowl of farro or rice, put an egg on it, or all of the above.

Garlic and Lemon Butter Smashed Potatoes (page 265). Put an egg on it.

Creamy Cilantro Dressing (page 266, from the Smoky Honey Shrimp Tacos).

- Drizzle over nachos or just eat it with tortilla chips.
- Toss it with roasted or boiled potatoes.
- Slather it on roasted or grilled corn, or use it to dress a corn salad with feta, cucumbers, and tomatoes (level up to a taco salad if you have a shell, beans, and a protein).
- Toss it with the fennel slaw as on page 266, but pair with a barbecued meat (or alternative) like pulled pork, chicken, or jackfruit.

Turkey Falafel Balls with Tangy Tomato Sauce (page 268). Serve over pasta or any grain. Add to a sandwich or pita with fresh vegetables.

Final Thought

This book is about the joys of imperfection. I knew for several years that I needed to write it. And if I look at all my former titles and drafts and ideas, they are just diluted and sidelong versions of this book. I knew that joy and peace in the kitchen come from being comfortable with imperfection. But I couldn't write it until I had lived it. This book could only blossom from the ashes of my own slain perfectionism.

Writing and sharing this book may be the hardest thing I've ever done in my life. It came to me at a time when I was in the midst of healing and transformation, learning to let go of shame and building a new life for myself. It is different from the books I have written before—different enough that I hear from others and my own inner voice, "Why are you writing this book?" It's deeply personal, and I have never done personal. It is creative and vulnerable and about *me*. The me before the last few years would have said, *No one wants to know about **me**, so I shouldn't do it.* The me now says, *I am more like everyone else than I ever imagined, and what is true about me can be true for others.* Everything that has ever been meaningful and transformative for me has come from others sharing their vulnerable experiences. I wanted to join all those brave people who have helped me so much and share in the hope that my vulnerability might reveal to you something about you.

This book also came along after I had a baby, at a moment when I suddenly had little time and energy to do creative work. Creative work requires vitality, emotional presence, bravery, discipline, and consistency, and yet here I was with less time, less attention span, less energy, and honestly more raw emotion than I had ever felt in my life. I thought all the time, *Why am I doing this to myself?*

One particularly hard afternoon, I was feeling disappointed with myself for procrastinating by doing the laundry and other chores. A maroon glove had accidentally made its way into a laundry load and had ruined many shirts, pajamas, and a cute white fluffy sweater that belonged to my daughter. I knew it didn't matter, but I felt terrible. I was overwhelmed with a wave of pain and fear that I couldn't do anything. *I can't get the laundry right? How will I write a decent book?* I lay on the floor and cried. After letting myself cry it out for a minute or so, I looked up and saw, reflected in the TV, a perfect beam of a rainbow. It was beautiful and vibrant. If I moved my head at all, it was gone. I could see it only from that one position, lying on the ground, crying.

I knew the rainbow was trying to tell me that it was going to be okay, and I could do this. But I fought it. Don't be so heavy-handed, universe! I didn't want it to be okay. I didn't want to get up. So I lay and looked at the rainbow through tears until I had the strength to get up.

Sometimes that beautiful something can only be seen from just the right angle while you're lying in the muck. This book is my rainbow, and it could only be born from this very specific, difficult time in my life. It is that much more precious to me for it.

Recipe Index

Conversion Tables

Please note that all conversions are approximate but close enough to be useful when converting from one system to another.

OVEN TEMPERATURES

Fahrenheit	Gas Mark	Celsius
250	½	120
275	1	140
300	2	150
325	3	160
350	4	180
375	5	190
400	6	200
425	7	220
450	8	230
475	9	240
500	10	260

NOTE: Reduce the temperature by 20°C (68°F) for fan-assisted ovens.

APPROXIMATE EQUIVALENTS

1 stick butter = 8 tbsp = 4 oz = ½ cup = 115 g

1 cup all-purpose presifted flour = 4.7 oz

1 cup granulated sugar = 8 oz = 220 g

1 cup firmly packed brown sugar = 6 oz = 220 g to 230 g

1 cup honey or syrup = 12 oz

1 cup grated cheese = 4 oz

1 cup dried beans = 6 oz

1 large egg = about 2 oz or about 3 tbsp

1 egg yolk = about 1 tbsp

1 egg white = about 2 tbsp

LIQUID CONVERSIONS

US	Imperial	Metric
2 tbsp	1 fl oz	30 ml
3 tbsp	1¼ fl oz	45 ml
¼ cup	2 fl oz	60 ml
⅓ cup	2½ fl oz	75 ml
⅓ cup + 1 tbsp	3 fl oz	90 ml
⅓ cup + 2 tbsp	3½ fl oz	100 ml
½ cup	4 fl oz	125 ml
⅔ cup	5 fl oz	150 ml
¾ cup	6 fl oz	175 ml
¾ cup + 2 tbsp	7 fl oz	200 ml
1 cup	8 fl oz	250 ml
1 cup + 2 tbsp	9 fl oz	275 ml
1¼ cups	10 fl oz	300 ml
1⅓ cups	11 fl oz	325 ml
1½ cups	12 fl oz	350 ml
1⅔ cups	13 fl oz	375 ml
1¾ cups	14 fl oz	400 ml
1¾ cups + 2 tbsp	15 fl oz	450 ml
2 cups (1 pint)	16 fl oz	500 ml
2½ cups	20 fl oz (1 pint)	600 ml
3¾ cups	1½ pints	900 ml
4 cups	1¾ pints	1 liter

WEIGHT CONVERSIONS

US/UK	Metric	US/UK	Metric
½ oz	15 g	7 oz	200 g
1 oz	30 g	8 oz	250 g
1½ oz	45 g	9 oz	275 g
2 oz	60 g	10 oz	300 g
2½ oz	75 g	11 oz	325 g
3 oz	90 g	12 oz	350 g
3½ oz	100 g	13 oz	375 g
4 oz	125 g	14 oz	400 g
5 oz	150 g	15 oz	450 g
6 oz	175 g	1 lb	500 g

Index

ACKNOWLEDGMENTS

The biggest thank-you to my editor, Liz Saunders, for patiently supporting this book through its many, many, many phases of development. The way you have understood and nurtured this book into being has meant the world to me. I don't think I could have made this with anyone else.

To Sarah Smith, whose incredible eye and taste made this book so dreamy I would just stare at it tearing up with amazement. And to Janet Vicario for her early support and sharp advice. To Allison Gore for her brilliant illustrations that brought so much of what was in my head into life.

Thank you so much to Hillary Leary, Kate Karol, Barbara Peragine, Doug Wolff, Rae Ann Spitzenberger, Becky Terhune, Anne Kerman, Evi Abeler, and Nora Singley for working so hard and with such tremendous attention to detail putting all the moving parts of this book into place. This was not standard stuff and you shone.

Thank you to Kim Daly for finding us the wisdom of Cristina Chua. And to Cristina for your generous and insightful reading.

Thank you to Kylie Foxx McDonald, Vaughn Andrews, and the inimitable Suzie Bolotin for believing in this project and for taking so much time to understand and foster its growth. Your faith means so much to me.

To the glorious Rebecca Carlisle: You pick me up when I am down and always tell the truth—could there be a better friend and colleague? And to Moira Kerrigan, Chloe Puton, and Kate Oksen, thank you for finding so many creative ways to connect these ideas to those who want to hear them, and for always being game to figure out what the hell I'm trying to say.

For Dan, who always has my back, always cheers me on, and knows I can do it long before I do; thank you for being here with me in it for real. And to my Io, for giving me courage to keep growing always, because what else can I do in the face of such inspiration? I love you both infinitely, and you mean everything to me.

Thank you to Mum and Dad for loving me without question and for knowing what I could do long before I did. To Em and Hannah for being so very fun to come home to, and welcoming and loving whatever I bring.

To Denise Clay for helping me come home to myself. To Sarah Chan for being my bestie and showing me what intimacy and safety in a relationship really feel like. To Brian Harris for being the parent-friend I needed most and so very much more. To Pato, who finds the sweetest, subtle ways to show he sees and values me. And to Heather Hogan for planting so many seeds in me that continue to sprout and grow.

Thank you to Anna Ellis Nesser, Eushavia Bogan, Preethi Sundaram, and Katrina Ceguera for listening without judgment and always making me feel like I am on the right track. To Matt Frehner for introducing me to your dad—kidding!—thank you for being my dear friend through so many iterations of growth and loving me always. To Lori for your sweetness and help with testing. To Hawa Hassan, for your friendship and honesty—you made me feel accepted for exactly who I am the moment we locked eyes.

To Lisa Hagen for always encouraging me and bringing wine. To Claire Dub for being so sensible and forthright when I need it. To Jhen Pabillano for being a wise, witty, and irascible role model and friend. To Katie for your long years of friendship; it means the world to me that we can still find new ways to connect over distance and time. To Rose, who has shown me how to embrace myself as an artist. To Dan Nielsen, for being such a reliable cheerleader and dear friend.

And to dearest Charlotte Masters, who is like a member of our family, whom I trust completely and feel so absurdly lucky to have found. Your empathy and good nature are irreplaceable; thank you for caring for Io and for all of us. And to all of the vast community of teachers, babysitters, and caregivers of all kinds who have held us up through Io's life so far—we are so rich and so lucky to have you supporting us.

Thank you to the white squirrel in Prospect Park for giving me confidence I am on the right path. Truly to anyone who listened to me talk about this project long before it became viable. To those who helped me test recipes, whether formally or informally! And finally to all the authors and artists and thinkers who populate my mind and heart and gave me courage in so many ways over so many years. I am standing on the plateau you built.

ABOUT THE AUTHOR

I'm Leanne Brown, your friend in the kitchen. I am here to send a calming deep breath into your body as you cook, so you can connect to the strength and ability that is already there waiting for you. Cooking has brought me profound healing,

and I want to share that with you. I have written some other cookbooks, most notably *Good and Cheap*. I live in Brooklyn with my partner, Dan, our daughter, Io, and our cat, Yoshimi. I was born in Canada and still think dill pickle is the best potato chip flavor. I also love to play, and sing, and talk to you about how you're feeling. I care about almost everything (except maybe the rules, or that line being straight). I am glad to be alive, and I hope you are, too.

ABOUT THE ILLUSTRATOR

Allison Gore is an illustrator and designer from California. Having previously worked in the live music industry, they now work in digital media and their work has appeared in *Bustle*, *Mic*, and *The Bold Italic*, among others. They live in upstate New York with their partner and cat.